Data Driven Systems Modeling

To my wife, for her loving support, and our family

Data Driven Systems Modeling

Remi Planche

Prentice Hall/Masson

First published in French by Masson, Paris, under the title
Maîtriser la modélisation conceptuelle
by Remi Planche

This edition first published in English by Prentice Hall International and Masson

Camera-ready copy for this book was prepared on a Macintosh II using Microsoft Word. Model examples were developed using Silverrun tools by Computer Systems Advisers Inc. Some graphic elements were added using MacDraw II by Claris Corporation.

Printed and bound in Great Britain by
BPCC Wheatons Ltd, Exeter

Library of Congress Cataloguing-in-Publication Data

Planche, Remi.
[Maîtriser la modélisation conceptuelle. English]
Data driven systems modeling/by Remi Planche.
p. cm.
Translation of: Maîtriser la modélisation conceptuelle.
Includes bibliographical references and index.
ISBN 0-13-201187-5
1. Electronic data processing. 2. System analysis. I. Title.
QA76.P5413 1991
004—dc20 90-7442
CIP

British Library Cataloguing-in-Publication Data

Planche, Remi
Data driven systems modeling.
1. Databases. Design
I. Title II. Maîtriser la modélisation conceptuelle.
English
005.74

ISBN 0-13-201187-5

1 2 3 4 5 95 94 93 92 91

Contents

List of Illustrations

PART I Systems Modeling

PART II The Data Foundation

PART III Building on the Foundation

5 The Logical Model

PART IV Conclusion

Foreword

This book presents a data driven approach to systems modeling. Over the years, the approaches and methods used to develop systems have evolved. In the 1960's and 70's a lot of emphasis was placed on specifying process logic. Data specifications were a by-product of process specifications. This led to the building of applications with each having their own files where the same or similar data was found in different files. The ensuing problems in systems maintenance and evolution are well documented. This led many to propose that data was a corporate resource which needed to be managed. We saw the emergence, in the 1980's, of database administration and data administration functions as well as an increase of data modeling activities within many organizations.

In many cases, the data and process specification activities were undertaken in parallel, often with separate teams responsible for each, resulting in a parallel/dual approach to systems modeling and development. This dual approach can lead to a number of coordination problems between process and data teams in a project. The underlying reason for the difficulty in applying the dual approach lies in a tight relationship between process and data. By separating what should be together, a lot of effort, energy and cost is expended to ensure the integrity of process and data. Thus a tighter coupling of data and process is required to avoid these problems.

What is proposed as a solution is a more data driven approach where process logic is linked or encapsulated with the data. This has also been called an 'object' approach to systems analysis and design. For business systems development, an 'object model' can be mapped to a data model. The objects of interest in an object model are in fact the entities of the conceptual data model. Therefore a data driven (or data centered) approach to systems development is an important factor in breaking the productivity bottleneck of either the process driven or the dual process/data driven approaches practiced today.

This book contributes to helping students as well as practitioners better understand the data modeling concepts required to apply such an approach. It uses a derivative of the *MERISE* data modeling notation developed in the mid-1970's and since established as a standard for conceptual data modeling in many public and private organizations in Europe and North America. The author also shows how, once the conceptual model is complete, it can be transformed into a logical and physical data model to be implemented in a database management system.

It is becoming increasingly clear that in order to improve the quality and the productivity of our systems development process we will need to develop the right methods and offer the right training to our students and systems development practitioners. This book contributes to both.

Robert W. Mantha, Ph.D.
Associate Professor of Information Systems
Faculty of Business Administration
Laval University
Quebec City, Quebec
and
Director of Planning and Technology
CSA Research Ltd.
Quebec City, Quebec

Preface

Data driven systems design and development is now recognized as the preferred approach to implement information systems. It is considered imperative when one uses state-of-the-art tools such as relational databases, fourth-generation languages or *CASE* tools.

This has not always been the case: process driven development, emphasizing control flow, had been the standard approach since the origin of computing. In the seventies, proponents of *Structured System Analysis* (*SSA*) such as Tom DeMarco and Chris Gane took a significant step toward emphasizing data, with the use of data flow diagrams. At the same time, conceptual data models were proposed by an *ANSI-SPARC* report and perfected by researchers such as Peter Chen and Hubert Tardieu. With James Martin, data modeling first found a high level niche in corporate systems planning, while development relied on *SSA*. Data modeling also became a key ingredient of the *MERISE* method for information systems development.

This book originates from research done in Quebec, which had access both to *SSA* and to *MERISE*, which Daniel Pascot had introduced there in the late seventies. This situation resulted in a demand from software houses for integrating both techniques into a unified method for analyzing systems. In addition, in the eighties, Normand Bouffard had incorporated Warnier/Orr data driven design concepts in a system generator. Thus the ingredients for a comprehensive data driven systems development approach were available.

1 What is this Book about?

This book views the development of a system as the process of constructing and refining specialized models that bridge the gap between the application domain and an implementation of the system. Part I, an overview, provides a digest of the book. It describes the fundamental aspects of such a modeling approach, its impact on a development life cycle extending from corporate systems planning to systems implementation, and its benefits.

Part II thoroughly investigates the conceptual model, which is the foundation of data driven methods. Too often, data modeling seems to be an obscure art, best left to specialists. This book attempts to show how much of it is a science, by presenting rules which apply to conceptual models and by demonstrating techniques by which models are put together. Indeed, the concepts of data modeling should be widely known and the techniques applied by all system developers.

The logical and physical models, which are process oriented, are used in succession to design information systems. They are introduced in Part III of the book. Their bond with the conceptual model is firmly established, by analyzing the structure of their components in terms of this model, and by demonstrating techniques to infer them from it. An alternate representation of the conceptual model, using a relational model, leads to examples of implementation with relational tools.

A short conclusion, in Part IV, emphasizes the need for a comprehensive perspective on systems development.

2 What is the Purpose of this Book?

This book is designed as a reference manual and a concise user guide. It follows a systematic plan which includes precise definitions, descriptions of applicable rules, and 'modeling' or 'approach' sections spelling out how to develop models.

It contains numerous examples, all drawn from the same case study, which establishes a consistent and meaningful context throughout the book. Illustrations show what models should look like and explanations demonstrate how to apply modeling rules, and how to actually develop models.

3 Who is this Book for?

This book is primarily intended for design teams in software houses and information systems departments who wish to improve their knowledge of modeling methods, particularly data modeling, and their use in systems development. Computer science and information technology students will also find it useful.

4 What Prior Knowledge is Needed?

In order to be able to make use of the techniques presented here, the reader should possess a general knowledge of systems development.

Part II on the conceptual model is complete in itself. All it requires from the reader is the ability to deal with things at this level of abstraction. Readers with a prior knowledge of database technology will benefit from it in that it sheds a different light on this field.

Part III normally requires prior knowledge of *Structured System Analysis* and relational technology. However, it may be used as an introduction to these subjects, from the perspective of the conceptual model. If this is the case, the reader should supplement it by studying some of the references suggested at the end of this book.

5 Acknowledgments

In developing the original French edition of this book, I was given encouragement and support by many individuals including Gérard Vahée, Jean-Pierre Delwasse, François Labrousse and Carmen Bernier. François Lustman and Jean-François Coulonval also read earlier drafts and contributed precious observations and insights.

This English edition includes several refinements to the subject matter, owing to modeling experience gained while applying the *Silverrun* and *Goldrun* software tools, and to discussions with their authors, respectively, Daniel Pascot and Robert Mantha, Normand Bouffard and Hector Filgueira. Using *Silverrun* in preparing the book greatly improved the process, as well as the appearance of the end result.

Special thanks go to my editors, Mike Cash and Viki Williams, for their guidance, and to the Prentice Hall staff who worked in producing this book.

PART I

Systems Modeling

Part I introduces several types of models which are useful in analyzing and designing information systems. It briefly shows how they fit into a data driven systems development life cycle and discusses the benefits of modeling for systems development.

Chapter 1

Overview

> Life is composed of so many interlocking and interwoven and often inconsistent 'systems' that it may seem simplistic to think of things in those terms. But it is often important to formulate simple ideas very clearly so that one can use them as models in thinking about more complex ideas.
>
> (D. Hofstadter, *Gödel, Escher, Bach*)

This chapter takes the reader to the heart of the matter.

First it proposes a few definitions of general import, and positions modeling activities within the development life cycle of an organization's information systems.

Then it succinctly presents each type of model, in its completed form. Models are illustrated by examples, all drawn from the same basic case used as a reference throughout this book.

Finally, it reviews the benefits derived from using a data driven modeling approach to develop information systems.

The reader who approaches this overview for the first time is invited to scan it, without focusing on details or seeking to master the vocabulary at once: this book attempts to integrate concepts from a variety of backgrounds, and borrows terms from all of them. More complete definitions and more progressive explanations are found in the remainder of this book; the reader will have a chance to return to this first chapter later.

1.1 General Definitions

1.1.1 Information systems

A *system* is a collection of components operating as a whole to reach a number of common objectives.

The objectives of any *information system* are to bring together, process, manipulate and distribute information required for carrying out some activities. Usually, an information system contains manual as well as automated components.

1.1.2 Models

Models of a system (Fig. 1-1) are representations with the specific purpose of helping to understand some aspects of the system, by emphasizing relevant features and de-emphasizing irrelevant ones.

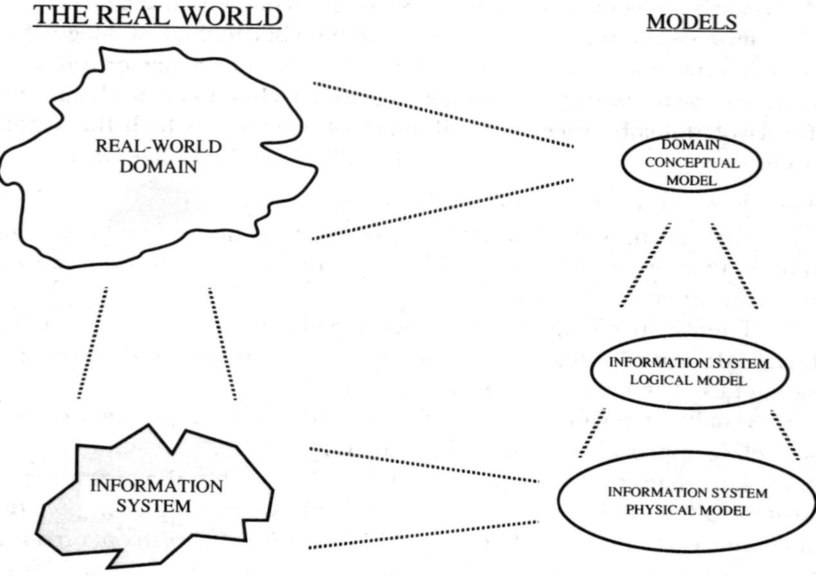

Figure 1-1 Types of models.

The more details of the real world a model hides, the more abstract it is. The approach set forth in this book uses three types of models, ranging from the more tangible to the more abstract:

- the *physical model,* which completely describes the system: data flows, processes, automated components, manual components;
- the *logical model,* which describes data and the processes which manipulate them; this model is the basis of the physical model and disregards any reference to material resources;
- the *conceptual model,* which describes the underlying contents of the logical model, that is, information and how it is connected; this model disregards the data manipulation described at the logical level.

The physical model – also called the *implementation model* – is the most complete but also the most complex model of a system. It is dependent on the resources used to implement the system.

The logical model – also called the *essential model* – is simpler. Being independent of material resources used, the same model could represent a manual or an automated version of a system. However, it still embodies choices regarding data and process organization.

The conceptual model – also called the *semantic model* – is the most synthetic and permanent of all models. Being independent of data and process organization, it represents not the system, but the fundamental substance of the domain of activity to which the system applies.

Each type of model is described with its own specific *components* (Fig. 1-2), but there is a correspondence between models. Some components are more directly related to *data*, while others are related to *processes*; others yet play an intermediate role and display both aspects. The data perspective of a system tends to be comprehensive, while the process perspective tends to remain local.

MODEL TYPE	DATA	<—>	PROCESSES	FOCUS
CONCEPTUAL	Entities Relationships Properties		Business rules	DATA
LOGICAL	Data stores	Data flows	Processes	DATA PROCESSES
PHYSICAL • AUTOMATED	Automated data stores	Screens, reports...	Automated processes	DATA PROCESSES RESOURCES
• MANUAL	Manual files	Manual documents	Manual processes	

Figure 1-2 Components of the various types of models.

1.1.3 Modeling

Modeling is the activity which consists of constructing models, either for describing an existing information system – analysis – or for developing a new information system – design.

To develop a system, an analyst will use both types of modeling. *Analysis* – or reverse engineering – of an existing system aims at rapidly reaching its foundation, by extracting a logical description from its physical description and then providing a conceptual description of the underlying domain. *Design* – or engineering – of the new system operates in the forward direction: it is based on the conceptual model, on which it progressively builds logical and physical models of the system.

1.1.4 Information systems development

However useful they are, modeling techniques alone cannot ensure the smooth development of information systems. There are feasibility and consistency issues which can be dealt with only within the framework of an overall approach. Generally, an effort is made to structure the organization's systems development cycle (Fig. 1-3) into levels and phases.

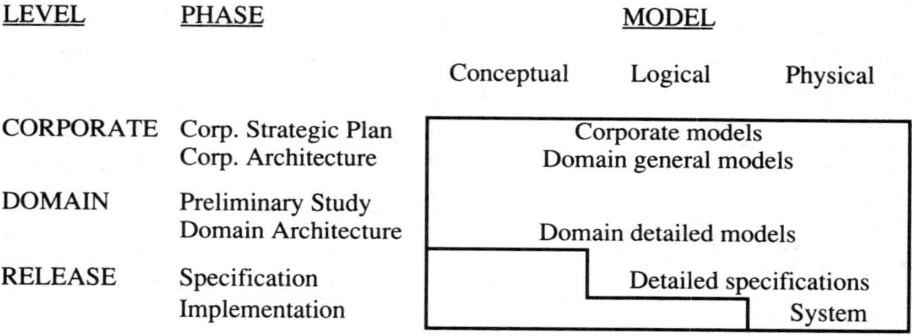

Figure 1-3 Modeling in the systems development life cycle.

Thus, at the corporate level, there may be an orientation phase: the *corporate systems strategic plan*, followed by – or combined with – a more thorough modeling phase: the *corporate systems architecture.*

At the level of each major functional domain, there may be an orientation phase: the *preliminary study*, followed by – or combined with – a more detailed modeling phase: the *domain systems architecture.*

For each systems *release*, there may be a *specification* phase, followed by an *implementation* phase.

During this cycle, progressively more refined versions of conceptual, logical and physical models are developed to support the objectives of each phase.

Thus overall *corporate models* provide high level overviews of systems and are the basis for developing long range systems plans.

General *domain models* are a refinement of corporate models for specific functional domains, and play similar roles at their own levels.

Detailed models help prepare the implementation of new information systems by identifying and relating all components to be developed and implemented.

Finally, *detailed specifications* describe these components with the degree of detail required to implement them.

This development life cycle provides a framework within which modeling activities and models may be positioned.

1.2 The Conceptual Model

1.2.1 Data

According to the *MERISE* diagramming technique, the conceptual model of a domain represents data, using an *entity-relationship diagram* (Fig. 1-4). The main components of this diagram are entities, relationships and properties.

Entities, drawn as rectangular boxes, represent different collections of individuals, things or events which are part of the domain.

Relationships, drawn as oval shaped boxes, represent different collections of interactions that exist between entities and are relevant to the domain. A relationship links a number of entities – at least two – which are its *participating entities.* Its meaning is obtained by forming a sentence with the verb which denotes it and the names of entities which are linked to it: an arrow is sometimes drawn near the verb to show in which way the sentence should be formed.

Collectively, entities and relationships are referred to as the *objects* of the model.

An entity and sometimes a relationship have properties which are written inside the corresponding box. A *property* is a piece of information that is part of the description of an object.

The different individuals or cases represented by a given object are called the *occurrences* of the object. Their number is the object *population;* it is sometimes written next to it.

Some properties – or property groups – enable one to uniquely distinguish each occurrence of a given object, sometimes in connection with occurrences of neighboring objects. They are called *identifiers.* The properties which are a constituting part of identifiers are underlined in the diagram.

In short, an entity-relationship diagram is a detailed and precise symbolic representation of a domain of activity (Fig. 1-5).

DISTRIBUTION OF SCHOOL SUPPLIES

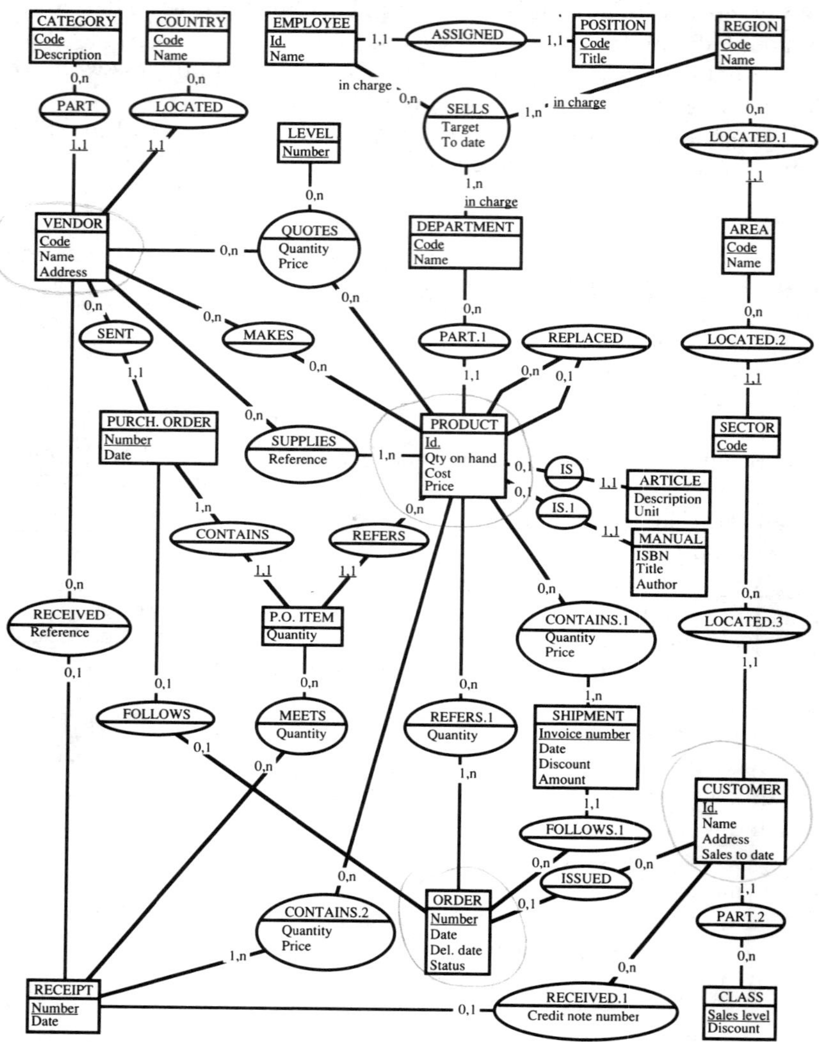

The entity-relationship diagram shows:

- Entities: VENDOR, PRODUCT, ORDER, CUSTOMER, etc;
- Relationships between entities: vendor SUPPLIES product, order is ISSUED by customer, etc;
- Properties of entities and relationships: Name and Address of vendor, Quantity of product in order, etc.

The model can be paraphrased to yield a description of the domain (Fig. 1-5).

Figure 1-4 Conceptual model of a domain: entity-relationship diagram.

Finalised as from pages 107 to 123 in detail

DISTRIBUTION OF SCHOOL SUPPLIES

OVERVIEW	For the organization examined, the distribution of school supplies involves purchasing products from vendors and selling them to customers.
PRODUCT	There are two main product lines: manuals and articles. Products are grouped by department. Some products may be replaced by others (when not available).
VENDOR	Vendors are categorized by country and category. Vendors supply products, sometimes make them and quote prices for them, depending on quantities ordered.
PURCH. ORDER	Purchase orders are sent to vendors (to replenish the inventory). They may directly follow customer orders. Purchase orders contain items which refer to products and state quantities ordered.
RECEIPT	Receipts may come from vendors. They contain products with stated prices and quantities, which more or less completely meet quantities in purchase orders. Receipts may also come from customers (returns).
CUSTOMER	Customers are categorized according to their location, by sector, area and region. They are also categorized according to their discount class, which is a function of their sales level.
ORDER	Orders are issued by customers. They refer to products and state quantities.
SHIPMENT	Shipments are sent out in response to orders. They contain products and state quantities and prices.
EMPLOYEE	There are employees (sales representatives) who sell products. They are given sales targets for specific departments and regions. Employees are assigned positions.

This interpretation of the entity-relationship diagram (Fig. 1-4) is based on relationships. It could be carried out further by using other information included in the diagram.
Modeling is the reverse process of preparing the conceptual model, starting with an informal description of the domain.

Figure 1-5 Conceptual model of a domain: interpretation of the entity-relationship diagram.

1.2.2 Business rules

In the conceptual model of a domain, data are constrained by *business rules,* which specify existence conditions for entity and relationship occurrences, and permissible property values.

Some of these rules are directly embodied in the structure of the entity-relationship diagram, that is, in the choice of entities and relationships, and the assignment of properties.

Other rules are also expressed in the entity-relationship diagram, using special symbols placed on relationship connectors: such is the case for *cardinality rules*, which indicate the conditions under which entity occurrences may participate in relationships.

Finally, there are business rules which are part of the definition of data and which cannot be easily represented in a graphic way: they must be stated separately (Fig. 1-6). In this book, such *explicit business rules* are considered an integral part of the conceptual model. The result is an extended model which covers not only data but also processes, insofar as they are represented by business rules.

DISTRIBUTION OF SCHOOL SUPPLIES

OBJECT	PROPERTY	BUSINESS RULE
CONTAINS.1	Quantity	= Max (Old Quantity on hand, REFERS.1.Quantity for ORDER - Sum of CONTAINS.1.Quantities for SHIPMENTS FOLLOWING ORDER)
	Price	= PRODUCT.Price (at time of shipping)
PRODUCT	Quantity on hand	= Old Qty on hand - CONTAINS.1.Quantity
and SHIPMENT	Amount	= Sum of (Qties x Prices) for SHIPMENT
(when preparing a shipment)	Discount	= CLASS.Discount for CUSTOMER CLASS x Amount
REPLACED (when entering an order)		PRODUCT.Qty on hand = 0 => A Replacement PRODUCT is proposed to the customer, if possible
ETC...		

Business rules make the conceptual model more precise by stating which conditions apply to properties and objects in the model.

Figure 1-6 Conceptual model of a domain: business rules.

1.2.3 Use of the conceptual model

Concepts introduced in the preceding summary are dealt with in more depth in Chap. 2 and 3, while Chap. 4 explains the approach to conceptual modeling. Before pursuing their study, the following points should be made.

First, the conceptual model of a domain represents data which may be processed by systems of the domain, in association with related business rules. However, a conceptual model represents only possible or permissible data, but not the actual values: entities and relationships are collections of things or interactions; properties denote collections of values; business rules are general conditions applicable to all members of these collections.

In fact, by displaying the connections between data and the constraints which apply to them, the conceptual model expresses their meaning (Fig. 1-6). Its structure is intuitively akin to the organization of mental representations that one might have of the domain.

Actual data are described by a *model implementation*, that is, a particular collection of object occurrences with specific values for their properties, complying with business rules. For a given model, there exists a potentially infinite number of implementations.

Second, the representation of a domain provided by the conceptual model is mostly static: the model specifies the existence of data without distinguishing whether the information is at rest or in motion; furthermore, there is no preferred order in which to read the entity-relationship diagram. The same is true for business rules: the conceptual model only states their existence, without imposing any particular sequence, thus leaving the task of determining the most efficient organization of data and processes, among those possible, to a logical modeling phase.

Third, the structure of a conceptual model obeys modeling rules which make it as modular as possible. Ideally, the resulting model is *normal*, that is, it displays as entities and relationships all the elementary objects contained in the domain being described; it also displays all elementary properties and assigns them directly to those objects to which they are most closely related. A normal model contains only essential objects, properties and rules, on which agreement is required prior to a more complete study of a system. In principle, a system designed on the basis of a normal model records only elementary facts, as independent as possible from each other. Thus it minimizes data redundancy and the resulting process duplications. It also makes system maintenance easier, when new objects or properties have to be taken into account. Moreover, a normal model shows as business rules all elementary interactions existing in the real world between those elementary facts, enabling the system to relate them in relevant ways and to derive any appropriate fact or conclusion.

Finally, by design, the conceptual model of a domain is independent from manual or automated systems which process domain data. This is an important benefit, since it ensures continuity between the analysis of an existing system and the design of a future system, by giving a stable vision of the domain of activity under study.

To summarize this discussion, the representation of a domain as a normal conceptual model is an especially synthetic one. On the one hand, it describes a fundamental aspect of a system, by entirely stating the 'what' and giving complete freedom with respect to the 'how' of the system. On the other hand, the graphic format of the entity-relationship diagram provides a comprehensive and detailed grasp of the data in a domain and their interrelationships, which is not as easily obtained with a narrative format or a list (Fig. 1-6). After some practice, it becomes an unequaled tool for understanding and communications.

1.3 The Logical Model

1.3.1 Components of the logical model

According to the Gane and Sarson diagramming technique, a system may be described, on the logical level, by three kinds of components: processes, data stores and data flows (Fig. 1-7).

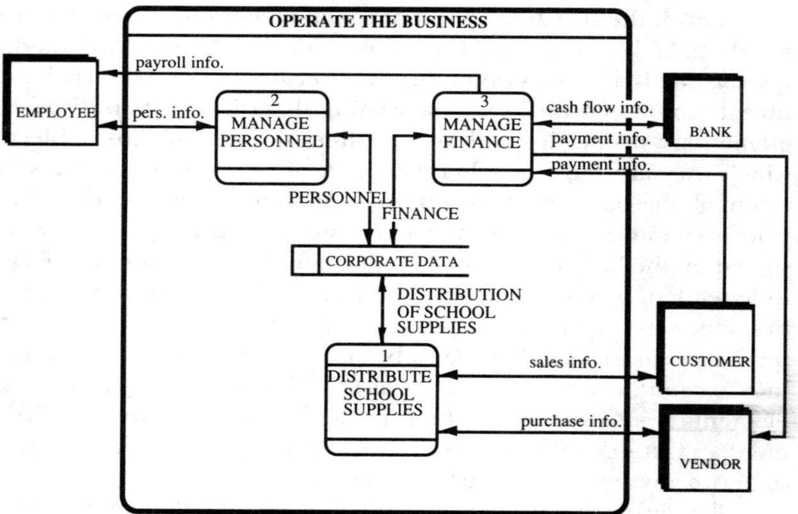

This diagram shows process Operate The Business as composed of:
• Processes: DISTRIBUTE SCHOOL SUPPLIES, MANAGE PERSONNEL and MANAGE FINANCE;
• Data store: CORPORATE DATA;
• Data flows between these components and between external entities: VENDOR, CUSTOMER, BANK and EMPLOYEE.

Figure 1-7 Logical model: corporate context diagram.

These logical components are the equivalent of physical components, that is: processes (data transformations), databases or files (data at rest), and data flows (data in motion). Links between these components and with the outside world are represented using *logical data flow diagrams* (DFDs).

By applying *top-down analysis,* a precept of *Structured System Analysis,* a process is broken down into sub-processes (Fig. 1-8) for which the same diagramming technique can be used.

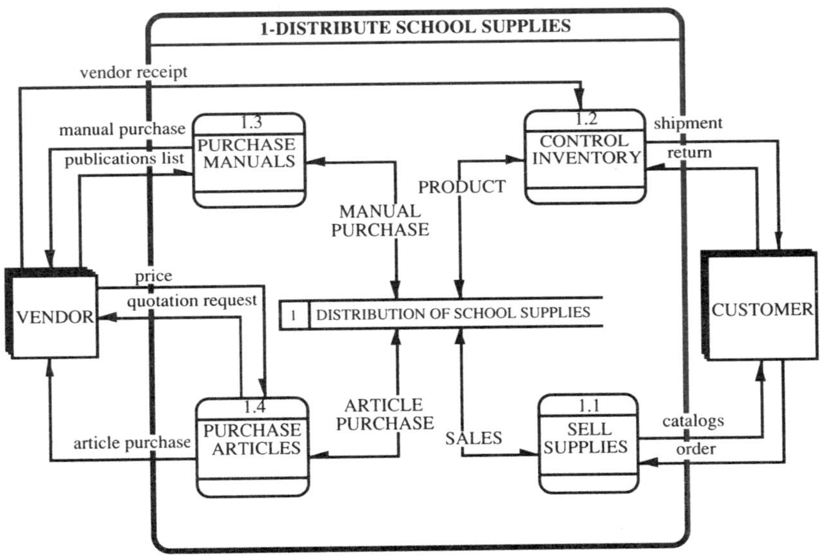

This domain context diagram shows process Distribute School Supplies as composed of:

- Processes: SELL SUPPLIES, CONTROL INVENTORY, PURCHASE MANUALS and PURCHASE ARTICLES;
- Data store: DISTRIBUTION OF SCHOOL SUPPLIES, a subset of data store CORPORATE DATA;
- Data flows between these components and between external entities: VENDOR and CUSTOMER.

Figure 1-8 Logical model: domain context diagram.

The logical model of a system consists of DFDs representing it at different levels of detail, together with detailed specifications of its components. As will be seen in the next section, specifications are based on the conceptual model, through views which represent particular uses of data.

1.3.2 Contribution of the conceptual model

When an existing system has been analyzed and the underlying conceptual model has been developed, a large measure of the information required to develop a new system is already at hand. Once the logical components have been identified, logical modeling starts with assigning data to data stores and data flows, and business rules to processes. The conceptual model supplies the materials which have to be integrated and distributed throughout the system logical model.

Indeed, a data store or a low level data flow may be described on the basis of a *view* (Fig. 1-9) containing the part of the conceptual model which is used, possibly after a suitable transformation. This description as a view offers the benefit of precisely showing the internal structure of data and their interrelations with other data, and is an incentive to maintaining the consistency of the whole model.

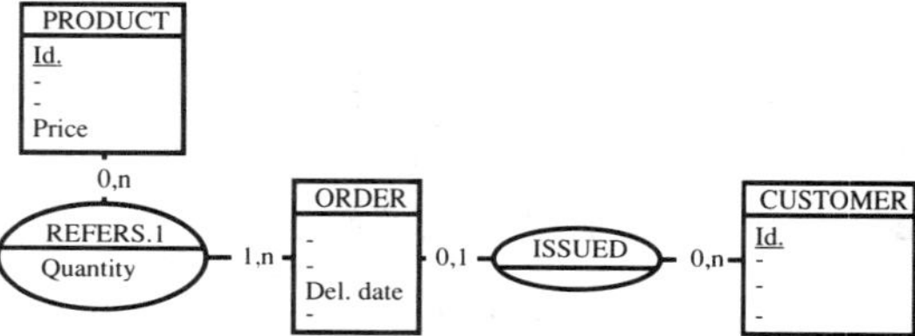

This view describes an input data flow to process Manage Orders.

Figure 1-9 Logical model: contents of a data flow.

A process may be described on the basis of an *access diagram* (Fig. 1-10) showing how it accesses stored data; and of an *action table* defining *access modules* and *procedures,* which respectively access and process data (Fig. 1-11).

1.3.3 Use of the logical model

The logical model of a system and the approach required to develop it are dealt with in Chap. 5.

Defining data flow and data store views as well as process access diagrams brings a high degree of modularity and accuracy to the logical model. While a conceptual model is static, the logical model of a system describes its dynamics. It specifies whether data are at rest or in motion. Business rules are gathered within procedures which help transform input flows into output flows.

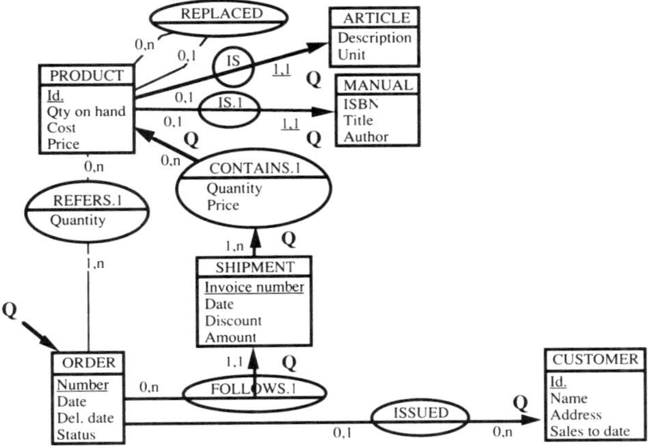

Arrows on this view show how process Query Order Shipments accesses ORDER and related CUSTOMER; SHIPMENT; CONTAINS.1, PRODUCT, ARTICLE and MANUAL.

Figure 1-10 Logical model: access diagram for a process.

MODULE	PRED.	ACC.	PROPERTY	PROCEDURE	CARD.
1 Order		Q	Number	If = Specified Number	0,1
			Date		
			Delivery date		
			Status		
1.1 Customer		Q	Id.	If ORDER ISSUED	0,1
			Name	by CUSTOMER	
			Address		
3 Shipment	1	Q	Invoice number	If SHIPMENT	0,*n*
			Date	FOLLOWS ORDER	
			Amount		
			Discount		
4 Contains.1	3	Q	(Product.Id.)	If SHIPMENT	1,*n*
			Quantity	CONTAINS PROD.	
			Price		
4.1 Product		Q	Id.	If SHIPMENT	1,1
			Price	CONTAINS PROD.	
4.2 Article		Q	Description	If PRODUCT IS	0,1
			Unit	ARTICLE	
4.3 Manual		Q	ISBN	If PRODUCT IS	0,1
			Title	MANUAL	
			Author		

This action table is based on the process access diagram (Fig. 1-10).

Figure 1-11 Logical model: action table for a process.

A system's logical model contains more information and detail than the underlying conceptual model, but it still allows different physical choices for its implementation.

1.4 The Relational Model

1.4.1 Components of the relational model

According to the relational approach, system data may be represented by *tables* containing data elements. In this book, a *relational diagram* (Fig. 1-12) also contains *links* between tables. Data elements are subject to *constraints*, which are the relational equivalent of business rules.

Some elements – or element groups – of a table may be defined as primary keys or indexes, allowing access to specific occurrences of tables. A *primary key* has its data elements underlined and points to a unique occurrence of the table. An *index* points to possibly multiple occurrences of the table it belongs to. Most indexes are in fact *foreign keys*, marked with a ¥, which are associated with links between tables.

As for system processes, following the relational approach, a significant portion of them – that is, the access modules – may be specified on the basis of a small number of primitive table operations, forming a relational language such as the *Structured Query Language (SQL)*.

1.4.2 Conversion of the entity-relationship diagram

System models prepared using the entity-relationship technique may be easily converted to relational diagrams. A table usually corresponds to an entity or a relationship, and sometimes to a group of neighboring objects. Primary keys and most indexes are defined on the basis of identifiers. The grouping of entities and relationships into tables and the choice of keys follow *derivation rules* based on the conceptual model structure. Constraints are derived from business rules.

1.4.3 Use of the relational model

The relational diagram may be used everywhere instead of the entity-relationship diagram, but it is especially useful at the physical level, since it readily translates into database definition language. The process required to develop the relational diagram is described in Chap. 6.

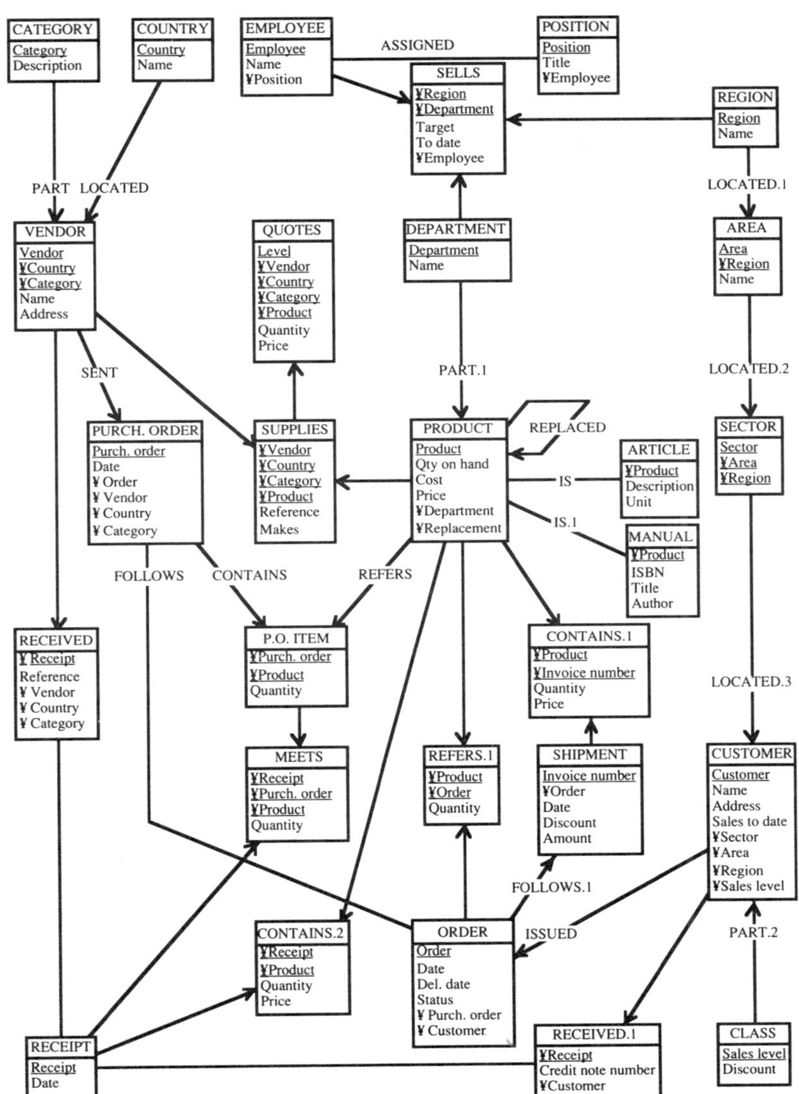

This relational diagram is derived and adapted from the Distribution of School Supplies entity-relationship diagram (Fig. 1-4). It includes:

- Tables, which more or less derive from model objects;
- Links, which more or less derive from relationship connectors.

Figure 1-12 Relational diagram: tables and links.

Relational diagrams with constraints convey in fact the same information as entity-relationship diagrams with business rules, although they are somewhat more redundant visually, due to foreign keys. Because of its more concise structure, the theory of the standard relational model – without links or constraints – is also more developed than the theory of entity-relationship models.

1.5 The Physical Model

1.5.1 Components of the physical model

On the physical level, a system may be described by *physical data flow diagrams*, similar to logical DFDs, but specifying resources used.

Likewise, physical data flow diagrams may be used to specify whether given physical data stores and data flows are manual or automated (Fig. 1-13).

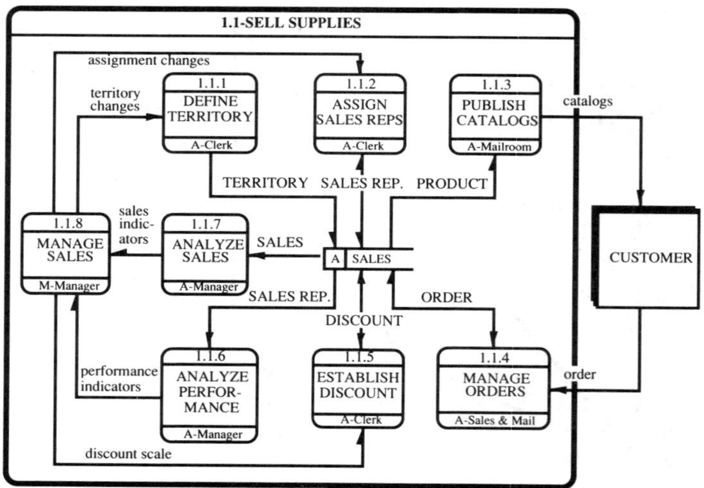

In addition to processes, data store and data flows, this physical data flow diagram shows:

- Organizational resources such as Manager, Clerk, Mail Room;
- Automated and Manual components.

Figure 1-13 Physical model: physical data flow diagram.

Thus the physical model of a system consists of physical DFDs together with specifications of their components (Fig. 1-14 and 1-15).

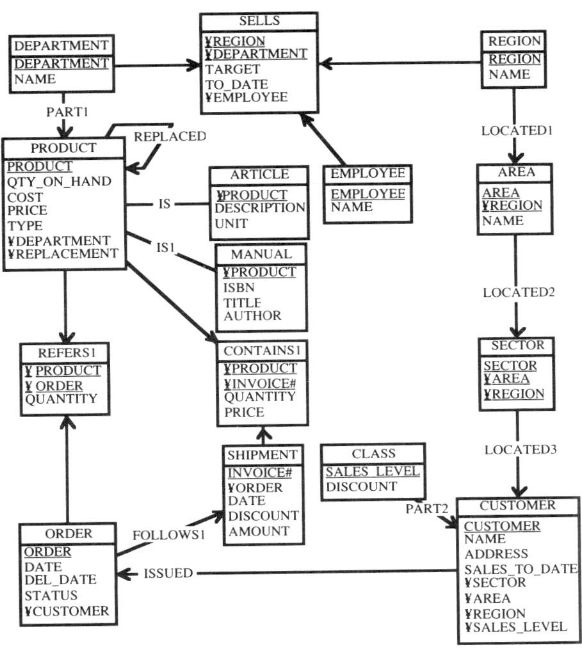

This relational diagram specifies the contents of the Sales data store.

Figure 1-14 Physical model: preliminary specification of an automated data store.

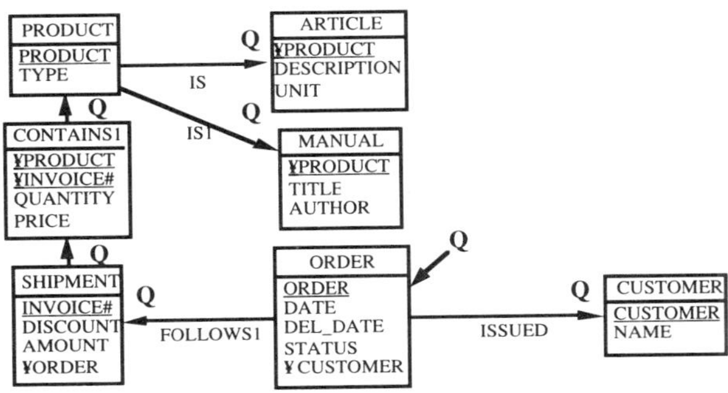

This physical access diagram helps specify the contents of Process QUERY_SHIPMENTS.

Figure 1-15 Physical model: preliminary specification of an automated process.

Automated components may be implemented based on their specifications, using a relational language (Fig. 1-16 to 1-18).

Create Table	ORDER		
	ORDER	Char (4)	
	DATE	Date	
	DEL_DATE	Date	≥ DATE + 2
	STATUS	Char (10)	= 'New', 'Back order', 'Filled'
	CUSTOMER	Char (3)	Null or in CUSTOMER table
Create Unique Index	ORDER_SEQ	On	ORDER (ORDER)
Create Index	ORDER_CUST	On	ORDER (CUSTOMER)

These statements implement the ORDER relational table using an *SQL*-like language.

Figure 1-16 Implementation of a table in an automated data store.

1.5.2 Contribution of the logical model

The logical model of a system deliberately ignores many real-world constraints. For this reason, it offers a somewhat idealized vision of the system, but one that is devoid of the complexities associated with the use of real-world resources. It permits a differentiation between two distinct issues: what the system should do, addressed by the logical level; and resources and performance, addressed by the physical level.

By breaking up the solution to this problem into two stages, this approach promotes the development of systems which suit requirements, both on the logical and physical levels.

1.5.3 Contribution of the relational model

A logical model expressed using a relational diagramming technique such as the one presented in this book may be converted more or less directly into a physical model. The conversion is easiest when a relational database, and especially a relational language, is used.

1.5.4 Use of the physical model

Chapter 7 summarily describes the physical model of a system as well as an approach to its design.

The physical model and the specifications which precisely describe its components are, in a way, the blueprints for implementing the information system.

```
Declare order module and associated screen form
Module          1_ORDER_MODULE_Q
Form            ORDER_TITLE (ORDER, DATE, DEL_DATE, STATUS,
                   CUSTOMER, NAME)
Enter order identifier
Accept From     ORDER_TITLE (ORDER)
         Values (ORDER)
On Query
Query order table
Select          DATE, DEL_DATE, STATUS
           From ORDER
          Where ORDER.ORDER = ORDER_TITLE.ORDER
If customer is specified, get customer information
If              ORDER.CUSTOMER Not Null
Select          NAME
           From CUSTOMER
          Where CUSTOMER.CUSTOMER = ORDER.CUSTOMER
EndIf
Display order title
Display Into    ORDER_TITLE
         Values (ORDER, DATE, DEL_DATE, STATUS, CUSTOMER, NAME)
EndOnQuery
Call shipment module
On Next
Call            3_SHIPMENT_MODULE_Q
EndOnNext
EndModule       1_ORDER_MODULE_Q
Declare shipment module and associated screen form
Module          3_SHIPMENT_MODULE_Q
Form            SHIPMENT_TITLE (INVOICE#, DATE, DISCOUNT, AMOUNT)
Query shipment table
Select          INVOICE#, DATE, DISCOUNT, AMOUNT
           From SHIPMENT
          Where SHIPMENT.ORDER = ORDER_TITLE.ORDER
For Each One
Display shipment title
Display Into    SHIPMENT_TITLE
         Values (INVOICE#, DATE, DISCOUNT, AMOUNT)
Call shipment detail module
On Next
Call            SHIPMENT_DETAIL_MODULE
EndOnNext
EndForEachOne
Return to order module
On Return
         Return
EndOnReturn
EndModule       3_SHIPMENT_MODULE_Q
                (Process continued)
```

These statements implement Mod. 1 and 3 of Process QUERY_SHIPMENTS.

Figure 1-17 Implementation of an automated process.

(Continuation)

```
Declare shipment detail module and associated screen form
Module          4_CONTAINS1_MODULE_Q
Form            SHIPMENT_DETAIL (PRODUCT, DESCR_TITLE,
                   UNIT_AUTHOR, PRICE, QUANTITY)
Query shipment detail table
Select          PRODUCT, QUANTITY, PRICE
           From CONTAINS1
          Where CONTAINS1.INVOICE# = SHIPMENT_TITLE.INVOICE#
For Each One
Query product table
Select          TYPE
           From PRODUCT
          Where PRODUCT.PRODUCT = CONTAINS1.PRODUCT
If product is an article, get article information and display shipment detail
If              TYPE = 'Article'
Select          DESCRIPTION, UNIT
           From ARTICLE
          Where ARTICLE.PRODUCT = PRODUCT.PRODUCT
Display Into    SHIPMENT_DETAIL
         Values (PRODUCT, DESCRIPTION, UNIT, PRICE, QUANTITY)
EndIf
If product is a manual, get manual information and display shipment detail
If              TYPE = 'Manual'
Select          TITLE, AUTHOR
           From MANUAL
          Where MANUAL.PRODUCT = PRODUCT.PRODUCT
Display Into    SHIPMENT_DETAIL
         Values (PRODUCT, TITLE, AUTHOR, PRICE, QUANTITY)
EndIf
EndForEachOne
Return to shipment module
On Return
         Return
EndOnReturn
EndModule       4_CONTAINS1_MODULE_Q
```

These statements implement Module 4 of Process QUERY_SHIPMENTS.

Process statements are derived from the process physical access diagram (Fig. 1-15), using an *SQL*-like language embedded in a procedural language.

Figure 1-18 Implementation of an automated process (continuation).

When appropriate tools are available, many components of the physical model may be directly implemented as prototypes. Prototypes may be viewed as dynamic specifications, taking the place of conventional static specifications. Sometimes, they may be enhanced and transferred to production when they are complete.

1.6 Benefits

Data driven systems modeling provides a sound, comprehensive and orderly framework for developing information systems. It yields a more efficient development process and systems which are easier to operate and to maintain.

The soundness of data driven systems modeling derives from its approach to system design and from the techniques it advocates. Systems are designed in stages, starting with a stable core and progressively adding secondary features. Modeling techniques ensure that the conceptual model satisfactorily captures the essence of a domain, and that subsequent logical and physical models suitably utilize the wealth of information present in the conceptual model.

Data driven systems modeling is comprehensive in more than one way. A data perspective promotes a comprehensive view of systems. Thus it is a most appropriate tool for investigating large scale systems integration. Data driven systems modeling also encompasses all systems development life cycle stages from higher level corporate planning to system implementation.

Data driven systems modeling provides an orderly and consistent framework throughout the systems development life cycle. The three types of models help one master systems complexity by focusing on relevant characteristics in turn, starting with the essential ones. Models are coordinated, thus providing continuity between analysis and design, and allowing one to progressively integrate the numerous requirements of a system into a common design.

A number of factors contribute to increased efficiency in the systems development process. Efforts expended in solving the most fundamental questions at the beginning facilitate subsequent stages. Models, especially graphical models, provide a common language which makes the deliverables of this process more visible, understandable and predictable, thus facilitating communications and control. Data driven models promote the modularity of systems components, thus minimizing interactions required to develop them. Lastly, model based development offers the opportunity to use *CASE* tools: their power is closely related to the level and degree of integration of the models that they support.

Systems developed using a data driven modeling approach tend to have a modular and consistent architecture. As a rule, data are stored in a manner independent of programs using them, thus favoring their re-utilization. Program design is based on the structure of the data which they access, and this brings a degree of uniformity. Interaction between data and between programs is minimized. Consequently, changes are localized and easier to implement. Users also benefit from program standardization and from the quality of documentation made possible by modeling.

PART II

The Data Foundation

The current view on information systems is that they start with data: understand the data, and you will understand the system. Part II of this book shows how one can fully understand the data foundation of systems, using a conceptual model. Chapter 2 presents a diagramming technique and related standards which can be used in documenting a conceptual model. Chapter 3 presents various ways of transforming such a model in order to obtain views, which may be used in later stages to describe the components of a system. It also presents the reverse transformations, which enable one to integrate and normalize a conceptual model. Chapter 4 describes a step-by-step approach which may be used to prepare conceptual models, within the organization's information systems development life cycle.

Chapter 2

The Conceptual Model

> When you confront a formal system you know nothing of, and if you hope to discover some hidden meaning in it, your problem is how to assign interpretations to its symbols in a meaningful way.
>
> (D. Hofstadter, *Gödel, Escher, Bach*)

This chapter presents the conceptual model. Why start with the conceptual level even though it is the most abstract one? The reason is that it is also the least complex one: the conceptual model does not call for any preliminary knowledge of information processing.

For readers already familiar with this topic, let us recall the main feature of this presentation. In addition to data, the conceptual model presented here includes all business rules which are part of the definition of data. This is a natural extension of conventional data models, and provides for a more complete and meaningful description of data. It is also in line with the trend of seeing systems as process-encapsulated data, as in the object-oriented approach.

A fully refined model is discussed here, to immediately convey to the reader the final outcome of conceptual modeling. In fact, such a model is not worked out in a single step, but is refined in stages, in which intuition is just as important as analysis. This will be explained in Chap. 4.

One last piece of advice: after completing this chapter, go back to the previous one, scrutinize the conceptual model given as an example and extract its meaning, then review the comments on its use.

2.1 Entity-Relationship Diagram

2.1.1 Definition

An *entity-relationship diagram* (Fig. 1-4) is a symbolic representation of a real-world domain (Fig. 1-5) which allows the structuring of information about categories of 'things' in the domain.

These categories are displayed as entities (rectangular boxes) and relationships (oval shaped boxes) – *objects* for short – and as properties (listed in the boxes). Objects which are connected to each other are called *neighbors*.

In the real world, and depending on how they are defined, 'things' are subject to existence conditions. Such conditions may be represented as *cardinality rules* (letters and figures on connectors of relationships); or they must be stated separately as explicit *business rules*.

In the real world, and also by selecting properties sensibly, it is possible to distinguish similar 'things' within the same category from one another. Such properties – or property groups – are called *identifiers* (underlined). Sometimes identification is done through a neighbor (underlined cardinalities on connector of relationship).

2.1.2 Modeling rules

(a) The entity-relationship diagram which represents a real-world domain usually consists of objects which are connected.

(b) The number of objects in the diagram and the number of properties are a function of the domain scope and of the precision with which it needs to be modeled.

2.1.3 Representation

The entity-relationship diagram is usually presented as a graphic, supplemented by a summary description of the domain.

2.2 Entities

2.2.1 Definition

An *entity* is a collection of similar individuals, things, facts or events which are of interest for the information system under consideration (Fig. 2-1 to 2-4).

Some entities are concrete: they denote persons or things. Some are abstract: they denote concepts, categories, more or less instantaneous events, more or less durable situations. They may denote self-standing 'things' or, on the contrary, parts of 'things' or various features of the same 'things'.

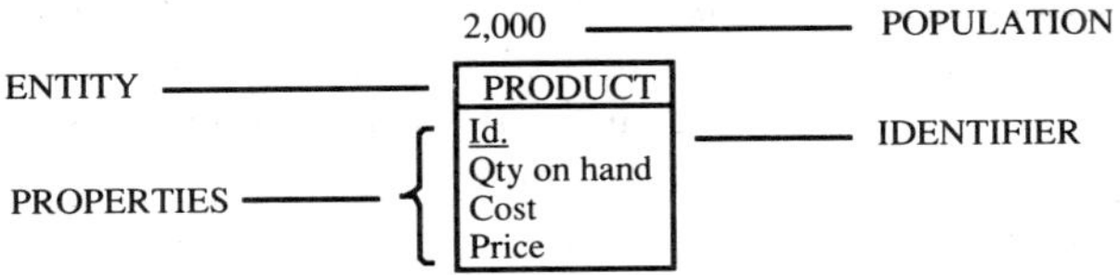

A PRODUCT, identified by an Id., has a Quantity on hand, a Cost and a Price.

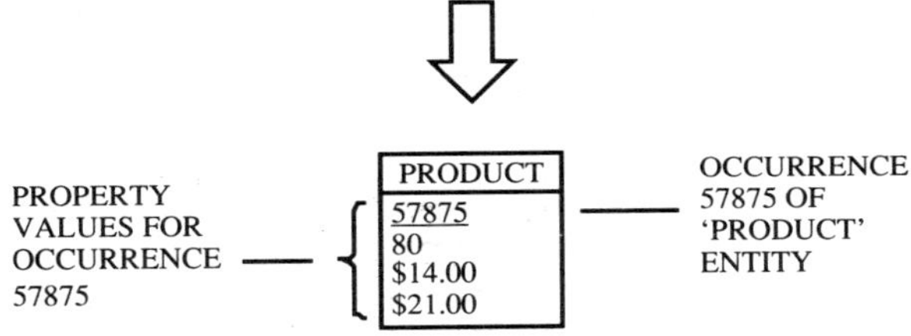

PRODUCT 57875, with a Quantity on hand of 80, has a Cost of $14.00 and a Price of $21.00.

Figure 2-1 Entity with a simple identifier.

2.2.2 Modeling rules

(a) *Occurrences* of an entity, that is, individual members of the collection represented by the entity, can be distinguished from one another and counted. The number of occurrences of an entity is called its *population*; it can be large or small, static or changing. Entities with a single occurrence are usually not represented.

(b) An entity possesses at least one property, otherwise it could not be described. Properties are common to all occurrences of the entity. More precisely, each property has a meaning for each entity occurrence and possesses a unique value.

(c) All properties of an entity are distinct from one another: there is no repetitive group of properties.

(Entities which comply with Rules (b) and (c) are said to be in *First Normal Form.*)

(d) An entity possesses an *identifier*, which consists of some of its properties – possibly including identifiers of neighboring entities. Since entity occurrences can be distinguished from one another, no two occurrences have exactly the same value for all their properties – including identifiers of neighboring entities as above. More precisely, there is a minimal group of such properties which takes different values for each entity occurrence, the identifier. It is *simple* if it consists of a single property (Fig. 2-1); *compound* if it consists of several properties (Fig. 2-2). For a given value of the identifier, it is possible to uniquely identify which specific occurrence it points to. It should be noted that the identifier makes it possible to distinguish between occurrences of the same entity; not between different entities.

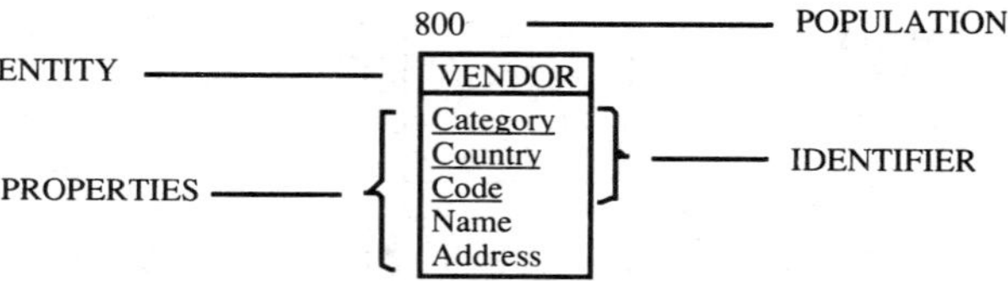

A VENDOR, identified by a Category-Country-Code combination, has a Name and an Address.

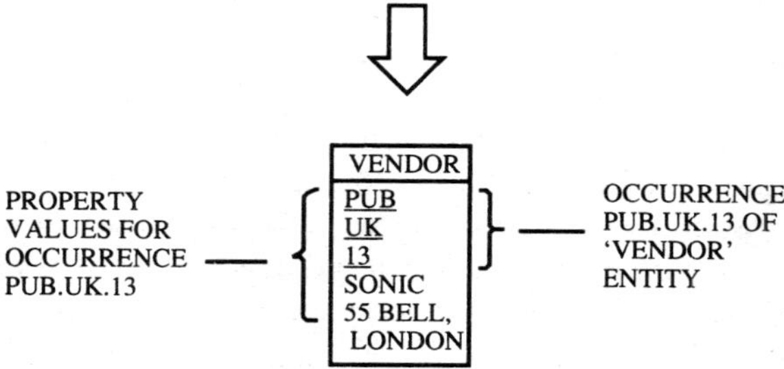

VENDOR PUB.UK.13 has Name SONIC and Address 66 BELL, LONDON.

Figure 2-2 Entity with a compound identifier.

(e) Some values of an entity identifier may not point to any occurrence of the entity. Nevertheless, when such an occurrence exists, it is unique, and the identifier value points to a unique combination of property values (Fig. 2-3). One expresses this by stating that there is a *dependency* between each entity property and the identifier, or that each property *depends* on the identifier.

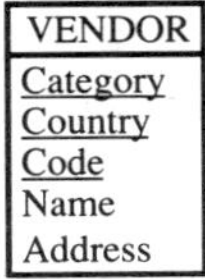

Occurrences of an entity depend only on identifier values.

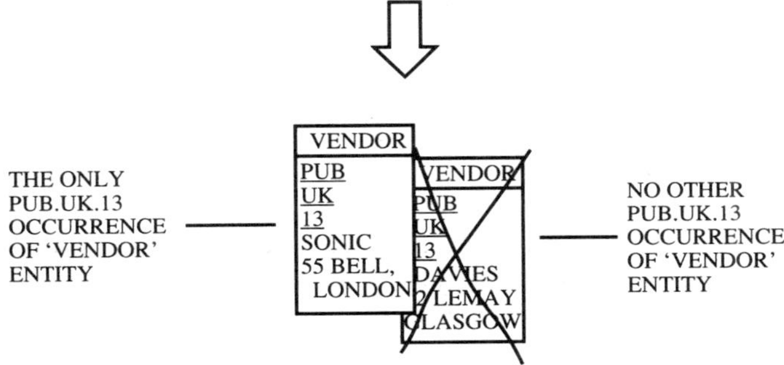

There cannot be another occurrence of VENDOR with the same PUB.UK.13 identifier value.

Figure 2-3 Entity whose occurrences depend only on identifier values.

(f) Conversely, it may easily be seen that, for each combination of property values which represents an existing entity occurrence, there is a unique occurrence of the entity and therefore a unique value of the identifier.

2.2.3 Representation

An entity is represented by a rectangular box. The title contains the name of the entity, and the body contains its properties; the properties included in the identifier are underlined. The entity population may be shown next to the box. Entity names are all different.

The graphic representation of an entity is supplemented by a definition and, if the case warrants it, by explanations which relate the entity to the context of the model, and by examples (Fig. 2-4).

ENTITY: PRODUCT

DEFINITION	A product which is included in the sales catalog.
COMMENTS	There are two product categories: articles and manuals, with different procurement rules. Only properties common to both categories are part of this entity.
EXAMPLES	The product with number 57875 and a cost of $14.00, i.e., the 'Drawing' manual, by B. Smith.

Figure 2-4 Description of an entity.

2.3 Relationships

2.3.1 Definition

A *relationship* – or *association* – is a collection of similar interactions which exist between occurrences of given entities and which are of interest for the information system under consideration (Fig. 2-5 to 2-12).

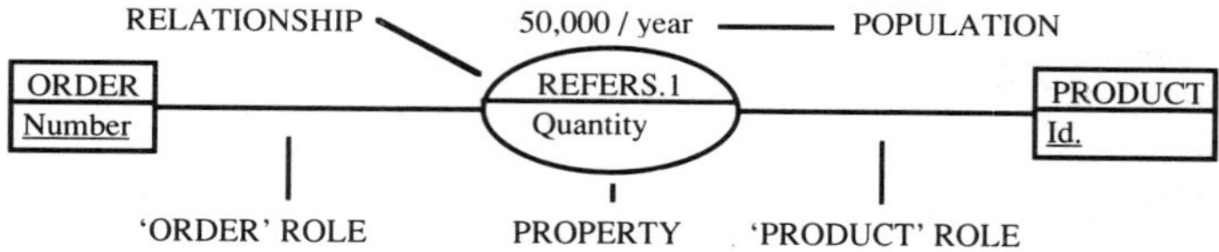

An ORDER REFERS to a Quantity of a PRODUCT.

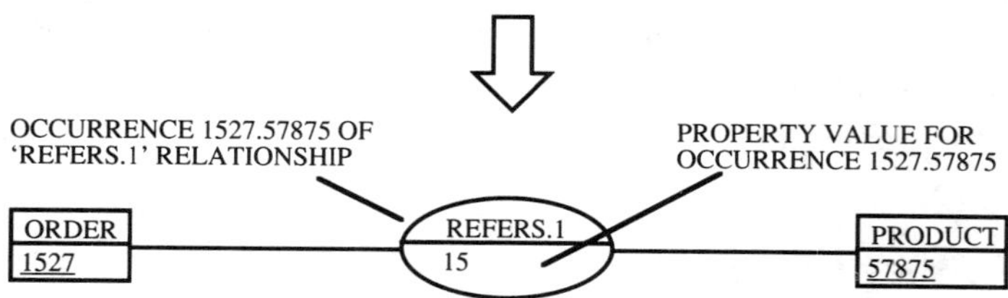

ORDER 1527 REFERS to 15 units of PRODUCT 57875.

Figure 2-5 Binary relationship.

A relationship connects two or more entities. Each of these entities is called a *participant* in the relationship; the connection with the relationship is called a *role*. A relationship with two roles is called *binary* (Fig. 2-5), one with three roles is called *ternary* (Fig. 2-6) and so on; a relationship with *n* roles is called *n-ary*.

A VENDOR QUOTES a Price for a Quantity of a PRODUCT (at some LEVEL).

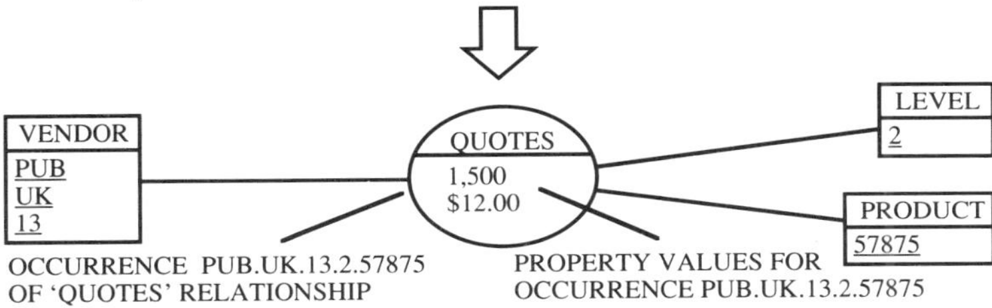

For PRODUCT 57875, VENDOR PUB.UK.13 QUOTES a Price of $12.00 for a Quantity of 1,500 (at LEVEL 2).

Figure 2-6 Ternary relationship.

An entity may participate in two or more relationships (Fig. 2-7).

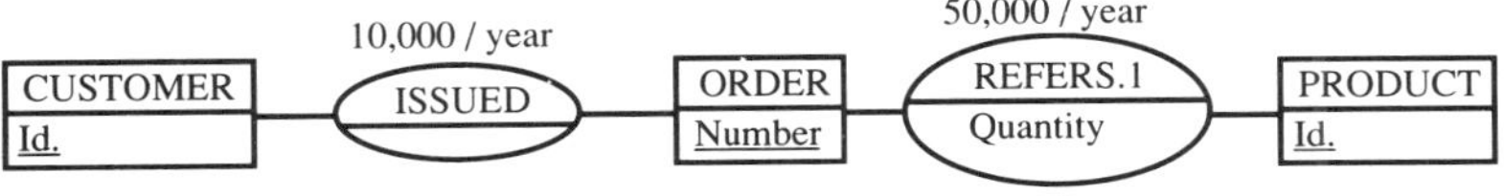

An ORDER is ISSUED by a CUSTOMER and it REFERS to a given Quantity of a PRODUCT.

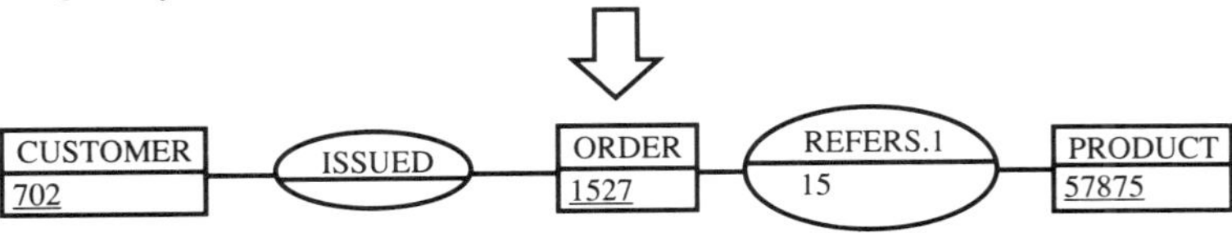

ORDER 1527 is ISSUED by CUSTOMER 702 and it REFERS to 15 units of PRODUCT 57875.

Figure 2-7 Distinct relationships with the same participating entity.

Conversely, a given relationship – called *recursive* – may have the same entity as participant more than once (Fig. 2-8); each role of the entity with respect to the relationship is distinct. Also, there may be more than one relationship between the same two entities (Fig. 2-9).

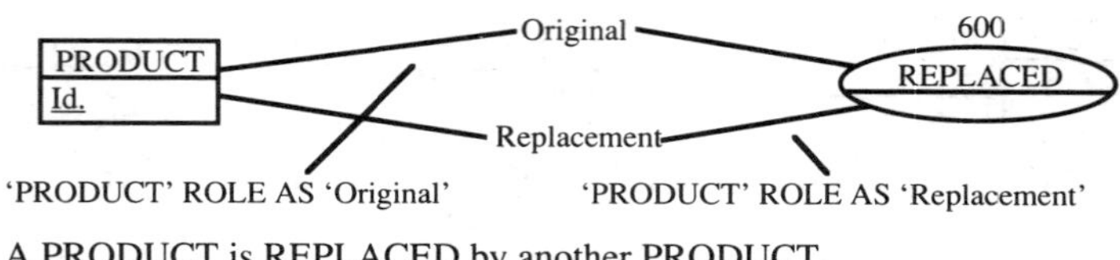

A PRODUCT is REPLACED by another PRODUCT.

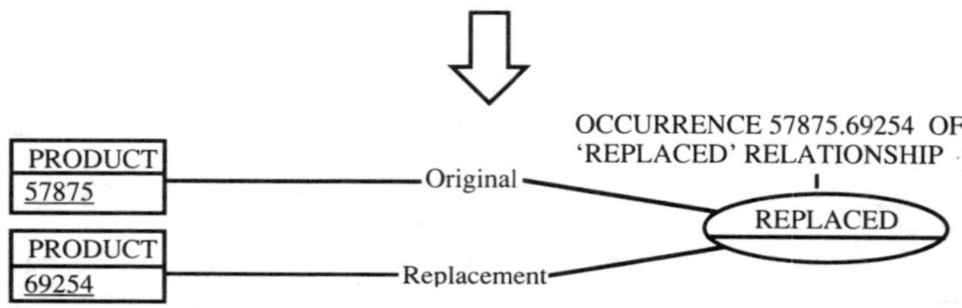

Original PRODUCT 57875 is REPLACED by Replacement PRODUCT 69254.

Figure 2-8 Recursive binary relationship.

Relationships denote more or less permanent associations between entities. They are more abstract and have different types such as: place, possession, part-whole relation, classification, exchange, etc.

2.3.2 Modeling rules

(a) *Occurrences* of a relationship, that is, individual associations from the collection that it represents, can be distinguished from one another based on occurrences of the participating entities, and they can be counted. The number of occurrences is called the relationship *population*; it can be large or small, static or changing.

(b) A relationship may possess any number of *explicit* properties, including none. In addition, each role of a relationship is considered an *implicit* (not shown) *property* of the relationship. Explicit and implicit properties are common to all occurrences of the relationship. More precisely, each explicit property has a meaning for each relationship occurrence and possesses a unique value. Similarly, each implicit property of a relationship has a meaning for each occurrence of the relationship, and points to a unique occurrence of the participating entity: its value is the value of the entity identifier for this occurrence.

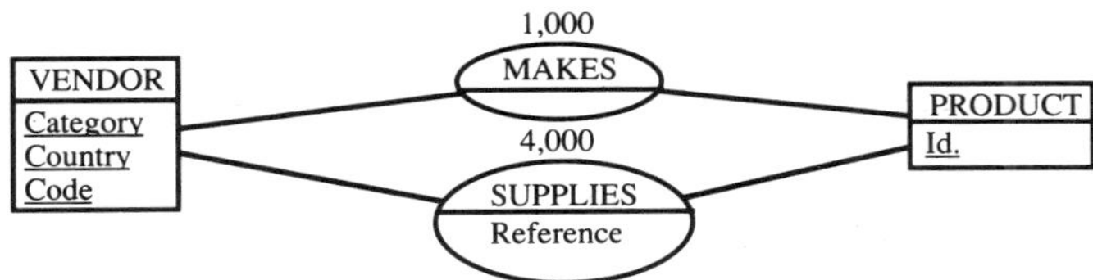

A VENDOR MAKES a PRODUCT.
A VENDOR SUPPLIES a PRODUCT under a Reference.

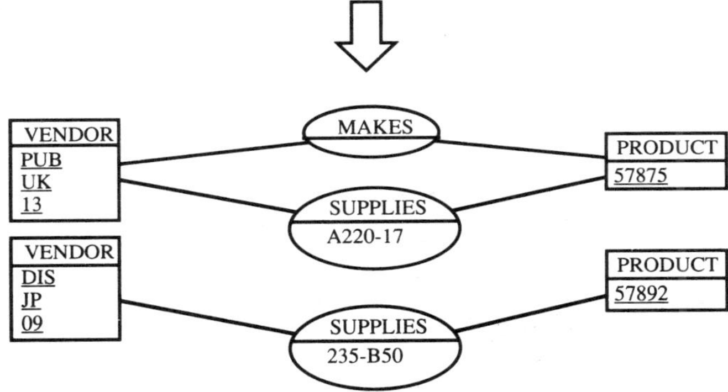

VENDOR PUB.UK.13 MAKES PRODUCT 57875 and SUPPLIES it under Reference A220-17.
VENDOR DIS.JP.09 SUPPLIES PRODUCT 57892 under Reference 235-B50 – and does not MAKE it.

Figure 2-9 Distinct relationships between two entities.

(c) All explicit and implicit properties of a relationship are distinct from one another: there is no repetitive group of properties.

(Relationships which comply with Rules (b) and (c) are said to be in *First Normal Form.*)

(d) A relationship possesses an *identifier*, which is composed of some – or all – of the identifiers of participating entities. Since relationship occurrences can be distinguished from one another based on occurrences of the participating entities, no two occurrences of the relationship have exactly the same value for all their roles.

More precisely, there is a minimal group of roles which takes different values for each relationship occurrence. This group is the relationship identifier. Some relationships possess a *simple* identifier, which consists of a single role; other relationships have a *compound* identifier, which consists of several roles. For a given value of the identifier, it is possible to precisely identify which specific occurrence it points to. It should be noted that the identifier makes it possible to distinguish between occurrences of the same relationship; not between different relationships.

(e) Some values of a relationship identifier may not point to any occurrence of the relationship. Nevertheless, when such an occurrence exists, it is unique, and the identifier value points to a unique combination of explicit and implicit property values (Fig. 2-10). One expresses this by stating that there is a *dependency* between each relationship property and the identifier.

Occurrences of relationships depend only on occurrences of participating entities.

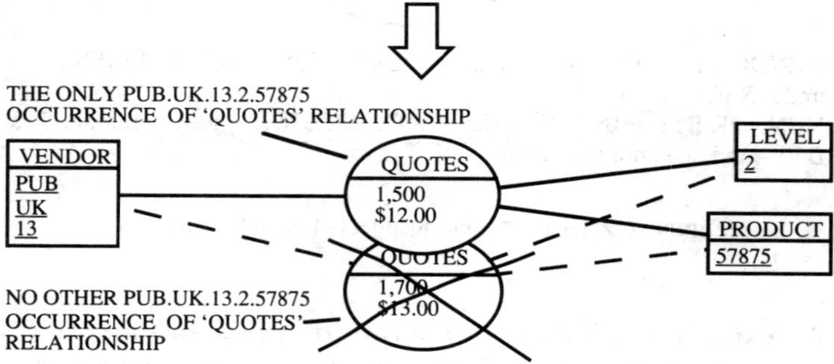

There cannot be another occurrence of QUOTES with the same occurrences of participating entities.

Figure 2-10 Relationship whose occurrences depend only on occurrences of participating entities.

(f) Conversely, it may easily be seen that, for each – implicit or explicit – combination of property values which represents an existing relationship occurrence, there is a unique occurrence of the entity and therefore a unique value of the identifier. However, this is not true for the explicit properties alone: two distinct occurrences of the relationship may have exactly the same values for these properties.

It is interesting to compare Rules (a) to (f) for entities in Sec. 2.2.2 and for relationships in Sec. 2.3.2. Entities are often self-standing, that is, first-order objects, whereas relationships are objects whose existence depends on the existence of two or more entities, that is, higher-order objects. Putting this difference aside, the same rules apply. This point is emphasized in the section on identifiers.

2.3.3 Representation

A relationship is represented by an oval shaped box linked by *connectors* to participating entities. Each connector corresponds to a different role of the relationship. The title contains the name of the relationship – usually a verb – and the body contains its explicit properties.

An arrow may be drawn near the relationship name to help decide in which direction the sentence corresponding to the relationship should be read. However this arrow does not denote a preferred direction: the relationship may be stated in a different way and a sentence may be read in the opposite direction (Fig. 2-11); it is still the same relationship.

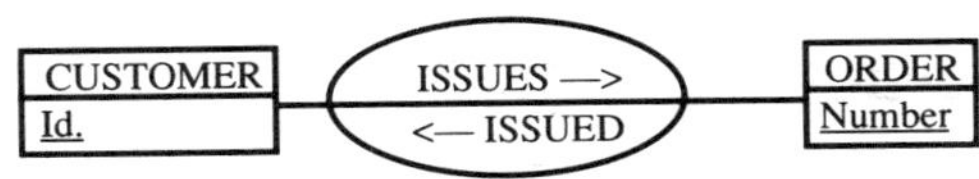

A CUSTOMER ISSUES an ORDER <=>
An ORDER is ISSUED by a CUSTOMER.

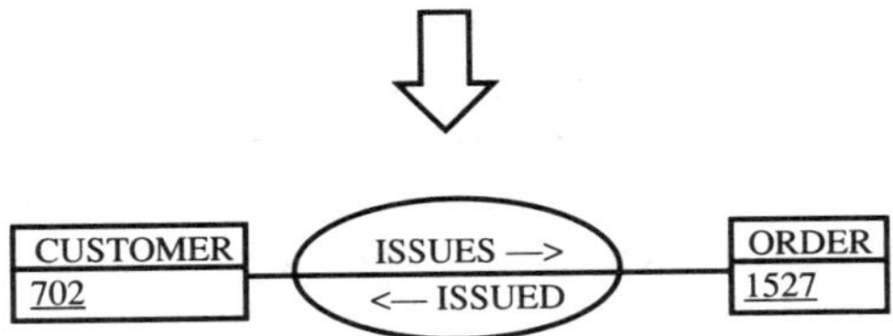

CUSTOMER 702 ISSUES ORDER 1527 <=>
ORDER 1527 is ISSUED by CUSTOMER 702.

Figure 2-11 Identical relationship stated in two different ways.

When distinct relationships are expressed using the same verb, they may be distinguished by adding distinct suffixes.

The roles of a relationship may be named and the names shown along the corresponding connectors; this is especially useful when the relationship has two roles involving the same entity.

The population of the relationship may be shown next to the box representing it.

The graphic representation of a relationship is supplemented by a definition if the case warrants it, by explanations which relate the relationship to the context of the model, and by examples (Fig. 2-12).

RELATIONSHIP: SUPPLIES

STATEMENT	A vendor supplies a product. A product is supplied by a vendor.
DEFINITION	A vendor who 'supplies' a product is a vendor which has been qualified to supply the particular product. As a result, buyers are authorized to procure the product from the vendor.
COMMENTS	This relationship is not to be confused with the 'makes' relationship. A vendor may supply a product without making it.
EXAMPLES	SONIC supplies product 57875, a manual entitled 'Drawing', by B. Smith.

Figure 2-12 Description of a relationship.

2.4 Properties

2.4.1 Definition

A *property* – or *attribute* – is a piece of information about the description of an entity or a relationship (Fig. 2-13 to 2-17).

A property which is listed in the body of an object is called *explicit*. Objects may also be considered as acquiring *implicit* properties through their connections with neighboring entities. Thus it has been seen that, for a relationship, each role may be considered an implicit property. It will also be shown that entities may acquire implicit properties through parent-child relationships.

A property denotes a collection of permissible cases, which is called its *domain* (Fig. 2-13); each individual case is called a *value* of the property.

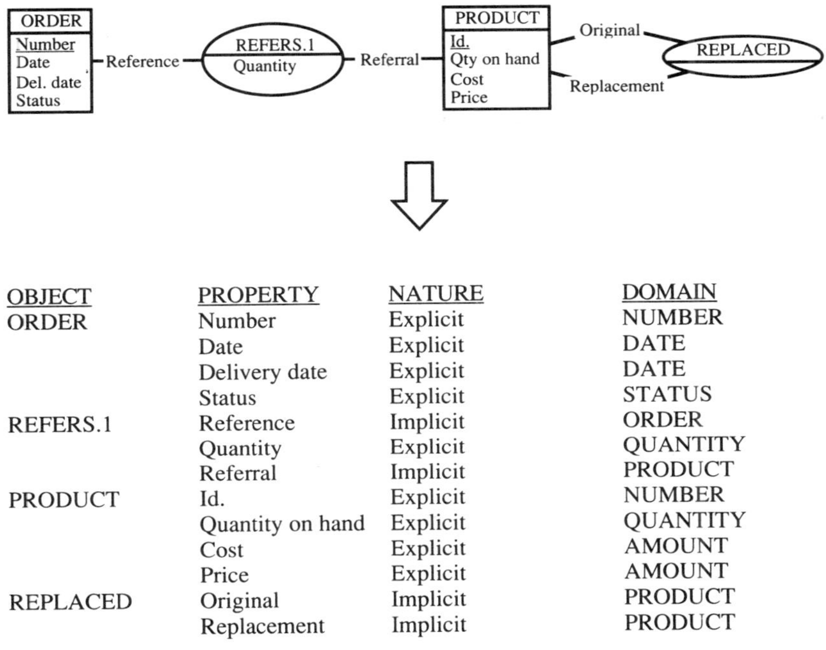

OBJECT	PROPERTY	NATURE	DOMAIN
ORDER	Number	Explicit	NUMBER
	Date	Explicit	DATE
	Delivery date	Explicit	DATE
	Status	Explicit	STATUS
REFERS.1	Reference	Implicit	ORDER
	Quantity	Explicit	QUANTITY
	Referral	Implicit	PRODUCT
PRODUCT	Id.	Explicit	NUMBER
	Quantity on hand	Explicit	QUANTITY
	Cost	Explicit	AMOUNT
	Price	Explicit	AMOUNT
REPLACED	Original	Implicit	PRODUCT
	Replacement	Implicit	PRODUCT

Figure 2-13 Entity and relationship properties.

In fact, a domain may be considered an entity in its own right; its occurrences are the values being distinguished and its population is the – often unlimited – number of such values (Fig. 2-14). Indeed, a domain complies with all the modeling rules pertaining to entities.

As a consequence, a property may be considered an association between an object of the model and a domain, that is, a shorthand for a particular type of relationship.

A property defined on a single domain is called *elementary*. In some cases, one is led to view a group of properties of a given object as a new *compound* property (Fig. 2-15). The domain of a compound property is obtained by combining the domains of each property in the group.

2.4.2 Modeling rules

The following rules apply to explicit as well as implicit properties.

(a) A domain – and consequently a property – possesses at least two distinct values; otherwise, it would not carry any information.

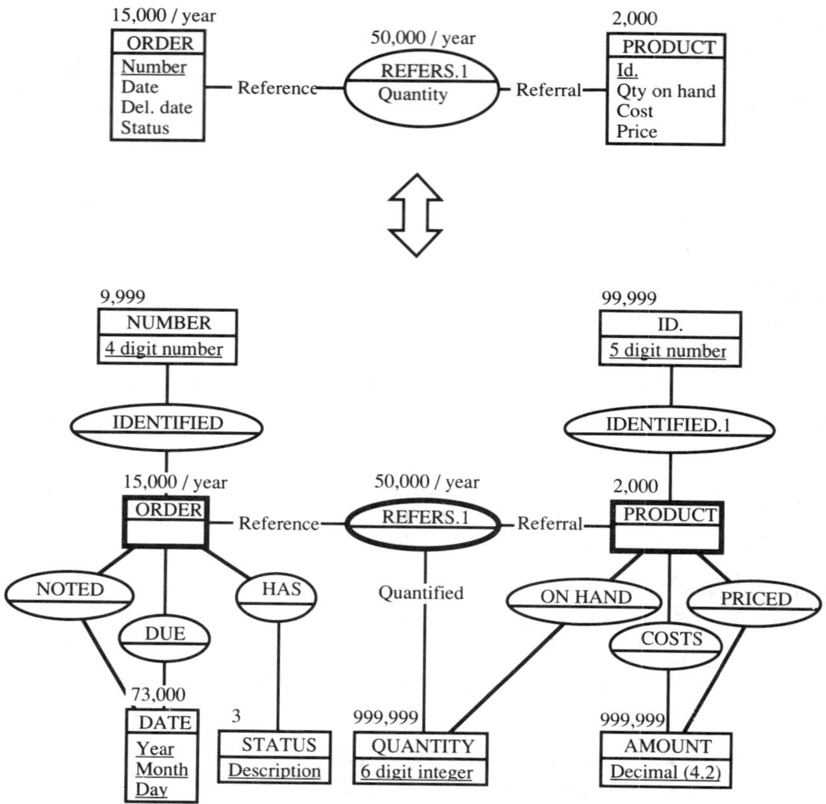

In the entity ORDER, Date and Delivery date share the domain DATE:
—> They are distinguished by the qualifier 'Delivery'.

In the relationship REFERS.1 and the entity PRODUCT, Quantity and Quantity on hand share the domain QUANTITY:
—> They belong to different objects and would not need a qualifier to be distinguished. Their full names are REFERS.1.Quantity and PRODUCT.Quantity on hand.

Figure 2-14 Distinct properties with the same domains.

(b) All properties of an object are distinct from one another. They often have distinct domains. When they have the same domain, they denote distinct ways of associating the object with the domain.

(c) Properties of distinct objects are distinct from one another. Even though some might have the same domain, they denote associations with distinct objects.

2.4.3 Representation

A property is usually named for its domain. Properties with the same domain generally use the same name. However, when two properties of the same entity have the same domain, it is best to distinguish them by adding a suitable qualifier.

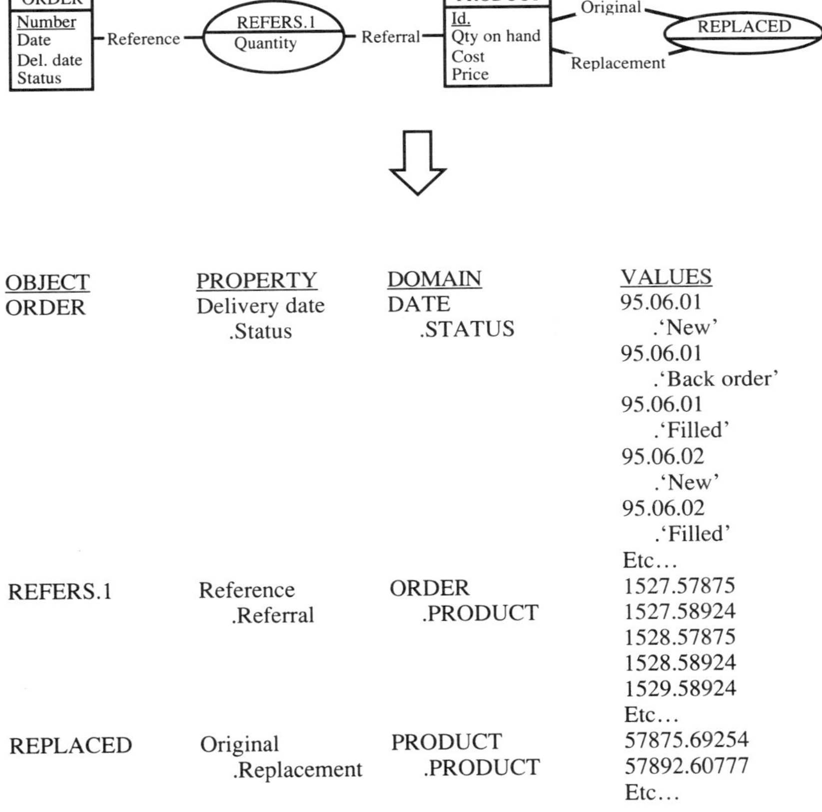

OBJECT	PROPERTY	DOMAIN	VALUES
ORDER	Delivery date .Status	DATE .STATUS	95.06.01 .'New' 95.06.01 .'Back order' 95.06.01 .'Filled' 95.06.02 .'New' 95.06.02 .'Filled' Etc...
REFERS.1	Reference .Referral	ORDER .PRODUCT	1527.57875 1527.58924 1528.57875 1528.58924 1529.58924 Etc...
REPLACED	Original .Replacement	PRODUCT .PRODUCT	57875.69254 57892.60777 Etc...

Figure 2-15 Compound properties.

When the context requires it, properties of distinct objects with the same domain may be distinguished by prefixing them with the object name.

The name of an explicit property is listed in the body of the object to which it belongs. It is usually not necessary to represent the domain of the property as a separate entity.

The name of an implicit property does not have to be written in the body of the object. When it is necessary to use a name, it may be formed in the same way as for an explicit property: for a relationship, it is the name of the participating entity, possibly qualified by its role in the relationship; for a child entity, it is the name of the parent entity, possibly qualified by the name of the relationship.

The graphic representation of the properties of an object is supplemented by definitions and, if the case warrants it, by explanations and examples (Fig. 2-16 and 2-17).

ENTITY: ORDER

PROPERTY	DEFINITION
Number	A sequential number assigned to the order as it is registered.
Date	The date on which the order is registered.
Delivery date	The date on which the customer expects the order to be delivered.
Status	Indicates whether a delivery has taken place or not, and if there is a back order.

Figure 2-16 Description of the explicit properties of an entity.

RELATIONSHIP: SUPPLIES

PROPERTY	DEFINITION
Reference	Code assigned to a product by a vendor and shown in its catalog.

Figure 2-17 Description of the explicit property of a relationship.

2.5 Cardinality Rules

2.5.1 Definition

A *cardinality rule* (Fig. 2-18 to 2-28) is a business rule which applies to a relationship role: such a rule states how many occurrences of the relationship are permissible for a given occurrence of the participating entity.

A cardinality rule states the permissible lower and upper limits for the relationship role, that is, usually:

- 0 or 1 for the lower limit;
- 1 or *n* – no limit – for the upper limit.

These limits are called the *minimum* and *maximum cardinalities* – or *connectivities* – of the role.

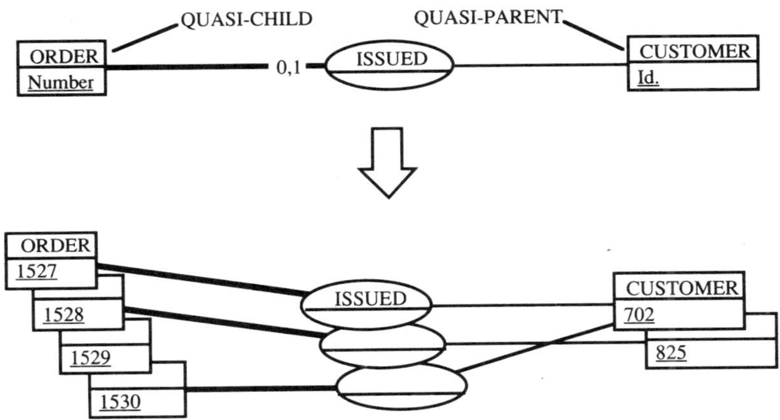

For 1 occurrence of ORDER:
—> 0 or 1 occurrence of CUSTOMER.

Figure 2-18 Cardinalities 0,1: quasi parent-child relationship.

Sometimes it is useful to consider the role *average cardinality*, that is, the average number of occurrences of the relationship in which an occurrence of the entity participates. Similarly, the role *maximal cardinality* is the practical limit on the number of occurrences of the relationship in which an occurrence of the entity may participate.

Cardinalities are essential components of a conceptual model: they contribute significantly to understanding the meaning of model objects, by stating existence conditions on their occurrences.

2.5.2 Modeling rules

(a) Each role is assigned two cardinalities usually combined as follows: 0,1; 1,1; 1,*n*; or 0,*n*.

(b) The 0,1 combination (Fig. 2-18) denotes an optional unique role: an occurrence of the participating entity may participate in a unique occurrence of the relationship, and possibly none.

(c) The 1,1 combination (Fig. 2-19) denotes a mandatory unique role: an occurrence of the participating entity must participate in exactly one occurrence of the relationship.

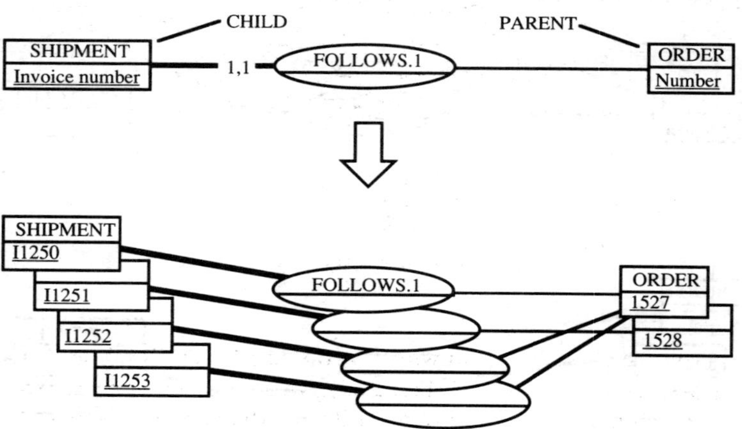

For 1 occurrence of SHIPMENT:
—> 1 occurrence of ORDER.

Through this parent-child relationship, SHIPMENT, the child entity, implicitly acquires the ORDER.Number property, with domain the ORDER entity.

Figure 2-19 Cardinalities 1,1: parent-child relationship.

(d) The 1,n combination (Fig. 2-20) denotes a mandatory multiple role: an occurrence of the participating entity must participate in at least one occurrence of the relationship, and possibly more.

(e) The 0,n combination (Fig. 2-21) denotes an optional multiple role: an occurrence of the participating entity may participate in any number of relationship occurrences, and possibly none.

(f) A given relationship may display any combination of cardinalities for its roles: thus, all combinations of 0,1; 1,1; 1,n; or 0,n cardinalities are permissible.

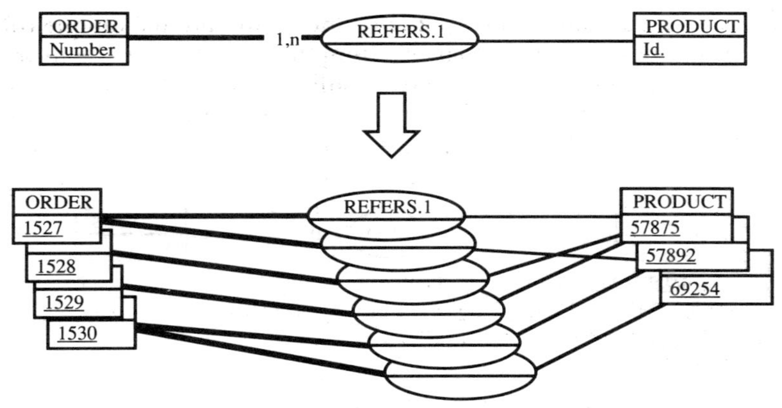

For 1 occurrence of ORDER:
—> 1 to *n* occurrences of REFERS.1;
—> 1 to *n* occurrences of PRODUCT.

Figure 2-20 Cardinalities 1,*n*.

(g) A binary relationship in which a role has 1,1 cardinalities is called a *parent-child relationship* (Fig. 2-19). In such a relationship, the entity with the 1,1 role is a *child,* and the other one is a *parent.*

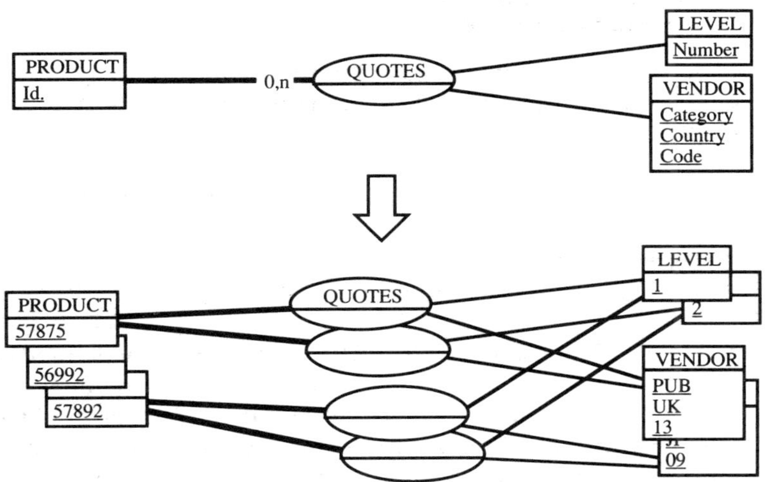

For 1 occurrence of PRODUCT:
—> 0 to *n* occurrences of QUOTES.

Figure 2-21 Cardinalities 0,*n*.

(h) The relationship between an object and the domain of one of its properties is a parent-child relationship; the domain is the parent, and the object is the child (Fig. 2-22). Similarly, the child of a parent-child relationship acquires an implicit property, with the parent as the domain (Fig. 2-19).

An ORDER has a unique STATUS;
For a given STATUS, there is any number of ORDERS.

Figure 2-22 Cardinalities of the relationship between an object and the domain of a property of the object.

(i) Similarly, a binary relationship in which a role has 0,1 cardinalities is called a *quasi parent-child relationship* (Fig. 2-18). In such a relationship, the entity with the 0,1 role is a *quasi-child,* and the other entity is a *quasi-parent.* The quasi-parent cannot be an implicit property of the quasi-child since it would be optional.

(j) A binary relationship with 0,1–0,1 cardinalities is an *optional assignment* relationship (Fig. 2-23): each occurrence of an entity is assigned one occurrence of the other entity or none, and vice versa. Each participant is a quasi-child – or quasi-parent.

A PURCHASE ORDER may FOLLOW a unique ORDER;
An ORDER may be FOLLOWED by a unique PURCHASE ORDER.

Figure 2-23 Cardinalities of an optional assignment relationship.

(k) A binary relationship with 0,1–1,1 cardinalities is a *semi-mandatory assignment* relationship (Fig. 2-24): each occurrence of the first entity is assigned one occurrence of the other entity or none, and each occurrence of the second entity is assigned exactly one occurrence of the first entity. The first entity is a quasi-child – or parent. The second entity is a child – or quasi-parent.

(l) The relationship between an object and the domain of its identifier is a 0,1–1,1 relationship (Fig. 2-25).

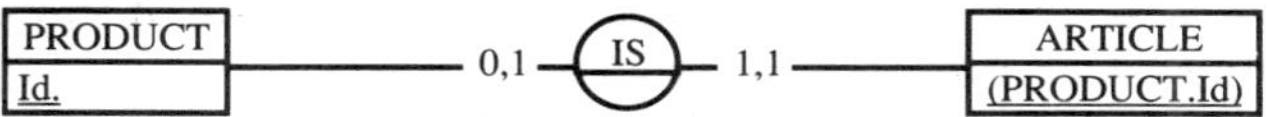

A PRODUCT may BE a unique ARTICLE;
An ARTICLE IS a unique PRODUCT.

NOTE: The identifier of ARTICLE is the implicit property PRODUCT.Id., acquired through IS, a parent-child relationship.

Figure 2-24 Cardinalities of a semi-mandatory assignment relationship.

An ORDER is IDENTIFIED through a unique NUMBER;
A NUMBER may IDENTIFY a unique ORDER.

Figure 2-25 Cardinalities of the relationship between an object and the domain of its identifier.

(m) A binary relationship with 1,1–1,1 cardinalities is a *mandatory assignment* relationship (Fig. 2-26): each occurrence of an entity is assigned exactly one occurrence of the other entity, and vice versa. Each participant is a child – or parent.

An EMPLOYEE is ASSIGNED a unique POSITION;
A POSITION is ASSIGNED to a unique EMPLOYEE.

Figure 2-26 Cardinalities of a mandatory assignment relationship.

(n) The average cardinality of a role (Fig. 2-27) is obtained by dividing the population of the relationship into the population of the entity.

2.5.3 Representation

Cardinalities are shown along the connector to which they apply. The cardinality rule may be stated by expressing that the participating entity:

- may participate in the relationship once or not at all – 0,1 cardinalities;
- participates in the relationship once – 1,1 cardinalities;
- participates in the relationship once or more – 1,*n* cardinalities;
- may participate in the relationship many times or not at all – 0,*n* cardinalities.

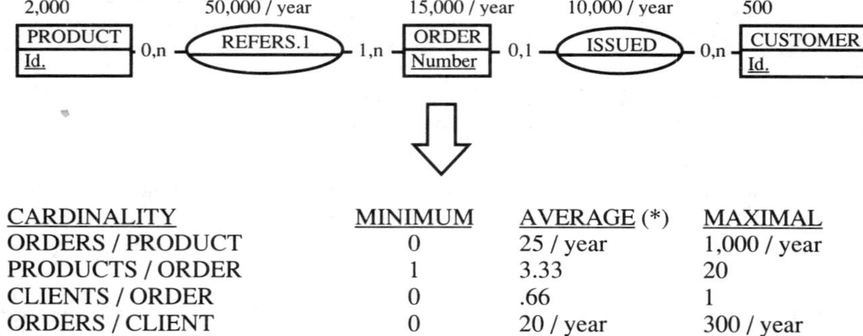

CARDINALITY	MINIMUM	AVERAGE (*)	MAXIMAL
ORDERS / PRODUCT	0	25 / year	1,000 / year
PRODUCTS / ORDER	1	3.33	20
CLIENTS / ORDER	0	.66	1
ORDERS / CLIENT	0	20 / year	300 / year

(*) Average cardinality = Relationship population / Entity population.

Figure 2-27 Minimum, average and maximal cardinalities.

Cardinalities are explained in the definition of participants in relationships (Fig. 2-28).

RELATIONSHIP: SUPPLIES

PARTICIPANT	CARDINALITY	
VENDOR	0	A vendor may supply no product at all: it has been identified to the company but none of its products have yet been recognized as acceptable.
	n	A vendor may supply several products.
PRODUCT	1	It is company's policy that every product has at least one recognized vendor who supplies it on a regular basis.
	n	It is company's policy that a product may have several recognized vendors.

Figure 2-28 Definition of participants and cardinalities for a relationship.

2.6 Explicit Business Rules

2.6.1 Definition

An *explicit business rule* is a rule which specifies existence conditions for the objects of the conceptual model and permissible values for properties (Fig. 2-29 to 2-32), and which is not expressed by the model structure, or by cardinality rules.

Explicit business rules add very valuable information, which is required for a full understanding of the meaning of the conceptual model, and which can be used to draw inferences about the possible implementations of the model.

OBJECT	PROPERTY	BUSINESS RULE
ORDER	Number	4 digit number
	Date	Year.Month.Day
	Delivery date	Year.Month.Day
	Status	'New', 'Back order', 'Filled'
REFERS.1	Quantity	6 digit integer
PRODUCT	Id.	5 digit number
	Quantity on hand	6 digit integer
	Cost	4 digit, 2 decimal amount
	Price	4 digit, 2 decimal amount
ETC...		

Figure 2-29 Domain rules.

Business rules may be more or less complex. For convenience, one may distinguish between:

- *domain rules*, which apply to individual properties;
- *integrity* and *calculation rules*, which apply to several properties of the same object, or of distinct objects; and
- *existence rules*, which apply to objects themselves.

2.6.2 Modeling rules

(a) A *domain rule* (Fig. 2-29) applies to a specific property, and states its collection of permissible values. Each property in a model is subject to such a rule. It can be expressed either by stating the conditions which the property must comply with, or by the list of permissible values.

(b) An *integrity rule* (Fig. 2-30) applies to two properties or more, and states the permissible combination of values for these properties. Such a rule may individually apply to each occurrence of an object, or it may simultaneously apply to several occurrences of the object, or all of them, or else to occurrences of distinct objects.

OBJECT	PROPERTY	BUSINESS RULE
PRODUCT	Price	≥ Cost x (1 + Profit rate)
ORDER	Delivery date	≥ Current date + 2 days
QUOTES	Quantity	Increases with LEVEL
	Price	Decreases with LEVEL for a PRODUCT.VENDOR combination
FOLLOWS	P.O. Date	PURCH. ORDER FOLLOWS an ORDER => P.O. date ≥ ORDER Date
ETC...		

Figure 2-30 Integrity rules.

(c) A *calculation rule* (Fig. 2-31) is a special kind of integrity rule: it expresses the fact that the value of some property is based on the values of other properties. Such a rule may introduce a dependency between the calculated value and the property values used for the calculation.

OBJECT	PROPERTY	BUSINESS RULE
CONTAINS.1	Quantity	= Max (Old Quantity on hand, REFERS.1.Quantity for ORDER - Sum of CONTAINS.1.Quantities for SHIPMENTS FOLLOWING ORDER)
	Price	= PRODUCT.Price (at time of shipping)
PRODUCT	Quantity on hand	= Old Qty on hand - CONTAINS.1.Quantity
and SHIPMENT	Amount	= Sum of (Qties x Prices) for SHIPMENT
(when preparing a shipment)	Discount	= CLASS.Discount for CUSTOMER CLASS x Amount
REPLACED (when entering an order)		PRODUCT.Qty on hand = 0 => A Replacement PRODUCT is proposed to the customer, if it is acceptable
ETC...		

Figure 2-31 Calculation rules.

(d) An *existence rule* (Fig. 2-32) applies to one object or more, and states under which conditions their occurrences may or must co-exist. It is usually expressed as a logical condition: exclusion, implication, equivalence, etc.

OBJECT	PROPERTY	BUSINESS RULE
PRODUCT		A PRODUCT IS either an ARTICLE or a MANUAL (Exclusion)
MAKES and SUPPLIES		VENDOR MAKES PRODUCT => VENDOR SUPPLIES PRODUCT (Implication)
PART.2		A CUSTOMER IS PART of the CLASS corresponding to its Sales last year (Implication)
ORDER	Status	No SHIPMENTS FOLLOW the ORDER <=> Status = 'New' Sum of Quantities CONTAINED in SHIPMENTS FOLLOWING the ORDER = Quantity REFERRED TO in ORDER (for each PRODUCT) <=> Status = 'Filled' Otherwise <=> Status = 'Back order' (Equivalence rule: definition of derived property Status)
*HAS SALES		DEPARTMENT *HAS SALES in REGION <=> In the current year there are SHIPMENTS CONTAINING DEPARTMENT PRODUCTS FOLLOWING ORDERS ISSUED by CUSTOMERS LOCATED in REGION (Equivalence rule: definition of derived relationship *HAS SALES)
	*Sales to date	= Sum of corresponding (Quantities x Prices)
SELLS		There is a unique EMPLOYEE who SELLS products of a DEPT in a given REGION (Dependency rule: dependency of EMPLOYEE on the DEPARTMENT .REGION combination)
P.O. ITEM		There is a unique PURCHASE ORDER ITEM for a given PURCHASE ORDER and PRODUCT (Dependency rule: dependency of P.O. ITEM on the PURCHASE ORDER .PRODUCT combination)
ETC ...		

Figure 2-32 Existence rules.

(e) In the same way that a calculation rule provides a definition for the value of a new property, based on the values of other properties, an *equivalence rule* (Fig. 2-32) is an existence rule which provides a definition for the occurrence of a newly derived property or object, based on occurrences of other objects (Fig. 2-33).

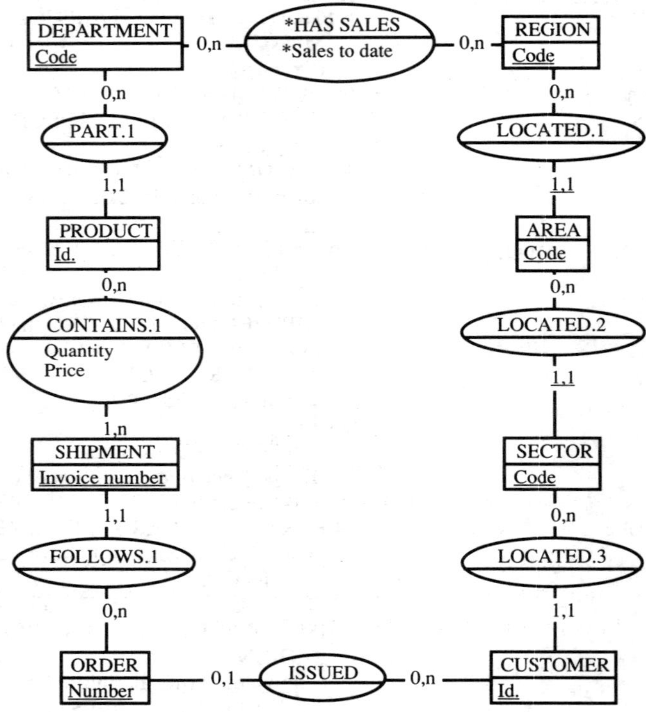

<u>EQUIVALENCE RULE</u>:
DEPARTMENT *HAS SALES in REGION
<=> In the current year, there are SHIPMENTS CONTAINING DEPARTMENT PRODUCTS FOLLOWING ORDERS ISSUED by CUSTOMERS LOCATED in the REGION.

<u>CALCULATION RULE</u>:
*Sales to date = Sum of corresponding (Quantities x Prices).

Derived relationship *HAS SALES is defined through an equivalence rule.
Derived property is obtained through a calculation rule.

Figure 2-33 Derived relationship defined through an equivalence rule.

(f) An explicit *dependency rule* (Fig. 2-32) is a special kind of existence rule which applies to an object and states that it depends on a combination of other objects, usually achieved through a relationship (Fig. 2-34) or through identifiers (Fig. 2-45).

'In charge' DEPENDENCY RULE:
For 1 occurrence of DEPARTMENT.REGION:
—> 1 occurrence of EMPLOYEE.

The name of the dependency rule is entered along the relationship connectors. It is underlined for the independent participants.

Figure 2-34 Relationship with a dependency rule.

2.6.3 Representation

Explicit business rules are presented separately from the diagram. They may be expressed in various ways: statements, mathematical formulas, logical conditions, decision tables, *IF-THEN* rules, etc. They may be linked to objects and properties which are verified, calculated or derived using these rules.

Simple rules, such as exclusion rules or dependency rules, are sometimes expressed directly in diagrams using special symbols. Calculated properties and objects may be marked with an asterisk.

2.7 Identifiers

2.7.1 Definition

According to definitions pertaining to entities and relationships (Sec. 2.2.2 and 2.3.2, Rules (d) to (f)), the *identifier* of an object in the conceptual model is a minimal group of properties of the object, the values of which make it possible to distinguish occurrences of the object (Fig. 2-35 to 2-54).

Identifiers are a fundamental component of a conceptual model. They completely determine the structure of the model: in fact, the values of all properties in the model depend only on the values of identifiers, within the limits stated by cardinality rules and explicit business rules.

Modeling rules stated in the above-mentioned sections in connection with identifiers of objects of the conceptual model are gathered here under Rule (a), the so-called First Normal Form. They are supplemented by Rules (b) to (d), the so-called Second, Third and Boyce-Codd Normal Forms. These rules – the *normalization rules* – as well as other more refined rules not mentioned here, were named by their inventor, E.F. Codd. They help represent a given real-world domain in a stable way, independent of the way the representation is to be used.

Other rules – the *construction rules* for identifiers – make it possible to build identifiers, based on existing identifiers and dependencies.

2.7.2 Modeling rules

Normalization rules

(a) Every object possesses an identifier such that, for each value of the identifier, there is at most one occurrence of the object; this occurrence has a unique value for each of its properties. Objects complying with Rule (a) are said to be in *First Normal Form.*

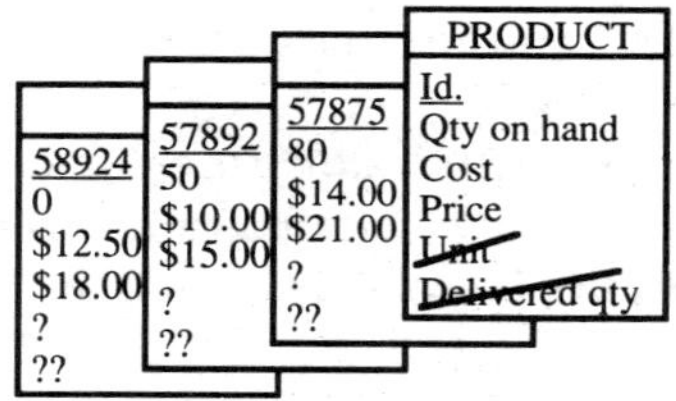

For 1 permissible value of Id.:
—> 1 occurrence of PRODUCT;
—> 1 value of each property.

For example:
57875 —> 57875, 80, $14.00, $21.00;
57900 —> Nothing;
58924 —> 58924, 0, $12.50, $18.00.

Unit, an optional property, is excluded.
Delivered quantity, a repetitive property, is excluded.

Figure 2-35 Entity with a simple identifier.

The identifier of an entity may be simple (Fig. 2-35) or compound (Fig. 2-36). It may be composed of explicit or implicit properties. Sometimes an entity may have additional identifiers:

in such a case, there is a one-to-one mapping between t.. identifier and *alternate* identifiers (Fig. 2-37).

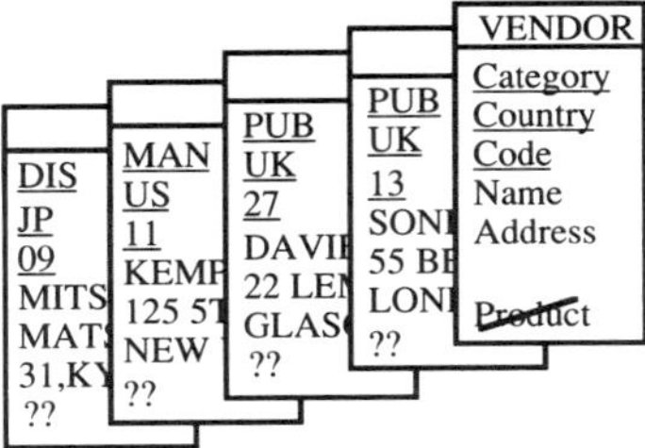

For 1 permissible combination of values of Category, Country, Code:
—> 1 occurrence of VENDOR;
—> 1 value of each property.

For example:
PUB.UK.27 —> PUB, UK, 27, DAVIES, 22 LEMAY GLASGOW;
PUB.UK.28 —> Nothing;
MAN.US.10 —> Nothing;
MAN.US.11 —> MAN, US, 11, KEMPF, 125 5TH AVE NEW YORK.

Product, a repetitive property, is excluded.

Figure 2-36 Entity with a compound identifier.

MANUAL
PRODUCT.Id.
ISBN (alt.)
Title
Author
57875
1-225-8
DRAW
SMITH
57892
1-523-9
PAINT
ZONG

The identifier of MANUAL is PRODUCT.Id.
Another identifier is the International Standard Book Number (ISBN).

For 1 value of PRODUCT.Id. identifying a MANUAL
<—> 1 value of ISBN, and vice versa.

For example:
57875 <—> 1-225-81203-9;
57892 <—> 1-523-92304-1.

Figure 2-37 Entity with an alternate identifier.

Similarly, the identifier of a relationship may be simple or compound (Fig. 2-38 and 2-39). It is always composed of some or all of the relationship implicit properties. Occasionally, a relationship may have an alternate identifier (Fig. 2-40).

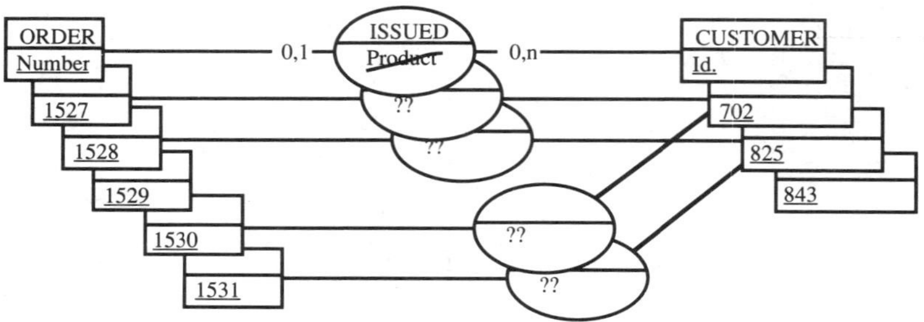

The identifier of ISSUED is ORDER.Number.

For 1 permissible value of ORDER.Number:
—> 1 occurrence of ISSUED;
—> 1 value of each property.

For example:
1527 —> 1527, 702;
1529 —> Nothing.

Product, a repetitive property, is excluded.

Figure 2-38 Binary relationship with a simple identifier.

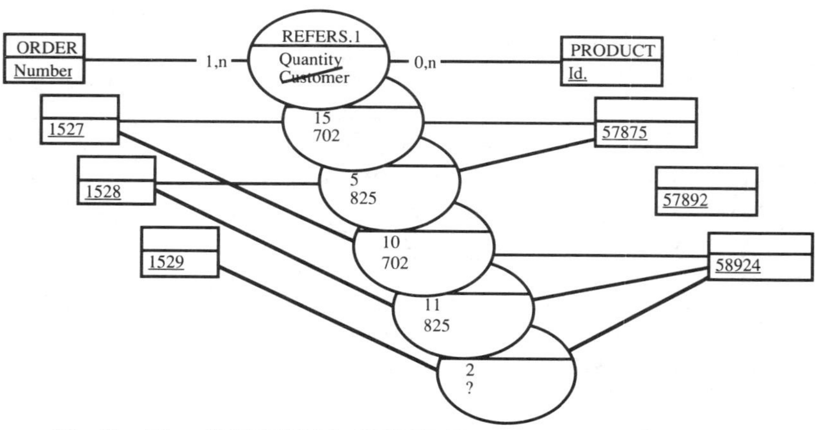

The identifier of REFERS.1 is (ORDER.Number).(PRODUCT.Id.).

For 1 permissible value of (ORDER.Number).(PRODUCT.Id.):
—> 1 occurrence of REFERS.1;
—> 1 value of each property.

For example:
1527.57875 —> 1527, 57875, 15;
1528.57892 —> Nothing.

Customer, an optional property, is excluded.

Figure 2-39 Binary relationship with a compound identifier.

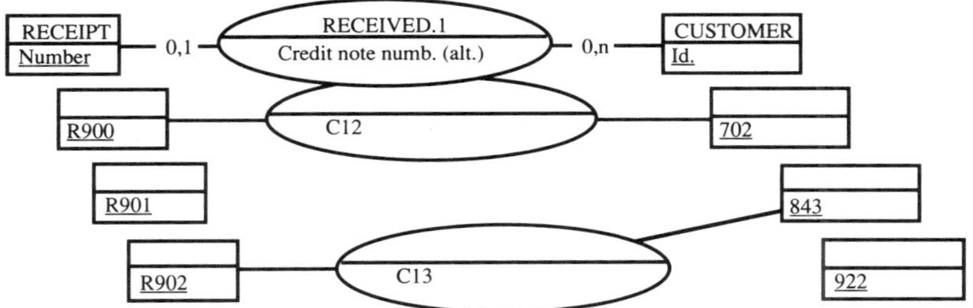

The identifier of RECEIVED.1 is RECEIPT.Number.
Another identifier is Credit note number.

For 1 permissible value of RECEIPT.Number
<—> 1 value of Credit note number, and vice versa.

For example:
R900 <—> C12;
R901 <—> Nothing;
R902 <—> C13.

Figure 2-40 Binary relationship with an alternate identifier.

(b) Each property of an object which is not part of the identifier depends on the whole identifier. In other words, the identifier cannot be broken down in such a way that object properties might depend only on a part of the identifier – unless they are a part of the identifier themselves. Objects complying with Rules (a) and (b) are said to be in *Second Normal Form.*

As a consequence, all explicit and implicit properties of an entity depend on the whole identifier (Fig. 2-41). Similarly, all explicit and implicit properties of a relationship depend on the whole identifier (Fig. 2-42).

P.O. ITEM
Purch. order
Product
Quantity
Purchase date

8432
57875
250
92.05.31

8432
58924
100
92.05.31

8433
59603
20
92.06.01

The property Purchase date does not depend on the whole identifier, composed of Purchase and Product, but only on Purchase:
—> It must be excluded.

The property Quantity depends on both Purchase and Product:
—> It may be included.

Figure 2-41 Entity whose properties depend on the whole identifier.

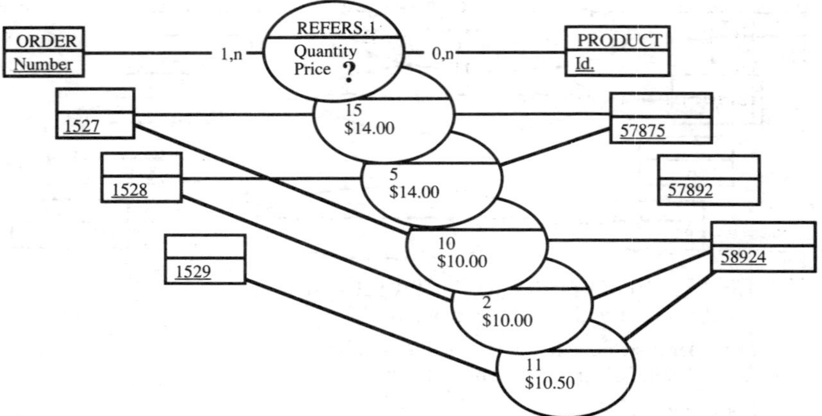

If Price means the product price at the time of the order, it depends on the whole identifier, composed of ORDER.Number and PRODUCT.Id.:
—> It may be included.

If Price means the product price in general, it depends only on part of the identifier, that is, PRODUCT.Id.:
—> It must be excluded.

Quantity depends on both ORDER.Number and PRODUCT.Id.:
—> It may be included.

Figure 2-42 Relationship whose properties depend on the whole identifier.

(c) Each property of an object which is not part of the identifier depends directly on the identifier. In other words, there is no intermediate property – or group of properties – on which such a property might be dependent. Objects complying with Rules (a) to (c) are said to be in *Third Normal Form.*

PRODUCT
Id.
Qty on hand
Cost
Price
~~Dept name~~

57875
80
$14.00
$21.00
ARTS

57892
50
$10.00
$15.00
ARTS

57924
0
$12.50
$18.00
LITTE

Department name does not depend directly on Id., but it depends on it through property Department code (not shown):
—> It must be excluded.

Other properties depend directly on Id.:
—> They may be included.

Figure 2-43 Entity whose properties depend directly on the identifier.

As a consequence, all explicit and implicit properties of an entity depend directly on its identifier (Fig. 2-43). Similarly, all explicit and implicit properties of a relationship depend directly on its identifier (Fig. 2-44).

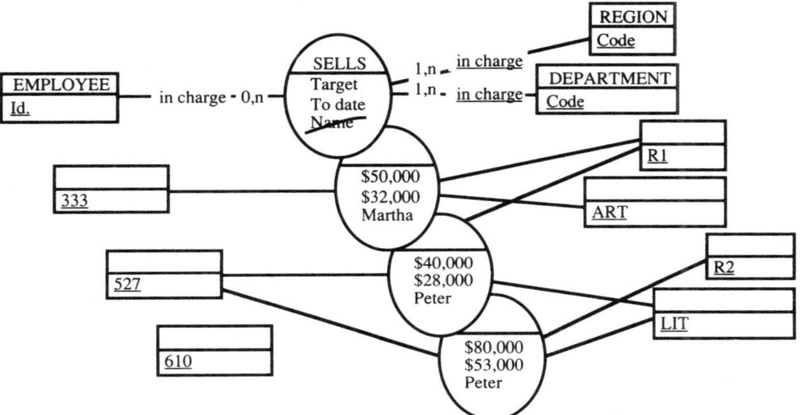

Name does not depend directly on the relationship identifier (REGION.Code) .(DEPARTMENT.Code), due to the dependency rule 'in charge'.
It depends on it through implicit property EMPLOYEE.Id.:
—> It must be excluded.

Other properties depend directly on the relationship identifier:
—> They may be included.

Figure 2-44 Relationship whose properties depend directly on the identifier.

(d) The only properties on which other properties are dependent are identifiers. Objects complying with Rule (d) are said to be in *Boyce-Codd Third Normal Form.* In practice, this rule is a condensed version of the first three rules, although it is somewhat more restrictive for objects with alternate identifiers.

Normalization rules may be summarized as follows:

> In a normal model, an object property is never repetitive or optional; it always wholly and directly depends on the object identifier.

Construction

(a) An entity may be identified directly, using a simple or a compound identifier. When the entity is the child of a parent-child relationship, it may also be identified indirectly, through an *identifier dependency*: the identifier of the parent entity, which is an implicit property of the child entity, may be used as part of the child identifier (Fig. 2-45). This is shown on the diagram by underlining the child 1,1 cardinalities.

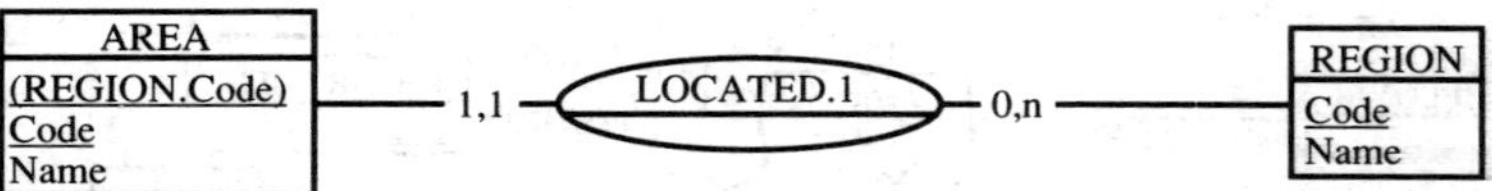

The identifier of AREA is (REGION.Code).(AREA.Code), which includes the identifier of the parent entity.

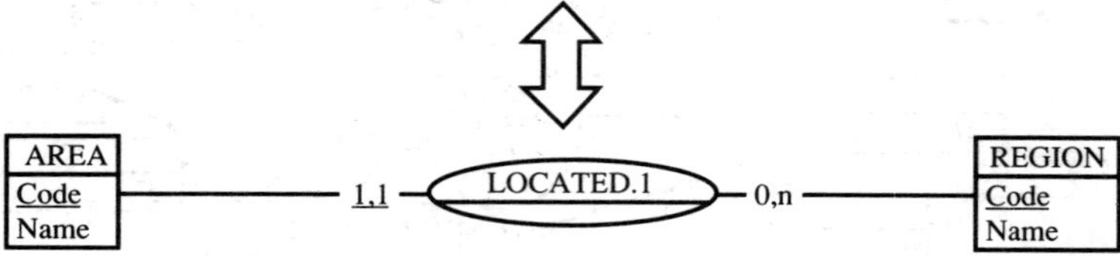

That is what is meant by the underlined 1,1 cardinalities.

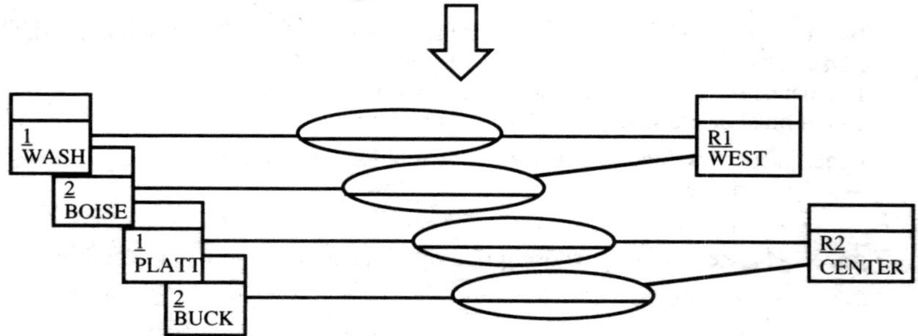

For 1 permissible value of (REGION.Code).(AREA.Code):
—> 1 occurrence of AREA;
—> 1 value of each property.

For example:
R1.1 —> R1, 1, WASH;
R2.1 —> R2, 1, PLATT;
R2.3 —> Nothing.

Figure 2-45 Identifier dependency.

(b) When the parent-child relationship is a semi-mandatory assignment – 0,1–1,1 cardinalities – the identifier of the parent may constitute the whole identifier of the child (Fig. 2-46). The child is called a *weak entity* to indicate that its existence is wholly dependent on the existence of the parent.

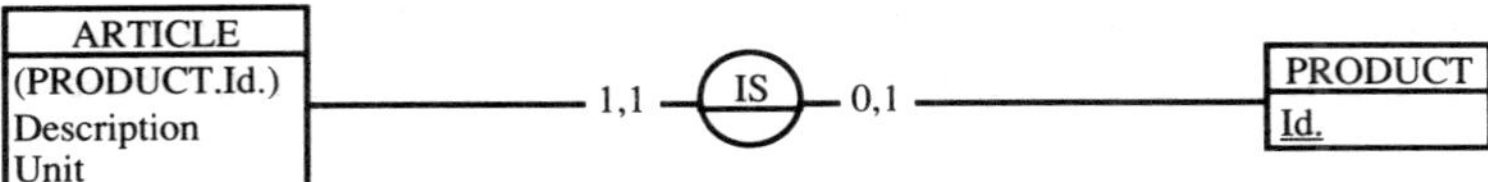

The identifier of ARTICLE is PRODUCT.Id., the same as the identifier of the parent entity. ARTICLE is called a weak entity.

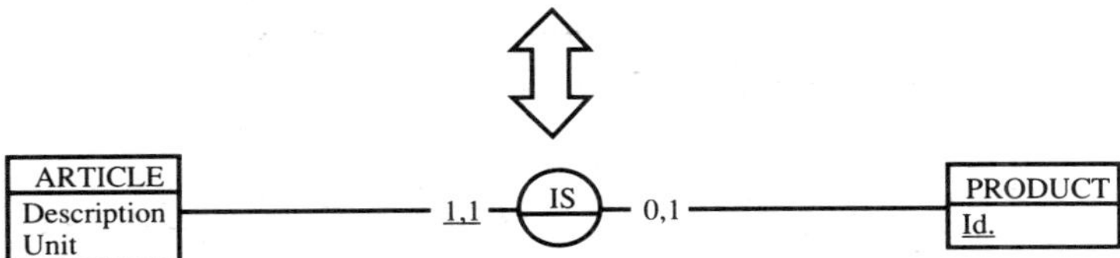

That is what is shown by the underlined 1,1 cardinalities and the lack of other identifier components.

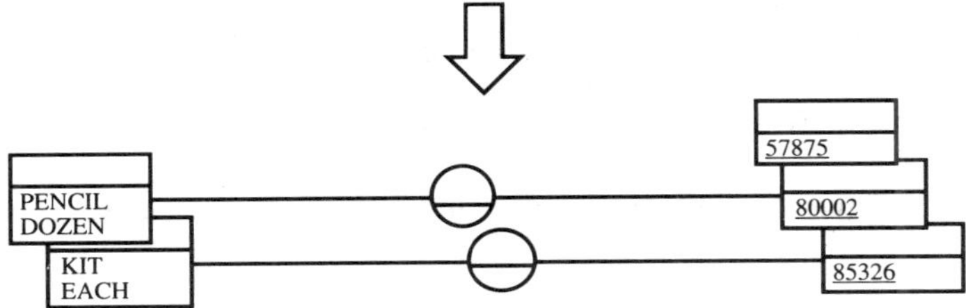

For 1 permissible value of PRODUCT.Id.:
—> 1 occurrence of ARTICLE;
—> 1 value of each property.

For example:
57875 —> Nothing;
80002 —> 80002, PENCIL, DOZEN;
85326 —> 85326, KIT, EACH.

Figure 2-46 Identifier for a weak entity.

(c) This method for building identifiers does not apply to quasi parent-child relationships (Fig. 2-18) or to optional assignments – 0,1–0,1 cardinalities (Fig. 2-23). The identifier of the quasi-parent does not qualify as an implicit property for the quasi-child: it is optional, and could not be used as its identifier.

(d) This method is generally not used for mandatory assignments – 1,1–1,1 cardinalities (Fig. 2-26) – because each participating entity has its own individuality, emphasized by its own identifier.

(e) When there is a family of parent-child relationships where children are also parents, identifiers may be built step by step, by extending the topmost entity identifier (Fig. 2-47). This is the system used in decimal classifications and hierarchical databases.

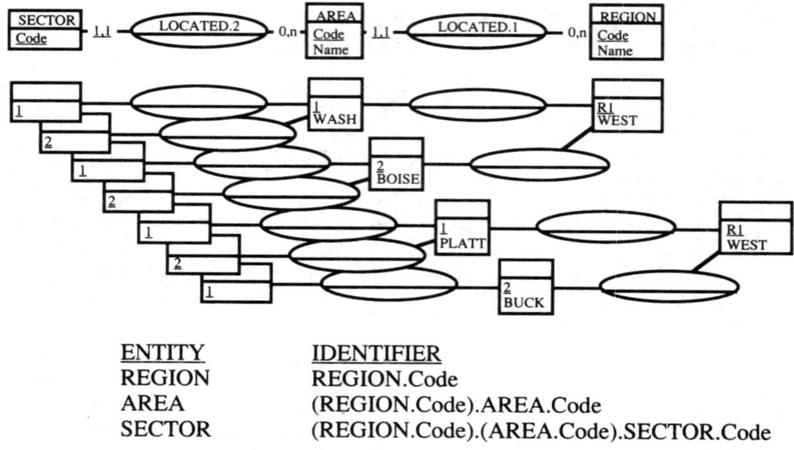

Figure 2-47 Identifiers for entities in a parent-child family.

(f) When an entity is the child of several parent-child relationships, it may be identified using all its parents identifiers (Fig. 2-48).

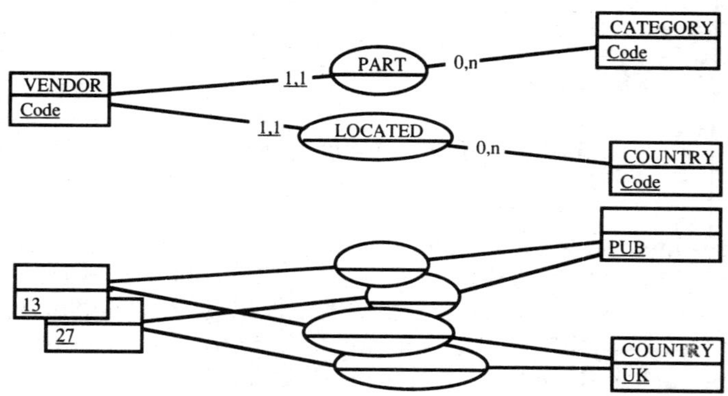

The identifier of VENDOR is
(CATEGORY.Code).(COUNTRY.Code).(VENDOR.Code).

For 1 CATEGORY.COUNTRY combination, there may be several occurrences of VENDOR. That is the reason why an additional VENDOR.Code is required.

Figure 2-48 Identifier for an entity with multiple parents.

(g) When an entity depends on the combination of its parents, its identifier consists of the combination of their identifiers. In fact, such an entity is a relationship in disguise (Fig. 2-49).

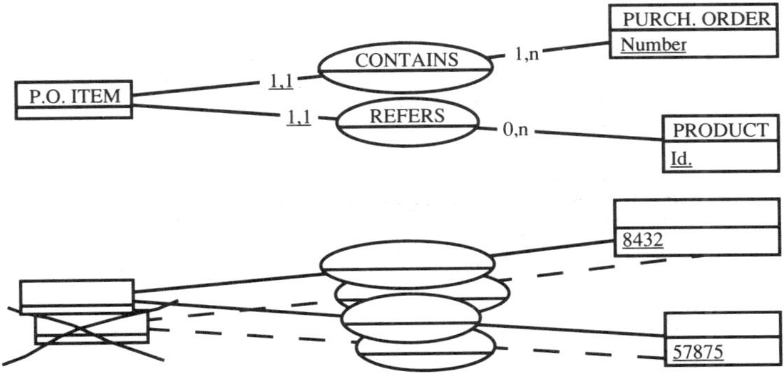

The identifier of P.O. ITEM is (PURCHASE ORDER.Number).(PRODUCT.Id.).

For 1 PURCHASE ORDER.PRODUCT combination, there may be only one occurrence of PURCHASE ORDER ITEM. That is the reason why an additional P.O. ITEM.Code should not be included.

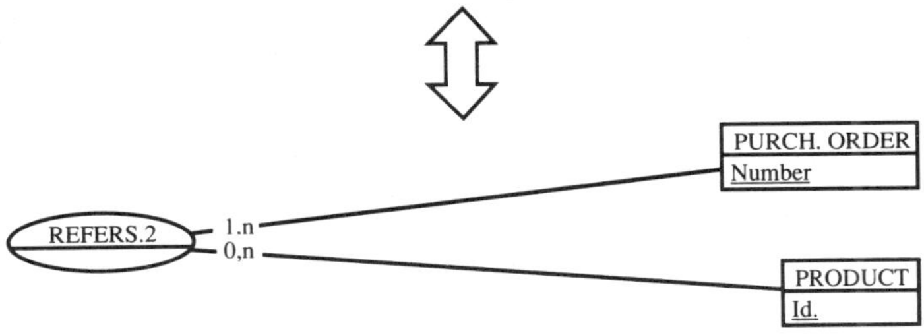

Relationship REFERS.2 has the same identifier as and is equivalent to the dependent entity P.O. ITEM.

Figure 2-49 Identifier for an entity depending only on its parents.

(h) The identifier of a parent-child relationship – or a quasi parent-child relationship – consists of the implicit property associated with the child (Fig. 2-50 and 2-51).

(i) The identifier of a relationship where one of the participants depends on the others excludes the implicit property associated with this participant (Fig. 2-52).

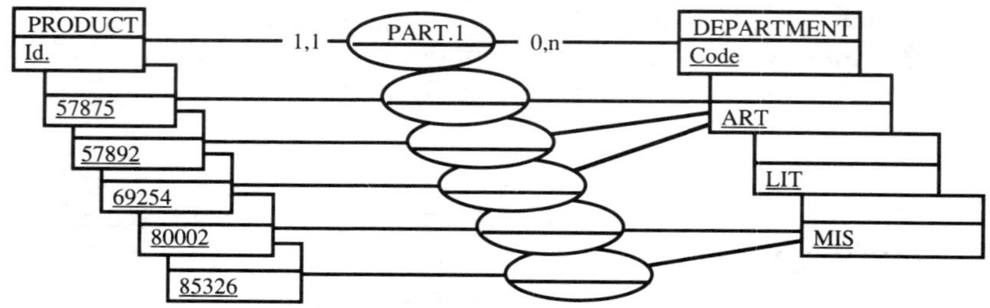

The identifier of PART.1 is PRODUCT.Id.

For 1 permissible value of PRODUCT.Id.:
—> 1 occurrence of PART.1;
—> 1 value of each property.

For example:
57875—> 57875, ART;
57876 —> Nothing.

Figure 2-50 Identifier of a parent-child relationship.

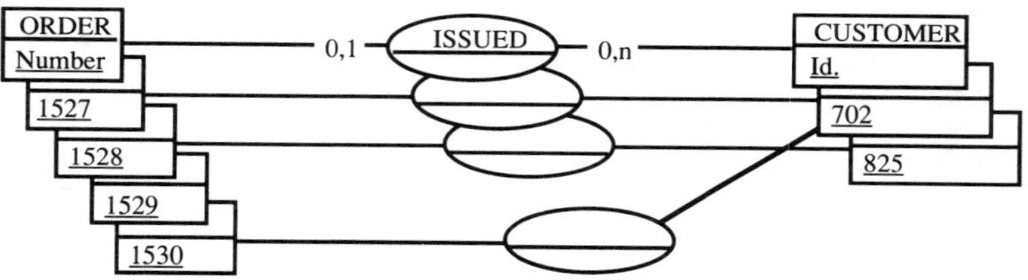

The identifier of ISSUED is ORDER.Number.

For 1 permissible value of ORDER.Number:
—> 1 occurrence of ISSUED;
—> 1 value of each property.

For example:
1528—> 1528, 825;
1529 —> Nothing.

Figure 2-51 Identifier of a quasi parent-child relationship.

(j) The identifier of a relationship with only 0,*n* or 1,*n* cardinalities consists of all its implicit properties (Fig. 2-53). Such a relationship is dependent on all its participants. For this reason, it is called *regular.*

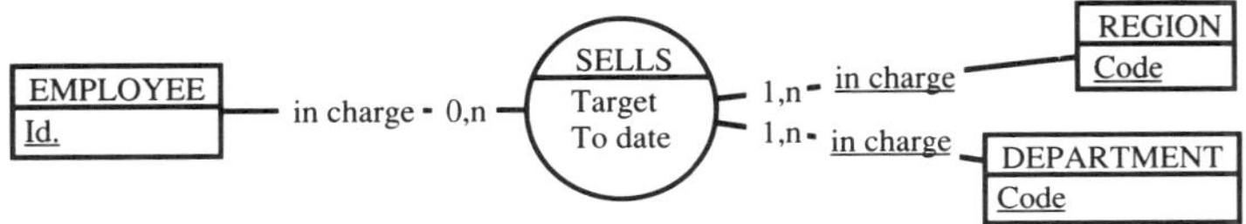

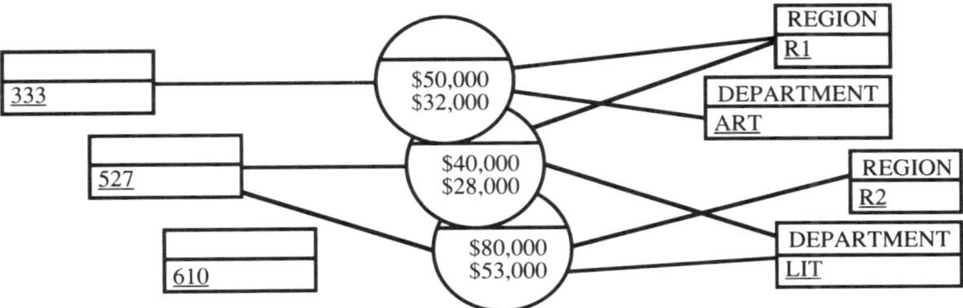

The identifier of SELLS is (REGION.Code).(DEPARTMENT.Code).

Indeed, the 'in charge' dependency rule states that, for 1 permissible REGION.DEPARTMENT combination, there is:
—> 1 occurrence of SELLS;
—> 1 value of each property.

For example:
R1.ART —> R1, ART, 333, $50,000, $32,000;
R2.ART —> Nothing;
R2.LIT —> R2, LIT, 527, $80,000, $53,000.

Figure 2-52 Identifier of a relationship with a dependency rule.

2.7.3 Representation

Explicit properties of an entity which are part of its identifier are underlined in the diagram.

Implicit properties of an entity which are part of its identifier are not shown, but the 1,1 cardinalities on the corresponding connectors are underlined. Such implicit properties may be underlined when documenting the identifier of the entity.

Implicit properties of a relationship which are part of its identifier are not shown in the diagram, since they may be inferred from its participants, cardinalities and the dependency rules which apply.

In the case of a relationship with a dependency rule, the underlined names indicate the independent – or key – participants. Such implicit properties may be underlined when defining participants in relationships (Fig. 2-54).

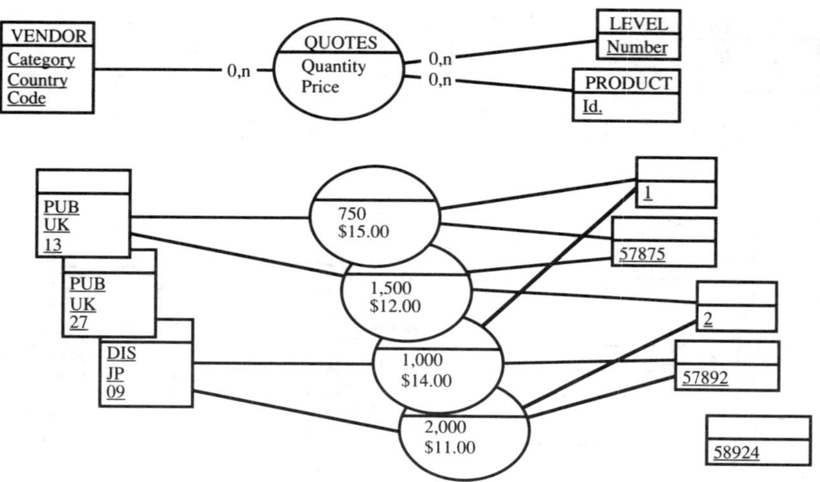

The identifier of QUOTES is
(VENDOR.Category.Country.Code).(PRODUCT.Id.).(LEVEL.Number).

For 1 VENDOR.PRODUCT.LEVEL combination:
—> 1 occurrence of QUOTES;
—> 1 value of each property.

For example:
PUB.UK.13.57875.1 —> PUB, UK, 13, 57875, 1, 750, $15.00;
PUB.UK.27.57875.1 —> Nothing;
DIS.JP.09.57892.2 —> DIS, JP, 09, 57892, 2, 2,000, $11.00.

Figure 2-53 Identifier of a regular relationship.

RELATIONSHIP: SELLS

PARTICIPANT (*)	CARDINALITY	
DEPARTMENT	1	All departments have at least one sales rep.
	n	Departments may be sold in several regions.
REGION	1	All regions have at least one sales rep.
	n	Regions may be selling several departments.
EMPLOYEE	0	Some employees are not sales representatives.
	n	An employee may sell several department region combinations.

(*) Participants which are part of the identifier are underlined.

Figure 2-54 Definition of the identifier of a relationship.

Chapter 3

Transformations and Views

> We keep on running up against 'sameness-in-differentness', and the question
>
> When are two things the same?
>
> (D. Hofstadter, *Gödel, Escher, Bach*)

This chapter analyzes the mechanisms which make it possible to proceed from a conceptual model – usually of a comprehensive nature – to more or less local views, and the reverse mechanisms, which lead from separate views to an integrated model.

This concept of view – or external model – has been put forward since the origin of data models. The specific contribution of this chapter is to propose a categorization of the transformations which produce them, in a manner somewhat similar to the relational approach.

However, the reader will not find rigorous notations and mathematics, only definitions and examples. The chief purpose here is to demonstrate more or less intuitive processes which are used by many modelers, whereas less experienced analysts continuously wonder which is the 'right' way to represent a given situation: should an entity, a relationship, a property, or several objects, be used? Those processes form the basis for developing modeling skills.

This chapter also offers a series of examples intended to provide guidance in recognizing whether representations are equivalent, in becoming familiar with representations which are not normal, and in knowing what to do to transform them. The goal of normalization, often considered difficult to achieve, will be seen instead as the natural outcome of thinking in terms of entities and relationships.

After perusing this chapter, the reader is invited to critically examine the model in Chap. 1, to assess the modeling choices made – which attempt to illustrate many different cases and are not necessarily the most natural ones – and to suggest alternate choices.

In addition to the objective of demonstrating the processes of conceptual modeling, this chapter proposes a mode of representation applicable to systems on the logical and physical levels. Indeed, concepts of views and transformations will reappear in following chapters, where they support the interpretation, not only of data stores and data flows, but also of processes.

3.1 Definition

A *transformation* is an operation which produces a new model based on one or more existing models.

In addition to equivalence transformations, which only change the way a model looks, without adding to or subtracting from its contents, there are two families of transformations which are, in a manner of speaking, the reverse of one another: derivations and integrations (Fig. 3-1).

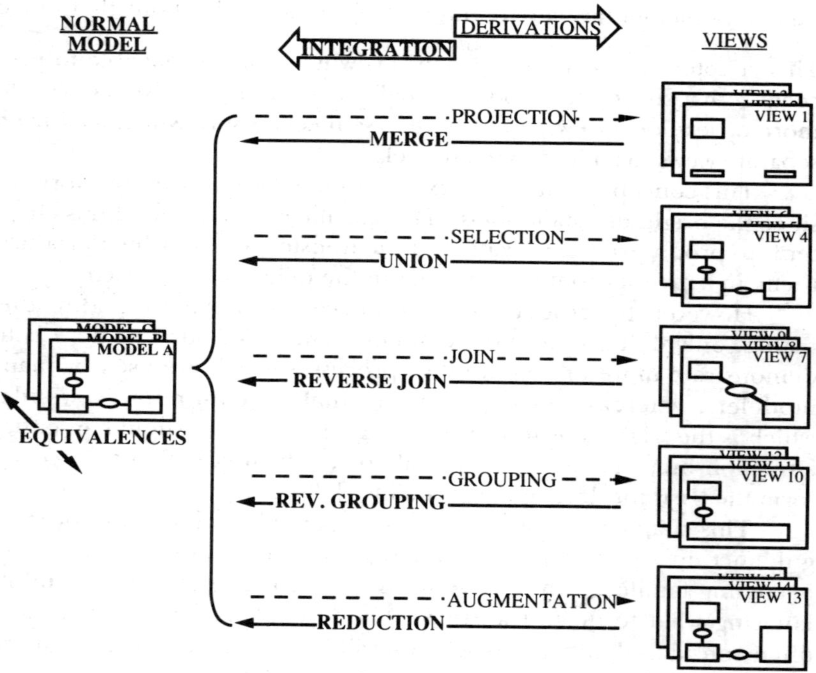

Figure 3-1 Families of transformations.

Derivations start with an existing model – or a part of a model – and present it in a new format. The result, which is called a *view,* is a consequence of the original model, and does not contain any new elementary facts.

In a system, a view often corresponds to the contents of an input document, a report or a file. Derivations are closely related to logical modeling.

On the other hand, *integrations* start with views and attempt to discover a common underlying model from which the views might be derived.

While derivations are deductive and relatively easy operations, integrations are constructive and more difficult operations: they start with models which are different and partial and which must be reconciled into a single model. Integrations are related to conceptual modeling, of which they are the main ingredient.

A model which complies with the rules stated in Chap. 2, especially the rules on identifiers, is called *normal*; every object in the model represents an elementary object in the real world; every property represents an elementary fact about an object and only about that object. This can be summarized as follows:

> In a normal model, every elementary fact appears once and only once, in the right place.

This quality of *non-redundancy* makes it easier to derive the logical model of a system, by supplying a concise and accurate representation for the system, which also simplifies update functions.

On the other hand, views derived from a conceptual model are not always normal. Indeed, redundancy is an appropriate feature of information produced by a system since it offers opportunities to look at it from different perspectives.

But when one has to rely on data flows and files of an existing system to develop the conceptual model, it is necessary to eliminate redundancy within and between the associated views in order to proceed back to the normal model on which they are based.

For this reason, integration transformations are closely related to normalization operations.

3.2 Equivalences

(a) *Equivalence* transformations change a normal model into another normal model with the same meaning. They may be carried out in both directions. When two models are equivalent, the simpler representation is preferable. But there are cases where the simplest model does not permit the expression of all relationships or properties involved. It is best to look for an equivalent model which does. Such a model usually contains more entities.

(b) A relationship is equivalent to an entity and a set of parent-child relationships of which it is the child (Fig. 3-2). The entity has the same properties as the initial relationship, and it is identified through all or part of the parent entities. Conversely, an entity whose identifier is a group of properties is equivalent to a relationship between the domains of those properties.

QUESTION: Given the following model, how can it be shown that a RECEIPT meets some PRODUCT requirements in a P. O., assuming that for 1 P. O. and 1 PRODUCT —> 0 or *n* occurrences of RECEIPT?

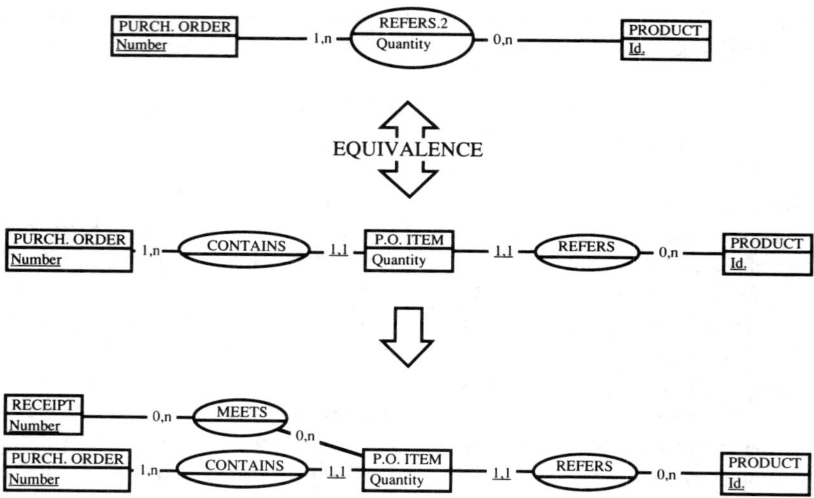

ANSWER: By representing relationship REFERS.2 as an equivalent entity PURCHASE ORDER ITEM with the same properties and identifier; by creating relationship MEETS.

Figure 3-2 Equivalence between a relationship and an entity.

(c) A property of an entity is equivalent to a parent-child relationship between the entity and the domain of the property (Fig. 3-3).

(d) A property of a relationship is equivalent to an additional role and an additional dependency rule with respect to the existing roles (Fig. 3-4).

(e) A property of a parent-child relationship may be equivalently assigned to the child entity (Fig. 3-5).

QUESTION: Given the following model, how can it be shown that an EMPLOYEE is in charge of a DEPARTMENT?

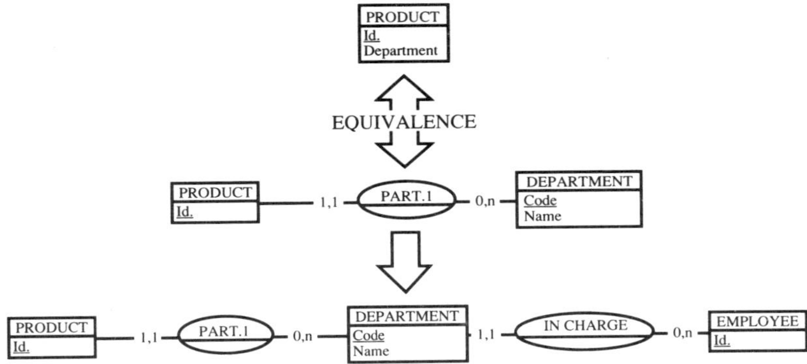

ANSWER: By representing property Department as the equivalent entity DEPARTMENT connected to PRODUCT through a parent-child relationship; by creating relationship IN CHARGE.

Figure 3-3 Equivalence between an entity property and a parent-child relationship.

QUESTION: Given the following model, how does one show an EMPLOYEE's POSITION?

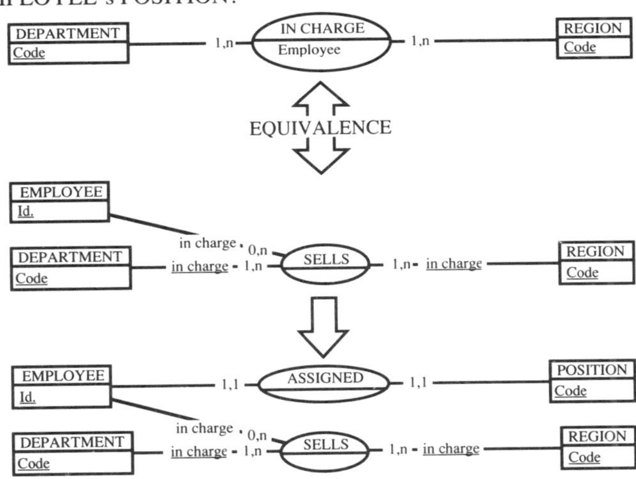

ANSWER: By representing EMPLOYEE as a third participant in IN CHARGE, renamed SELLS; by making explicit the dependency rule implicit in the original relationship; by creating ASSIGNED.

Figure 3-4 Equivalence between a relationship property and an additional participant and dependency rule.

QUESTION: Can this model be simplified?

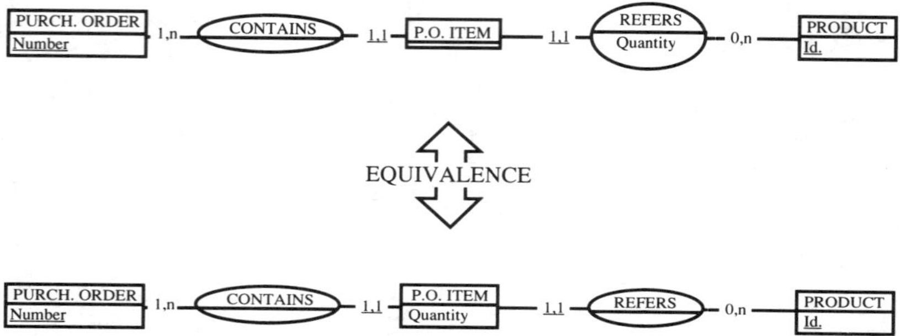

ANSWER: Yes, by using the equivalent representation where Quantity is a property of entity PURCHASE ORDER ITEM, a simpler object than a relationship.

Figure 3-5 Equivalence between the property of a parent-child relationship and the property of a child entity.

(f) A business rule may result in a relationship (Fig. 3-6).

RULE: A CUSTOMER is assigned the CLASS with the highest Sales level less than or equal to the CUSTOMER's year-end Sales to date.

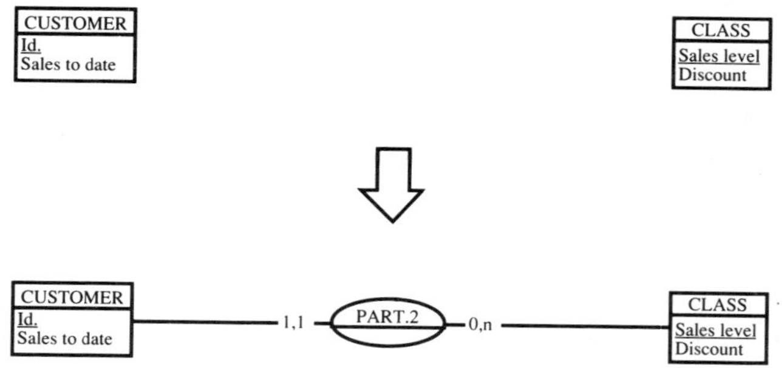

This business rule creates a relationship between the entities.

Figure 3-6 Creation of a relationship through a business rule.

(g) A model equivalent to a normal model is usually normal.

Additional cases of equivalences are mentioned in the following sections.

3.3 Derivations

3.3.1 Projections

(a) *Projection* transformations isolate parts of a model. They allow for verification of a comprehensive model by verifying its parts.

(b) A projection of an object (Fig. 3-7) is obtained by removing some properties from the object. The occurrences and population of the new object are the same as those of the original object.

This representation contains all properties of objects being considered. It is complete.

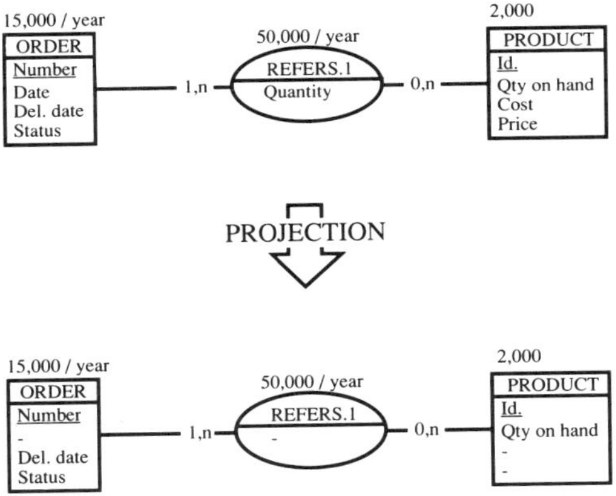

This projection contains only properties of interest for order follow-up.

Figure 3-7 Projection of an object.

(c) A projection of a model – or *sub-model* – is obtained by removing some objects and properties and the business rules which concern them (Fig. 3-8).

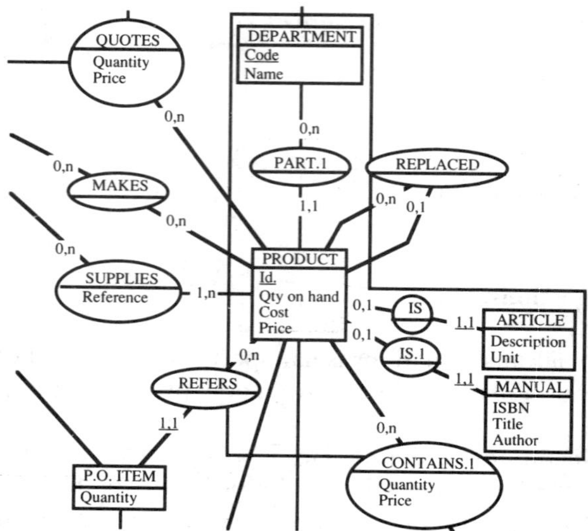

RULES: A PRODUCT IS either an ARTICLE or a MANUAL.
Quantity on hand = Old Qty on hand - CONTAINS.1.Quantity.

PROJECTION

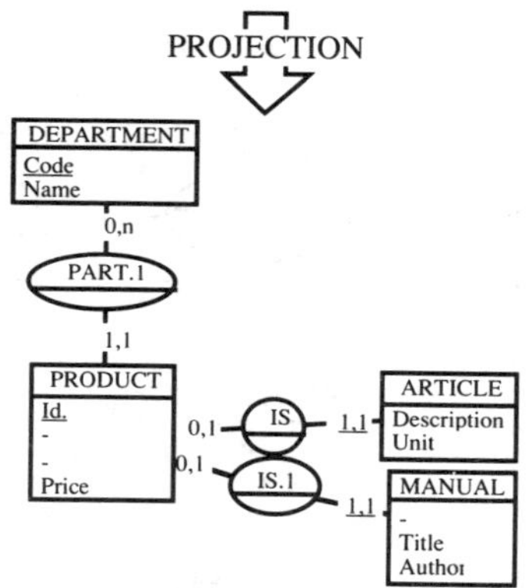

RULE: A PRODUCT IS either an ARTICLE or a MANUAL.
This projection highlights the sub-model of interest for printing a catalog.

Figure 3-8 Projection: sub-model.

(d) The *model of primary properties* is the sub-model obtained by removing all properties whose values could be derived again from properties in the model and all objects whose occurrences could be derived again from objects in the model (Fig. 3-9), as well as business rules which define them. This sub-model is the simplest model which contains all the primary facts included in the source model, and it cannot be made smaller without losing part of the information.

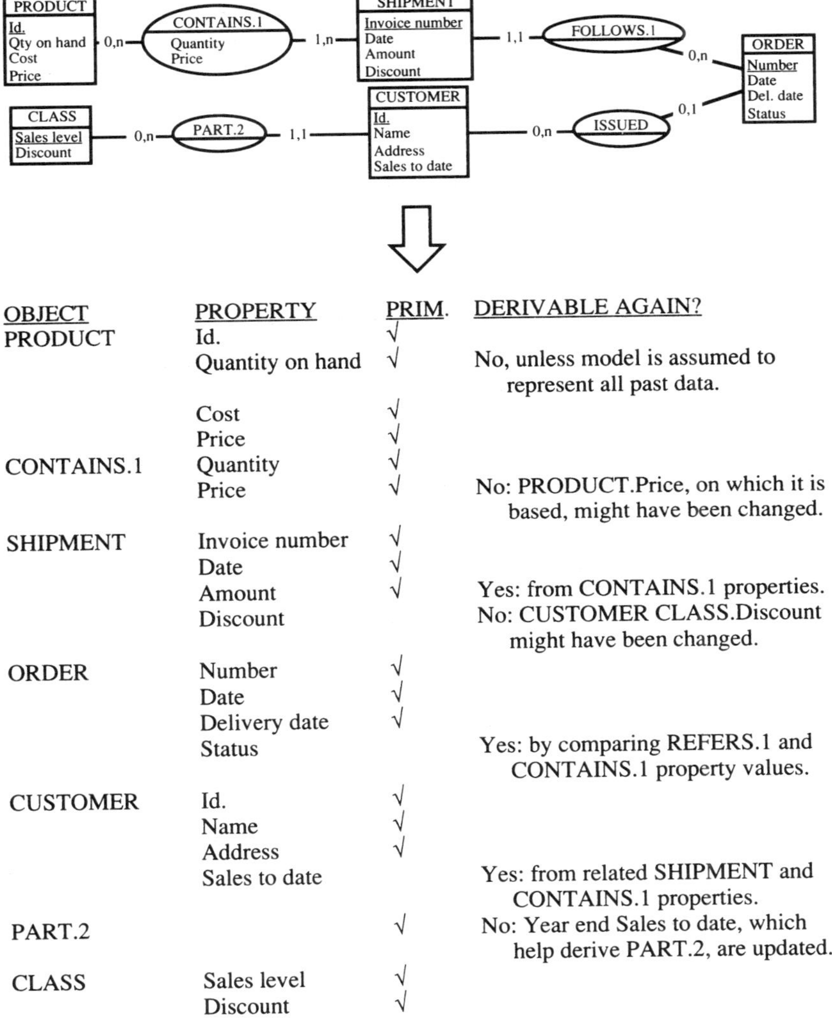

OBJECT	PROPERTY	PRIM.	DERIVABLE AGAIN?
PRODUCT	Id.	√	
	Quantity on hand	√	No, unless model is assumed to represent all past data.
	Cost	√	
	Price	√	
CONTAINS.1	Quantity	√	
	Price	√	No: PRODUCT.Price, on which it is based, might have been changed.
SHIPMENT	Invoice number	√	
	Date	√	
	Amount	√	Yes: from CONTAINS.1 properties.
	Discount		No: CUSTOMER CLASS.Discount might have been changed.
ORDER	Number	√	
	Date	√	
	Delivery date	√	
	Status		Yes: by comparing REFERS.1 and CONTAINS.1 property values.
CUSTOMER	Id.	√	
	Name	√	
	Address	√	
	Sales to date		Yes: from related SHIPMENT and CONTAINS.1 properties.
PART.2		√	No: Year end Sales to date, which help derive PART.2, are updated.
CLASS	Sales level	√	
	Discount	√	

Figure 3-9 Primary properties.

(e) The *model of identifiers* is the sub-model obtained by keeping only identifiers (Fig. 3-10) and related business rules. This sub-model describes the fundamental structure of the original model, to which all facts concerning the system may be related.

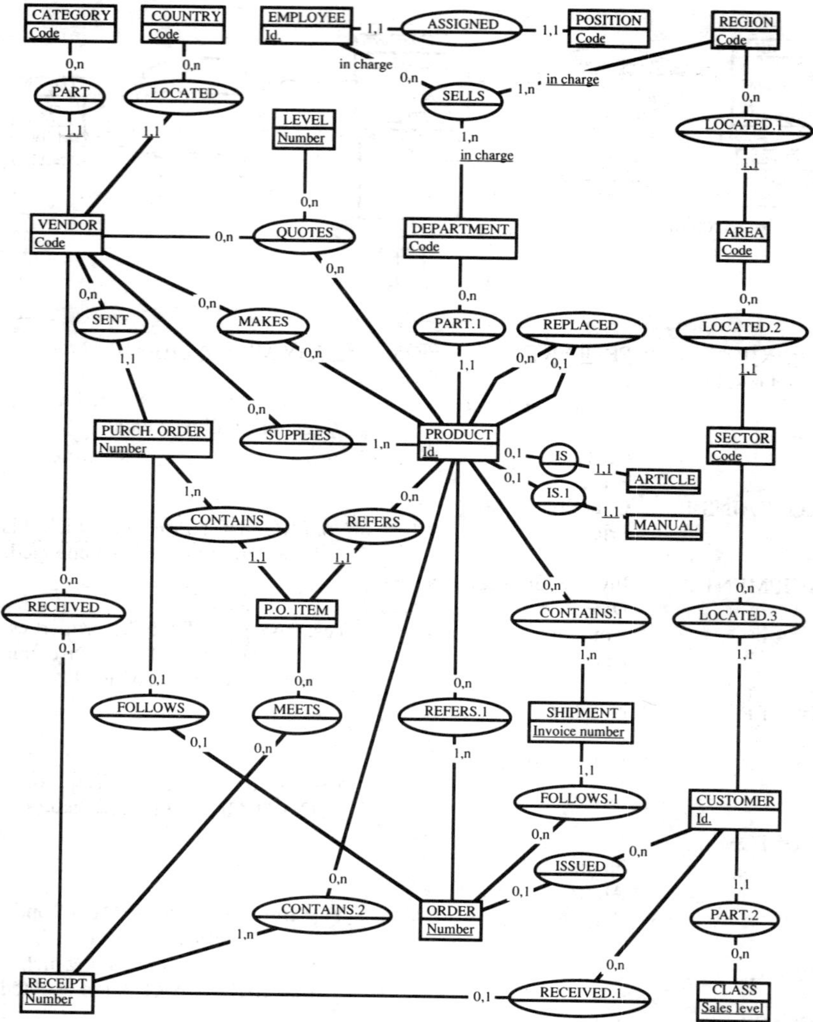

The model of identifiers highlights the fundamental structure of a conceptual model:

- All properties depend on identifiers shown or implied in this sub-model;
- This is the smallest sub-model for which this statement is true.

Figure 3-10 Model of identifiers.

(f) A view obtained by projecting a normal model is normal as long as each projected object keeps its identifier. If this is the case, cardinalities are unchanged.

3.3.2 Selections

(a) *Selection* transformations restrict the application context of a model. They make it possible to verify a comprehensive model, by auditing its interpretation in a variety of more restrictive contexts.

(b) An object's selection (Fig. 3-11) is effected by choosing occurrences of the object which comply with a business rule called a *selection criterion.* The new object has the same properties as the original, but its population is smaller.

These representations apply to all occurrences of objects being considered.

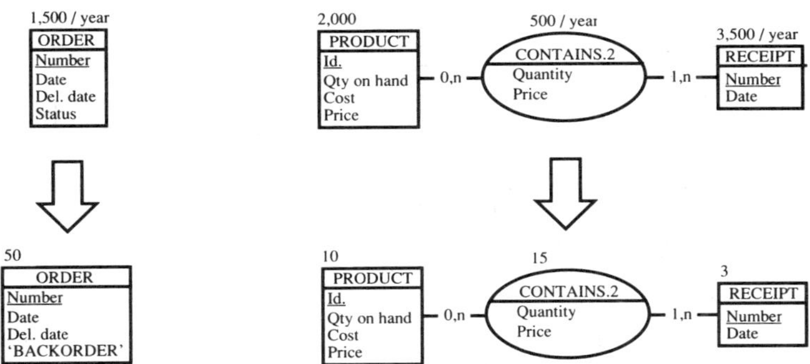

These selections describe the result of queries with specific criteria:

- ORDERS with Status = 'BACK ORDER';
- RECEIPTS of the day with Sum (Quantities x Price) < $1,000.

Figure 3-11 Selection of objects.

(c) A set of selections based on all the values of the same selection criterion yields several derived objects whose populations add up to the original population. Each of those objects is called a *sub-object,* or a *specialization* of the original object with respect to the selection criterion used. The source object is called a *super-object* or a *generalization.*

(d) Specializations of an entity are *sub-entities.* Generalizations of entities are *super-entities* (Fig. 3-12 to 3-14). A super-entity may be represented with its sub-entities in the same model: properties and relationships must be assigned at the proper level.

The representation of vendors as a super-entity VENDOR is preferred because it is sufficient to express all considered relationships.

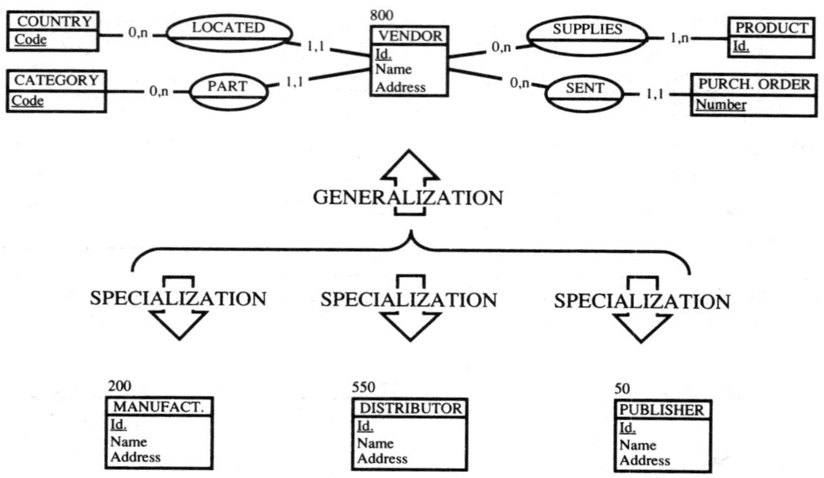

These selections describe the result of applying the following criteria:
- VENDORS with Category = 'MAN';
- VENDORS with Category = 'DIS';
- VENDORS with Category = 'PUB'.

This representation of vendors as various sub-entities is redundant because sub-entities have similar properties and participate in the same relationships.

Figure 3-12 Super-entity and sub-entities: super-entity preferred.

(e) Specializations of a relationship are relationships with the same roles or a subset of such roles (Fig. 3-15), that is, *sub-relationships.* Generalizations are *super-relationships.*

(f) A selection of a model – or *partial model* – may be obtained by adding business rules which limit the permissible implementations of a model: stricter cardinalities, additional domain rules, integrity rules or existence rules (Fig. 3-16).

The representation of third parties as a super-entity COMPANY requires that type specific business rules be added to the model.
Type dependent properties Sales to date, Reference and Credit note number become optional, resulting in non-normal objects.

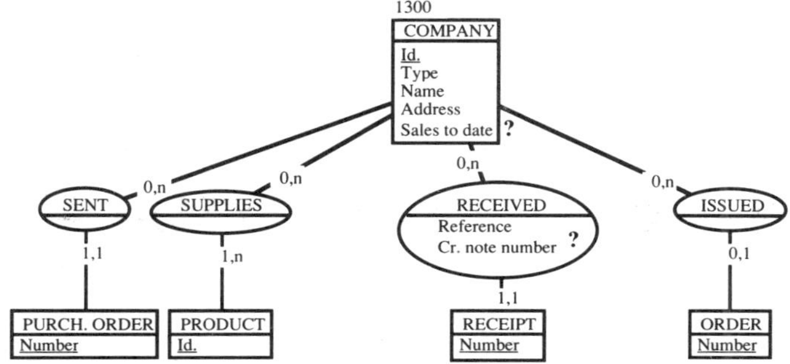

RULES: A P.O. is SENT to a COMPANY of Type 'VENDOR'.
A PRODUCT is SUPPLIED by a COMPANY of Type 'VENDOR'.
An ORDER is ISSUED by a COMPANY of Type 'CUSTOMER'.

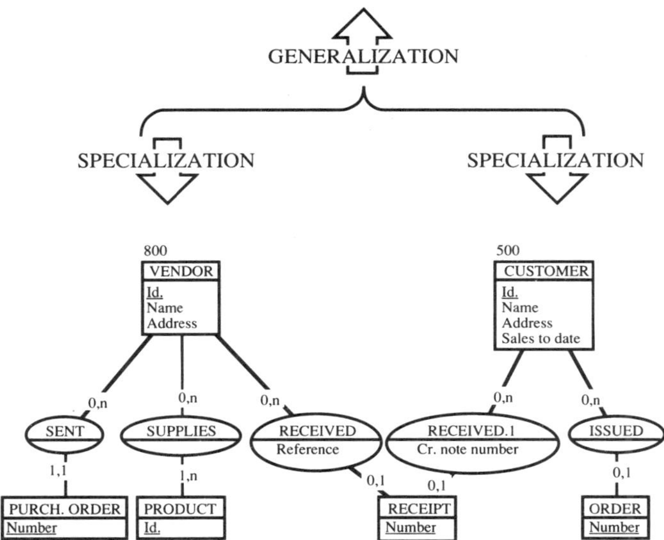

RULE: A RECEIPT is RECEIVED either from a VENDOR or a CUSTOMER.

The representation of third parties as sub-entities VENDOR and CUSTOMER is preferred because it allows for a simpler expression of properties and relationships specific to each sub-entity.

Figure 3-13 Super-entity and sub-entities: sub-entities preferred.

The representation of third parties as the modified super-entity COMPANY connected with its own modified sub-entities VENDOR and CUSTOMER provides maximum flexibility: properties and relationships may be assigned at the proper level.

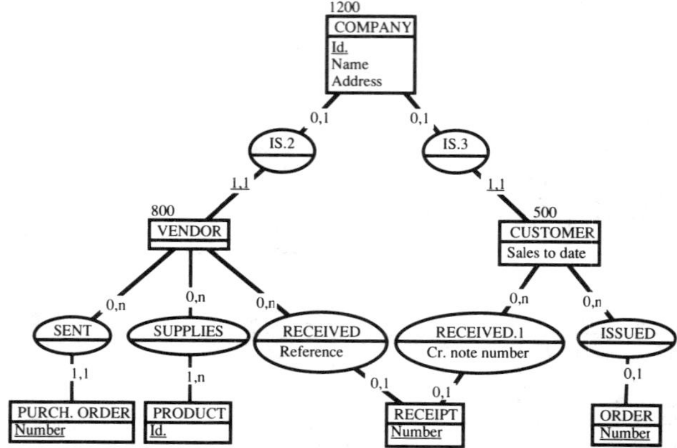

RULE: A RECEIPT is RECEIVED either from a VENDOR or a CUSTOMER.

NOTE: No rule states that a COMPANY IS either a VENDOR or a CUSTOMER. Indeed, some COMPANIES are both and their population is less than the sum of populations of VENDORS and CUSTOMERS.

Figure 3-14 Super-entity and sub-entities: a synthesis.

The representation of QUOTES as a generalized relationship is preferred because it is sufficient to express all considered situations.

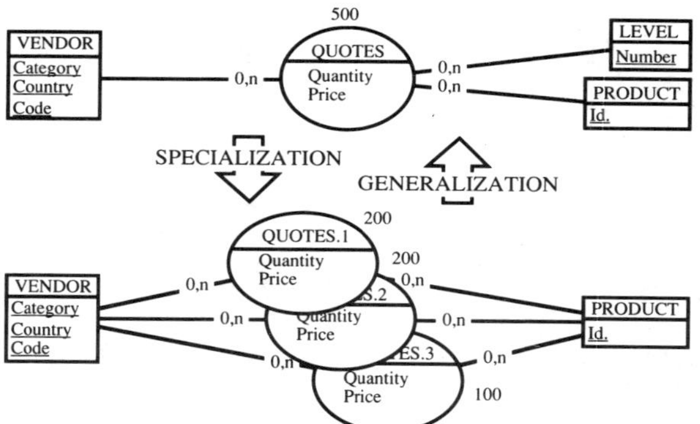

The representation of QUOTES as relationships specialized by levels is redundant: meanings, participants and properties are similar.

Figure 3-15 Generalized and specialized relationships.

This representation applies to ARTICLES and MANUALS: it is more complete.

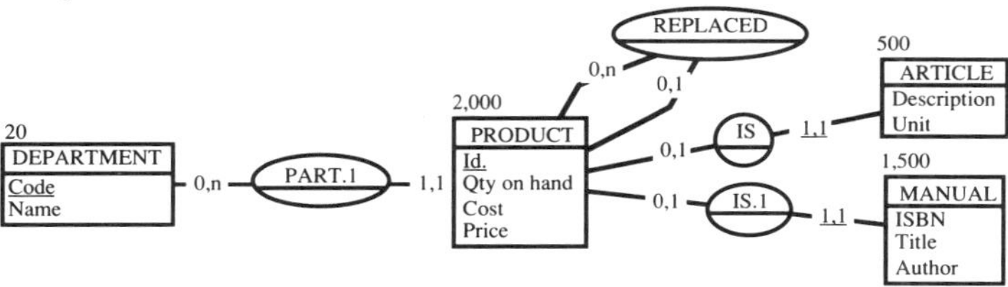

RULES: A PRODUCT IS either an ARTICLE or a MANUAL.
A MANUAL is not REPLACED.

SELECTION

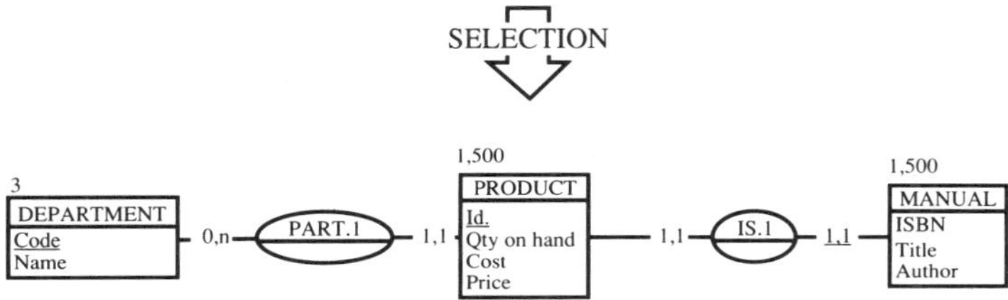

CRITERION: PRODUCT must BE a MANUAL.

This representation applies only to PRODUCTS which ARE MANUALS: their population is 1,500 in 3 DEPARTMENTS.
Note that some cardinalities are changed.

Figure 3-16 Selection: partial model.

(g) A view obtained by selection from a normal model is usually normal.

3.3.3 Joins

(a) *Join* transformations simulate a way in which objects are frequently associated on the logical level. Their usefulness for conceptual modeling is derived from the reverse transformation – the reverse join – which helps in normalizing a model.

(b) When two objects have a property with the same domain, it is possible to form a new object by joining them: to each occurrence of the first object, one joins each occurrence of the second object for which the property has the same value, which yields the occurrences of the new object (Fig. 3-17). The property which is used in the join may be simple or compound.

NORMAL VIEW: To be used for the conceptual model.

PRODUCT
Id.
Qty on hand
Cost
Price
0,n
50,000 / year
REFERS.1
Quantity
1,n
ORDER
Number
Date
Del. date
Status
0,n
FOLLOWS.1
1,1
0,1
ISSUED
0,n

JOIN
REVERSE JOIN

PRODUCT
Id.
Qty on hand
Cost
Price
0,n
CONCERNS
1,1
50,000 / year
ITEM
Number
Date
Del. date
Status
Quantity
0,n
FOLLOWS.1
1,n
0,1
ISSUED
0,n

NON-NORMAL VIEW: Date, Del. date and Status depend only on Number.

Join of ORDER and REFERS.1 on the common property Number results in a set of occurrences of ITEM in which ORDER properties are repeated.

Figure 3-17 Join of an entity and a relationship.

(c) The resulting join has the properties of objects joined. It has an identifier which is obtained by grouping the identifiers of the original objects. Its population depends on the original distribution of values of the property used in the join.

NORMAL VIEW: To be used for the conceptual model.

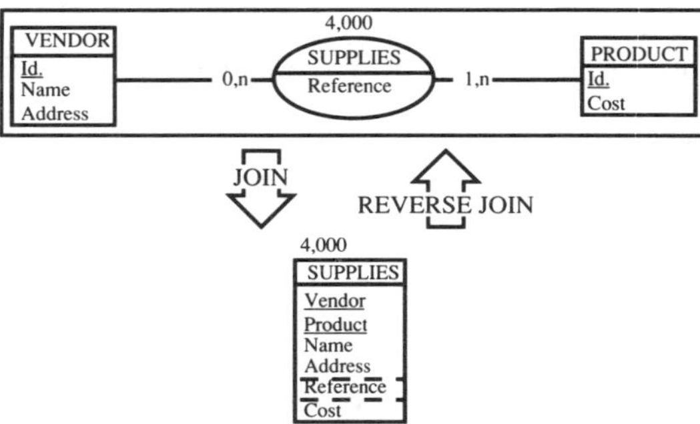

NON-NORMAL VIEW: Name and Address depend only on Vendor; Cost depends only on Product.

Double join of SUPPLIES on properties VENDOR.Id. and PRODUCT.Id.: the resulting object is a set of occurrences of SUPPLIES in which VENDOR and PRODUCT properties are repeated.

Figure 3-18 Join of a relationship and two entities.

(d) In the conceptual model, one may think of the resulting join as taking the place of the original objects and participating in the same relationships with other objects. Cardinalities must be adjusted accordingly.

(e) Various types of objects may be joined: entities, relationships or derived objects (Fig. 3-18). Most often, joins are performed on neighboring objects and are based on relationships, through implicit properties.

(f) An object obtained by join is usually not normal, since some of its properties depend on a part of the identifier.

(g) A view in which an object is obtained by join is usually not normal.

3.3.4 Groupings

(a) *Grouping* transformations simulate a way in which objects are frequently associated on the logical level. Their usefulness for conceptual modeling is derived from the reverse transformation – the reverse grouping – which helps in normalizing a model.

(b) When two objects are neighbors, it is possible to form a new object by grouping them: with each occurrence of the first object, one associates all occurrences of the second object which are connected to the first object, which yields one occurrence of the new object (Fig. 3-19).

(c) The resulting grouping has the properties of objects grouped, that is, the properties of the first object plus a certain number of times those of the second object: this number is determined by the cardinalities of the relationships involved. The resulting object has the same identifier and the same population as the first object.

(d) In the conceptual model, one may think of the resulting grouping as taking the place of the original objects and participating in the same relationships with other objects. Cardinalities must be adjusted accordingly.

(e) Various types of objects may be grouped: entities, relationships or derived objects (Fig. 3-20).

NORMAL VIEW: To be used for the conceptual model.

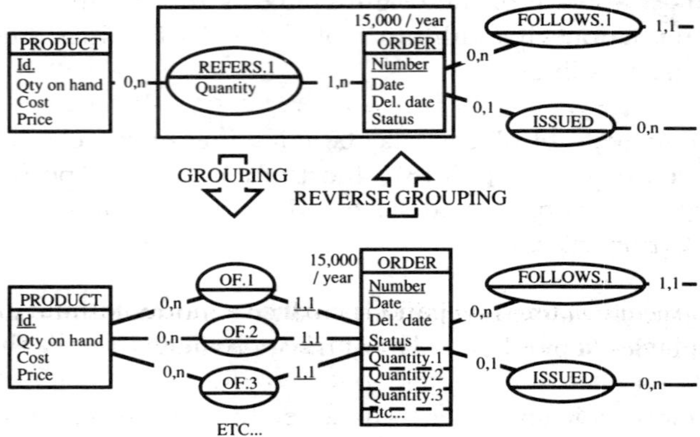

NON-NORMAL VIEW: Quantity and OF relationship are repeated.

Grouping of ORDER and REFERS.1: the resulting object is an occurrence of ORDER in which a variable number of occurrences of REFERS.1 are repeated.

Figure 3-19 Grouping of an entity and a relationship.

NORMAL VIEW: To be used for the conceptual model.

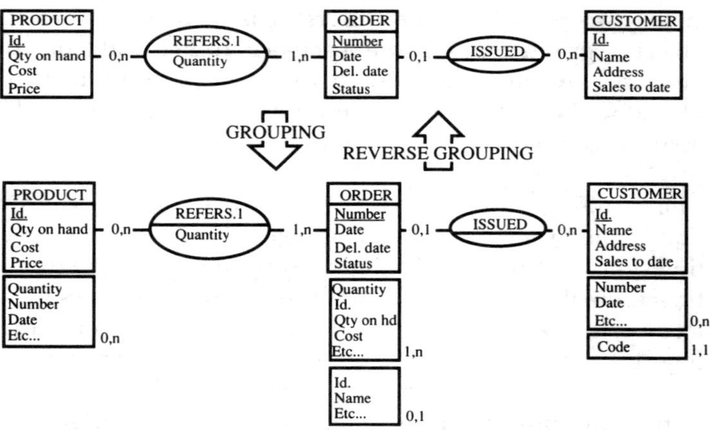

NON-NORMAL VIEWS: These various groupings present the same information in different ways. Each one is built around a different entity. Cardinalities entered next to each property group indicate how many times the group is repeated; they are the same as cardinalities of relationships in the model.

Figure 3-20 Groupings of several objects.

(f) An object obtained by grouping is usually not normal, since some of its properties are optional, repetitive or do not directly depend on the identifier.

(g) A view in which an object is obtained by grouping is usually not normal.

3.3.5 Augmentations

(a) *Augmentation* transformations enlarge a model without altering its fundamental contents. They make it possible to verify that a model is able to meet a variety of information requirements and thus are also useful on a logical level.

(b) An *augmented model* is obtained by adding new objects to the original model, with existence rules which define them, or new properties with the calculation rules which define them. New objects and properties are said to be *derived,* whereas original objects and properties are called *primary.*

QUESTION: Where should the derived properties be assigned?

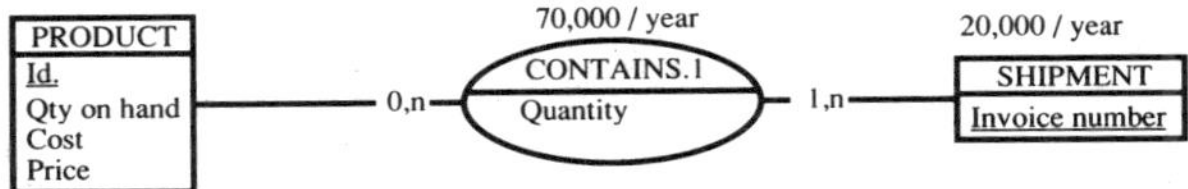

RULES: Shipped price = PRODUCT.Price.
Amount = Sum of (Quantities x Shipped prices).
Discount = CUSTOMER CLASS.Discount.

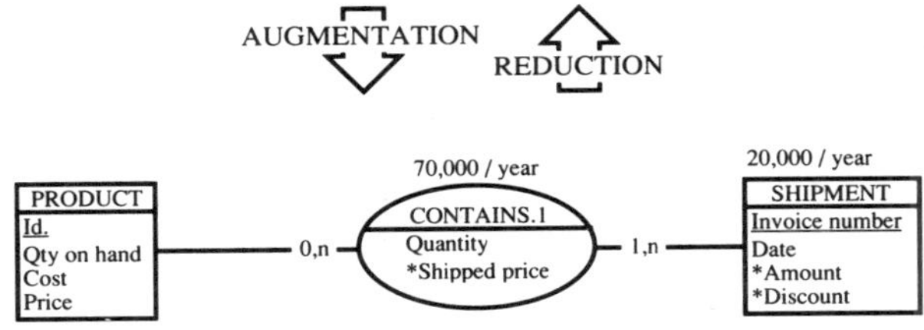

ANSWER: Property Shipped price is assigned to CONTAINS.1 since it has one value for each occurrence of CONTAINS.1.
Properties Amount and Discount are assigned to SHIPMENT since they have one value for each occurrence of SHIPMENT.

Figure 3-21 Augmentation: derived properties.

(c) A calculated property is assigned to an object in the same way as a primary property, that is, by following the same modeling rules (Fig. 3-21). Sometimes a new object must be introduced to the model to carry that property (Fig. 3-22).

QUESTION: Where should the derived properties be assigned?

RULES: *Sales to date by DEPARTMENT, by REGION = Sum of sales of DEPARTMENT PRODUCTS to REGION CUSTOMERS.
*Company sales to date = Sum of all sales of PRODUCTS to CUSTOMERS.

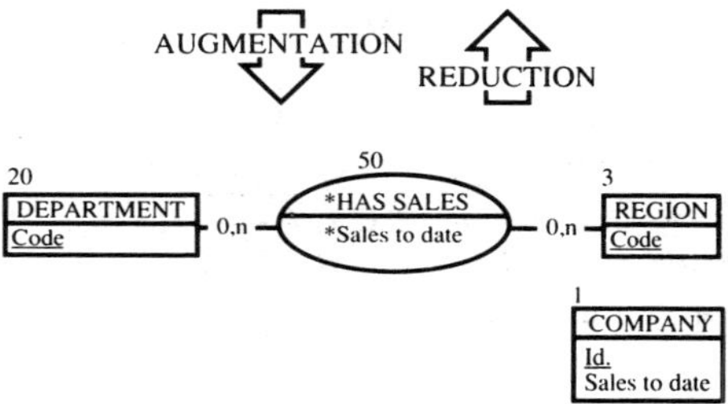

ANSWER: Relationship *HAS SALES between DEPT and REGION is created to carry property *Sales to date, which depends on both of them. There is one occurrence of *HAS SALES each time that *Sales to date are not zero.

Entity COMPANY, with a single occurrence, is created to carry property COMPANY.*Sales to date, which in fact does not depend on any identifier. All such properties may be assigned to COMPANY.

Figure 3-22 Augmentation: derived properties and objects.

(d) A model may be augmented unrestrictedly. An augmented model is usually represented without showing the additional dependencies introduced by the calculation rules.

3.3.6 Combining derivations

Derivation transformations, that is, projections, selections, joins, groupings and augmentations, as well as transformations obtained by combining them, provide many ways of transforming a given model into a great variety of views, which are usually not normal. On the logical level, a view provides a way to represent a data flow or a data store; therefore, the derivation which produces this view can represent the process which produces the data flow, or which accesses the data store.

3.4 Integration

3.4.1 Merges

(a) *Merge* transformations simplify a model by decreasing the number of required objects. A merge is a transformation which consists of retrieving a normal model from projections of that model. It is somehow the reverse of a set of projections. It is feasible only if the sub-models to be merged originate – through projections – from the same model.

(b) A property may be merged with an object if it has a unique value for each occurrence of the object (Fig. 3-23 and 3-24).

QUESTION: Where should properties Quantity on hand and Author be assigned?

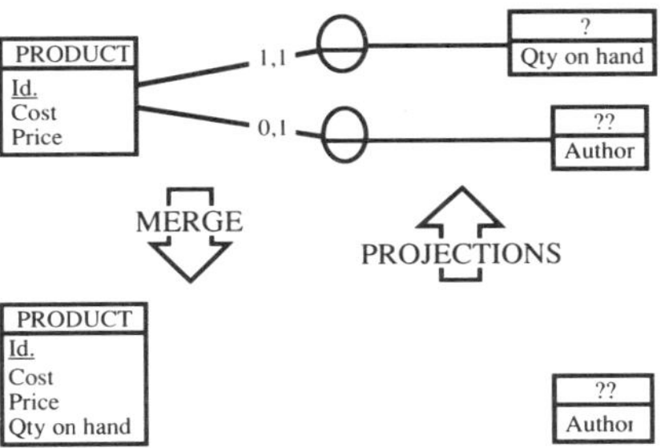

ANSWER: Property Quantity on hand may be merged with PRODUCT, assuming that there is a unique value for each occurrence of PRODUCT. Property Author cannot be merged with PRODUCT because there are occurrences of PRODUCT without a value for Author. Creating another object might be required.

Figure 3-23 Merge of a property and an entity.

(c) Two entities may be merged if there is a one-to-one correspondence – a mandatory assignment relationship – between their occurrences (Fig. 3-25). This yields an equivalent model.

QUESTION: Where should property Shipped quantity of a product be assigned?

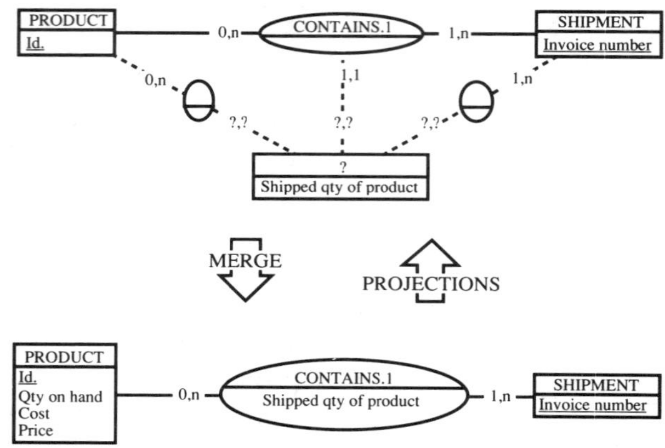

ANSWER: It may be merged with CONTAINS.1 because it has a unique value for each occurrence of CONTAINS.1.
It cannot be merged with SHIPMENT (or with PRODUCT) because there might be occurrences of SHIPMENT (or PRODUCT) with more than one value of Shipped quantity.

Figure 3-24 Merge of a property and a relationship.

QUESTION: Can this model be simplified?

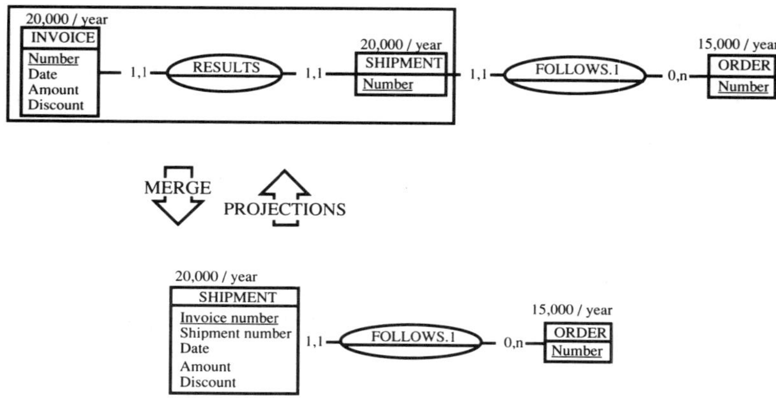

ANSWER: Yes, INVOICE and SHIPMENT may be merged (but not SHIPMENT and ORDER).
But don't if the rule: 1 INVOICE <—> 1 SHIPMENT, may change.

Figure 3-25 Merge of entities.

(d) Two relationships may be merged if there is a one-to-one correspondence between their occurrences, which also means that they have the same participating entities and cardinalities (Fig. 3-26). Thus the resulting relationship has the same occurrences, participating entities and cardinalities. The new model is equivalent to the original model.

<u>QUESTION</u>: Can this model be simplified assuming that:
For 1 occurrence of CONTAINS.1 <—> 1 occurrence of INVOICED.
For 1 occurrence of SUPPLIES —> 0 or 1 occurrence of MAKES?

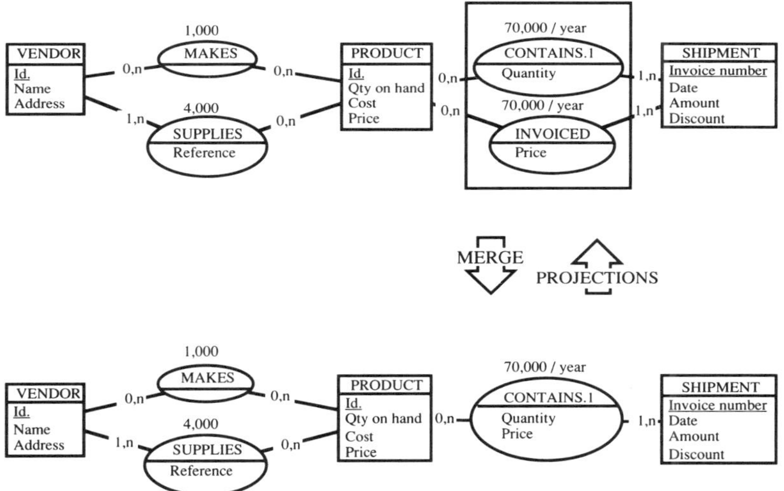

<u>ANSWER</u>: Yes, CONTAINS.1 and INVOICED may be merged (but not SUPPLIES and MAKES).

Figure 3-26 Merge of relationships.

(e) The object resulting from the merge has the properties of both original objects: distinct properties remain distinct; common properties are preserved only once (Fig. 3-27). Its population is the same as the population of each of the merged objects.

(f) Two views having a common entity with the same occurrences may be merged through this entity (Fig. 3-28). The resulting entity keeps all its participations in the relationships of the original views.

QUESTION: Can this model be made less redundant?

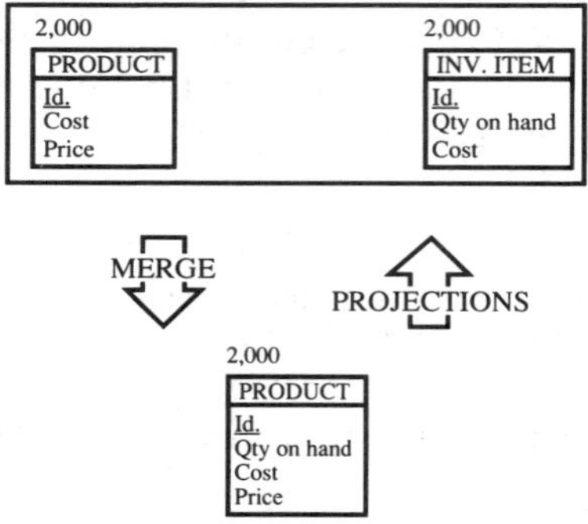

ANSWER: Yes, by merging INVENTORY ITEM and PRODUCT which are two views of the same entity. Properties Id. and Cost, which are common to merged entities, are preserved once. Properties Quantity on hand and Price are preserved just as they are.

Figure 3-27 Merge of objects and properties.

QUESTION: How to integrate these views?

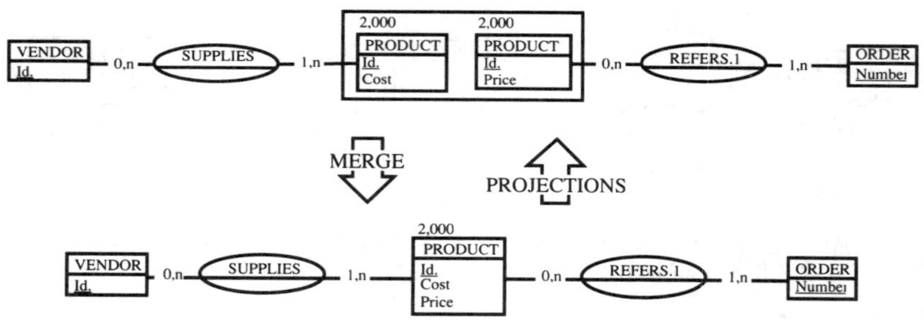

ANSWER: By merging the common entity PRODUCT.

Figure 3-28 Merge of views with a common entity.

(g) Two views which do not have a common entity may be merged if there exists a relationship between their entities (Fig. 3-29). The resulting model includes the relationship.

(h) A merge of two views may be performed step by step – when it is feasible.

QUESTION: How to integrate these views?

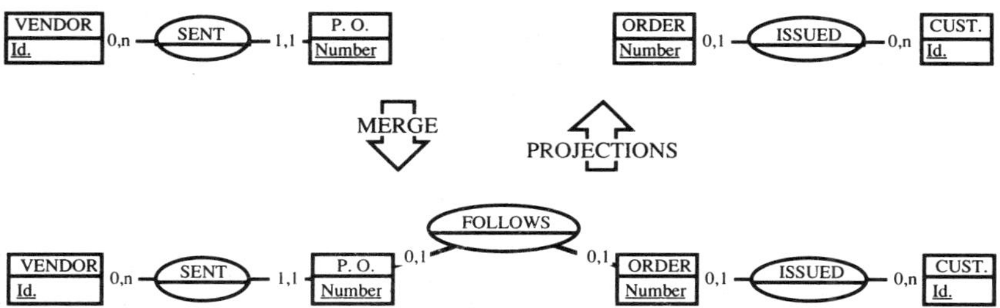

ANSWER: By merging them using relationship FOLLOWS.

Figure 3-29 Merge of views without a common entity.

3.4.2 Unions

(a) *Union* transformations simplify a model by decreasing the number of required objects. A union is a transformation which consists of retrieving a normal model from selections of that model. It is, in a manner of speaking, the reverse of a set of selections. It is feasible only if the partial models to be united originate – through selections – from the same model.

(b) A new occurrence may be united with an object if it has the same properties as the object (Fig. 3-30).

QUESTION: Where should occurrence 'WHOLESALER' be included?

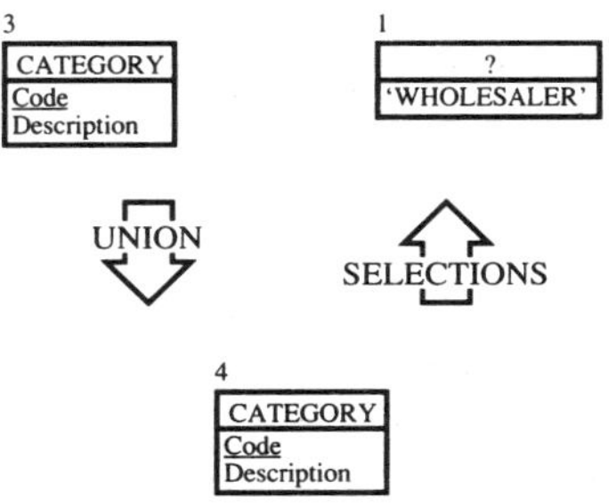

ANSWER: It may be united with CATEGORY, with a new Code value.
—> A model can represent new occurrences: only populations are changed.

Figure 3-30 Union of an occurrence and an object.

(c) Two entities may be united if they have the same properties or may be assigned the same properties (Fig. 3-31 and 3-32).

QUESTION: How to make this model less redundant?

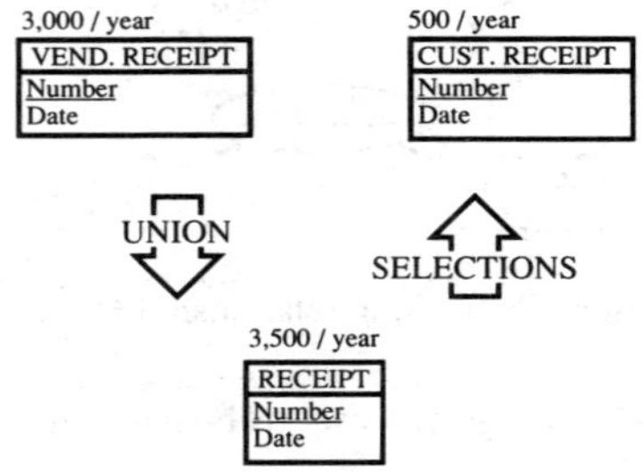

ANSWER: By uniting VENDOR RECEIPT and CUSTOMER RECEIPT:
• They have similar properties;
• They are views of the same entity RECEIPT.
A common identifier must be defined.
Occurrences of source entities are distinct:
—> Pop. of RECEIPT = Pop. of VEND. RECEIPT + Pop. of CUST. RECEIPT.

Figure 3-31 Union of entities without common occurrences.

QUESTION: How to make this model less redundant?

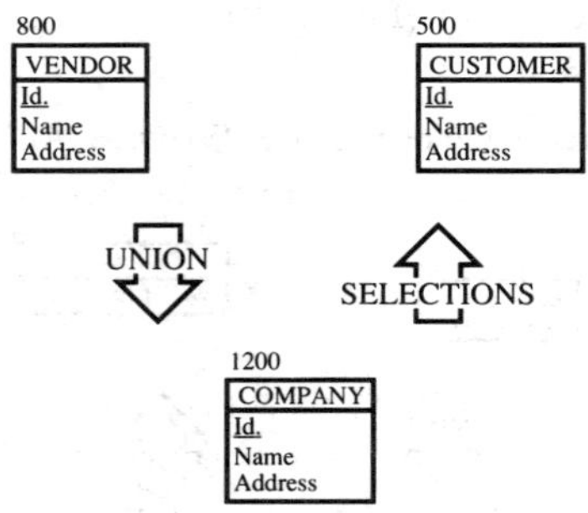

ANSWER: By uniting VENDOR and CUSTOMER:
• They have similar properties;
• They are views of the same entity COMPANY.
A common identifier must be defined.
A number of occurrences of source entities are common:
—> Pop. of COMPANY < Pop. of VENDOR + Pop. of CUSTOMER.

Figure 3-32 Union of entities with common occurrences.

(d) Two relationships may be united if the resulting relationship generalizes their meaning: they should have the same participating entities and the same properties (Fig. 3-33). It is not necessary that cardinalities be the same. In addition, cardinalities of the resulting relationship may be different.

QUESTION: Can this model be simplified?

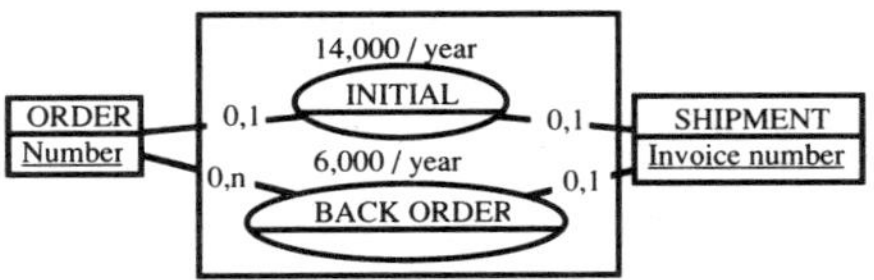

RULE: A SHIPMENT is either an INITIAL shipment for an ORDER or a BACK ORDER.

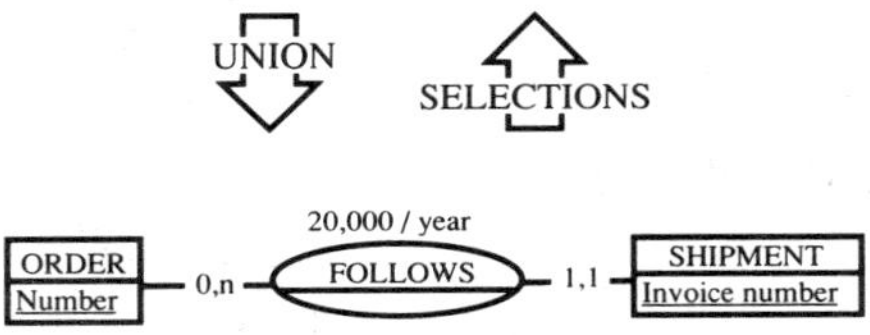

ANSWER: Yes, relationships INITIAL and BACK ORDER may be united in a new relationship FOLLOWS which generalizes their meaning. Some resulting cardinalities are different.

Figure 3-33 Union of relationships.

(e) The object resulting from the union of two objects unites their occurrences: distinct occurrences remain so, common occurrences are preserved once each. Thus its population (Fig. 3-31 to 3-33) is equal to, or less than, the sum of the populations of each of the united objects. The resulting object has the same properties as each of the united objects.

(f) Several objects with the same properties may often be united in a single object, called a *super-object* or a *generalization* of the original objects. Generalization is the reverse of a set of specializations.

(g) The *super-entity* associated with a set of entities includes the same properties as each of them (Fig. 3-12 and 3-14), plus possibly an additional property to distinguish the original entities (Fig. 3-13). This new property may be part of the identifier.

(h) The *super-relationship* associated with a set of relationships includes the same properties and roles as each of them, plus an additional role and participating entity to distinguish the original relationships from each other (Fig. 3-15).

(i) Two views may be united through an entity if it is a generalization of entities found in both views (Fig. 3-34). The resulting entity keeps all its participations in relationships of the original views. Cardinalities may change. Additional business rules might be required.

QUESTION: How to integrate these views?

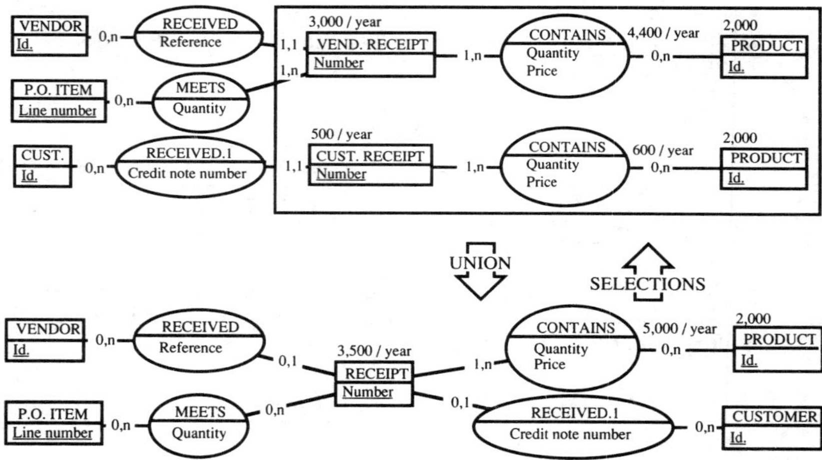

RULES: A RECEIPT is RECEIVED either from a VENDOR or a CUSTOMER. Only a VENDOR RECEIVED RECEIPT can MEET a P.O. ITEM.

ANSWER: By uniting entity PRODUCT, present in both views;
by merging VENDOR RECEIPT and CUSTOMER RECEIPT;
by merging relationship CONTAINS, present in both views:
• Same participants and properties;
• Similar meaning.
RECEIPT participates in the same relationships as source entities, but:
• Some resulting cardinalities are different;
• Business rules must be added to specify participation conditions.

Figure 3-34 Union of views.

(j) A union of two views may be performed step by step – when it is feasible.

3.4.3 Reverse joins

(a) *Reverse join* transformations simplify and normalize a model by creating objects which are more modular than objects observed on the logical level. A reverse join is a transformation which consists of retrieving a normal model from a composite object. It is feasible only if the object to be reverse joined really originates – through a join – from a normal model.

(b) A view where some property partially depends on the identifier (Fig. 3-35) – thus violating Second Normal Form – must be reverse joined.

QUESTION: How to normalize view PRODUCT.1, assuming that:
For 1 value of Product —> 1 value of Quantity on hand;
—> 1 or *n* values of Reference.
For 1 value of Product.Vendor —> 1 value of Reference.

NON-NORMAL VIEW

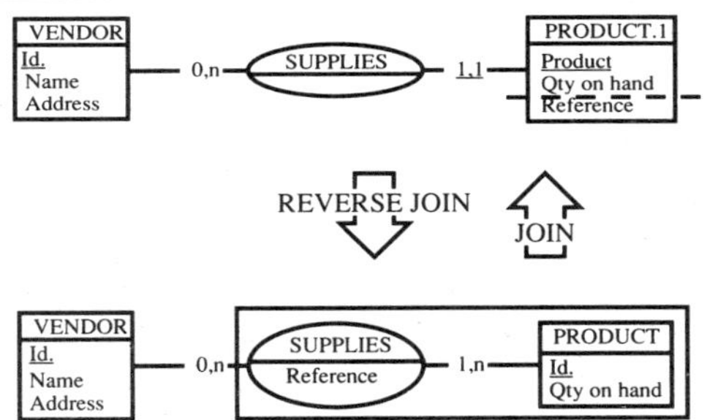

NORMAL VIEW

ANSWER: By reverse joining the view into two objects:
• Entity PRODUCT with property Quantity on hand;
• Relationship SUPPLIES with property Reference.

Figure 3-35 Reverse join of a view into an entity and a relationship.

(c) A view where some property indirectly depends on the identifier (Fig. 3-36) – thus violating Third Normal Form – must be reverse joined.

(d) The model resulting from a reverse join usually consists of connected objects. It may include an entity and a relationship (Fig. 3-35), two entities connected by a relationship (Fig. 3-36), or a relationship with a new role and participating entity (Fig. 3-37).

Properties are assigned to the resulting objects according to their dependencies with respect to identifiers.

QUESTION: How to normalize view PRODUCT.2, assuming that:
For 1 value of Department —> 1 value of Department name;
—> 0 or *n* values of Product;
For 1 value of Product —> 1 value of Product cost;
—> 1 value of Department.

NON-NORMAL VIEW

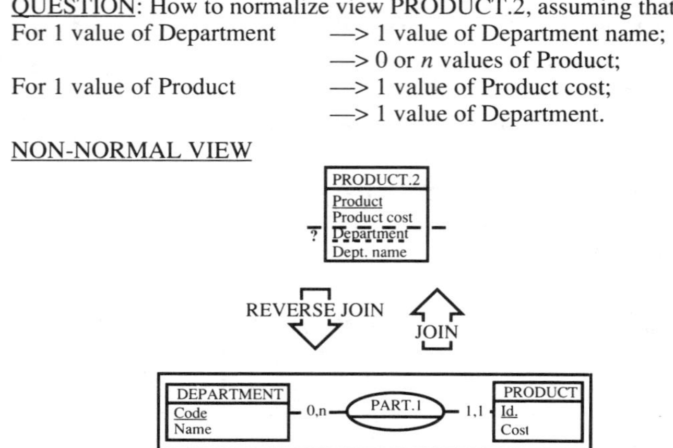

NORMAL VIEW

ANSWER: By reverse joining the view into two entities and a relationship.

Figure 3-36 Reverse join of a view into two entities and a relationship.

QUESTION: How to normalize view TARGET, assuming that:
For 1 value of Employee —> 1 value of Employee name;
—> 0 or *n* values of Sales target;
For 1 value of Dept.Region —> 1 value of Employee;
—> 1 value of Sales target.

NON-NORMAL VIEW

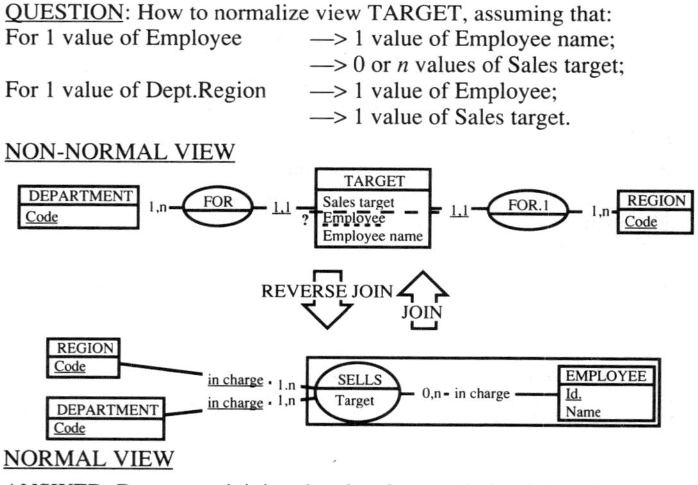

NORMAL VIEW

ANSWER: By reverse joining the view into a relationship and an entity, and stating the 'in charge' dependency rule implicit in the source view.

Figure 3-37 Reverse join of a view into a ternary relationship and an entity.

(e) A relationship with three roles or more and 1,1 cardinalities may be reverse joined into parent-child relationships (Fig. 3-38). This yields an equivalent model.

QUESTION: Can the ternary relationship BELONGS, in which VENDOR participates with 1,1 cardinalities, be simplified?

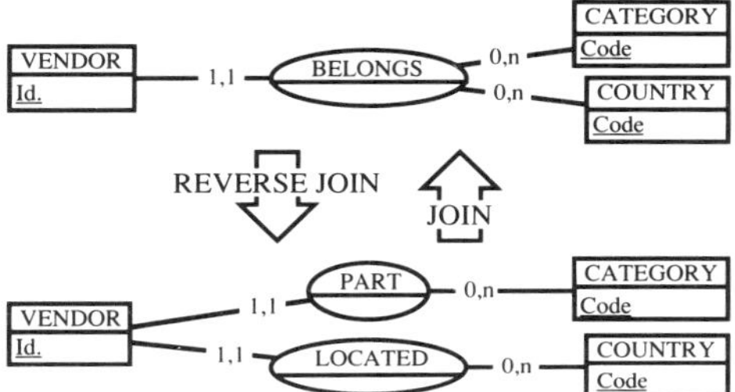

ANSWER: Yes, by reverse joining it into two parent-child relationships which express the same cardinality rules.

Figure 3-38 Reverse join of a ternary relationship with 1,1 cardinalities.

(f) A ternary relationship which is the join of two binary relationships must be reverse joined (Fig. 3-39).

QUESTION: Can SELLS be simplified, assuming that an EMPLOYEE (non-exclusively) sells a set of DEPARTMENTS in a set of REGIONS?

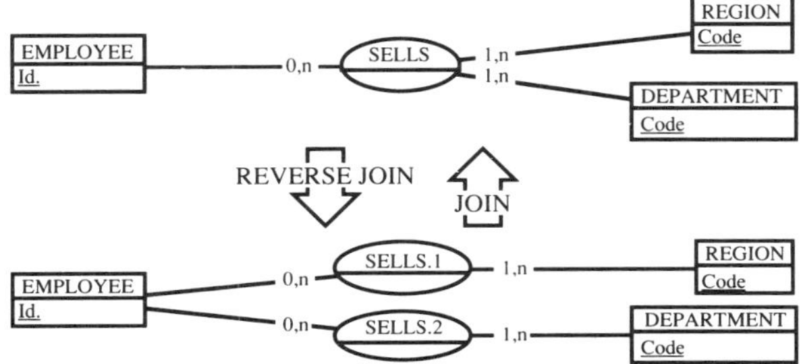

ANSWER: Yes, by reverse joining it into the two binary relationships which express the stated assumption (No, if it carries properties which depend on the DEPARTMENT.REGION combination).

Figure 3-39 Reverse join of a ternary relationship.

(g) The reverse join of a view may be performed step by step – when feasible.

3.4.4 Reverse groupings

(a) *Reverse grouping* transformations simplify and normalize a model by creating objects which are more modular than objects observed on the logical level. A reverse grouping is a transformation which consists of retrieving a normal model from a composite object. It is feasible only if the object to be reverse grouped really originates – through a grouping – from a normal model.

(b) A view where some property is optional or repetitive – thus violating First Normal Form – must be reverse grouped (Fig. 3-40).

QUESTION: How to normalize view ORDER.1, assuming that:

For 1 value of Number	—> 1 or *n* values of Product;
	—> 1 value of each date;
For 1 value of Product	—> 1 value of Cost;
For 1 value of Number.Prod.	—> 1 value of Quantity.

NON-NORMAL VIEW

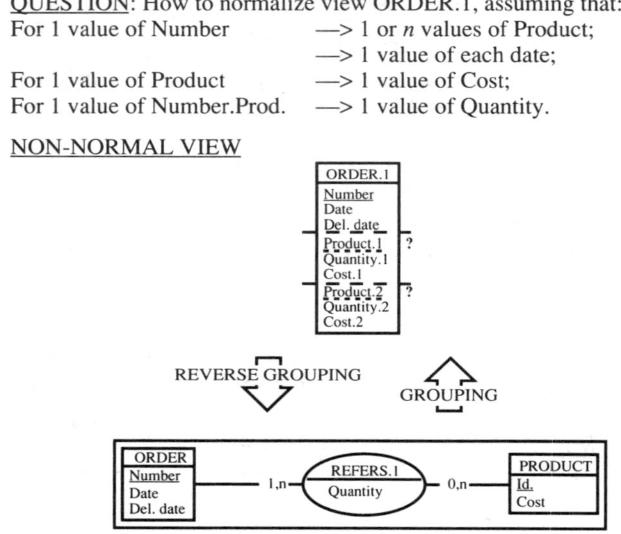

NORMAL VIEW

ANSWER: By reverse grouping it into two entities and a relationship.

Figure 3-40 Reverse grouping of a view into two entities and a relationship.

(c) The model resulting from a reverse grouping usually consists of connected objects. It may include an entity and a relationship (Fig. 3-19), two entities connected by a relationship (Fig. 3-40), or a relationship with a new role and participating entity (Fig. 3-41).

(d) The reverse grouping of a view may be performed step by step – when feasible.

<u>QUESTION</u>: How to normalize view PRODUCT PRICE, assuming that:
For 1 value of Vendor.Product —> 0 or *n* values of Quantity;
For 1 value of Vend.Prod.Qty —> 1 value of Price.

<u>NON-NORMAL VIEW</u>

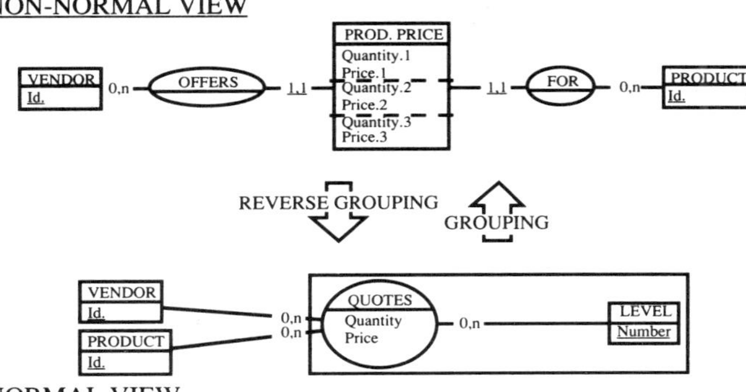

<u>NORMAL VIEW</u>

<u>ANSWER</u>: By reverse grouping it into entity LEVEL and relationship QUOTES which shows Qty and Price LEVELS for VENDOR PRODUCTS.

Figure 3-41 Reverse grouping of a view into a relationship with a new participant.

3.4.5 Reductions

(a) *Reduction* transformations simplify a model by keeping only fundamental objects and properties. A reduction is a selection which eliminates derived objects and properties from a view, as well as corresponding business rules. It is the reverse of an augmentation (Fig. 3-42).

<u>QUESTION</u>: Can this model be simplified, assuming that an EMPLOYEE SELLS.1 the PRODUCTS of the DEPARTMENT that he or she SELLS?

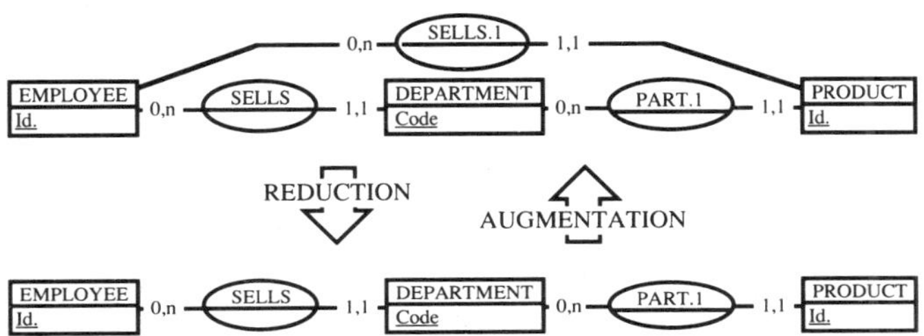

<u>ANSWER</u>: Yes, by reduction: derived relationship SELLS.1 is removed.
(No, if SELLS.1 has a different meaning.)

Figure 3-42 Reduction.

(b) The primary properties model does not include any derivable object or property; it cannot be reduced.

3.4.6 Combining integrations

It is often necessary to combine integration transformations, that is, merges, unions, reverse joins, reverse groupings and reductions, to simplify a model.

For example, this is the case when candidate sub-entities cannot be directly united because they do not have exactly the same properties (Fig. 3-14): the combined integrations result in a model which includes both a super-entity and modified sub-entities, linked by a collection of 0,1–1,1 relationships. A similar situation may involve entities and relationships (Fig. 3-43).

QUESTION: Can this model be made less redundant?

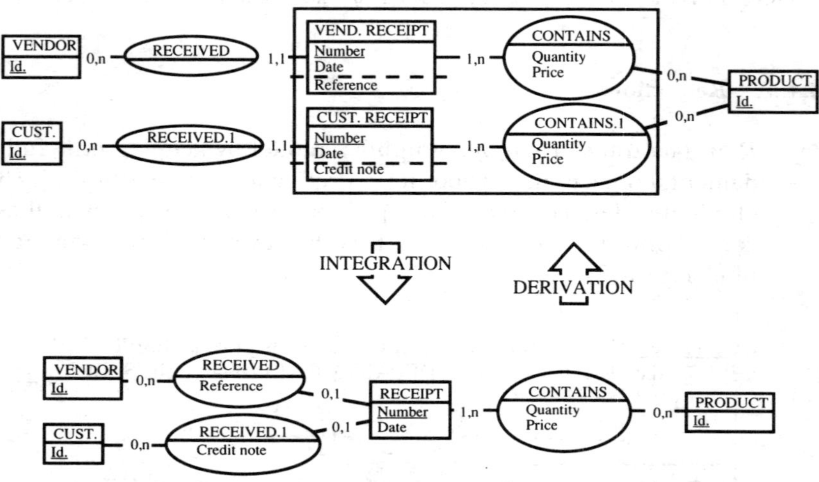

RULE: A RECEIPT is RECEIVED either from a VENDOR or a CUSTOMER.

ANSWER: Yes, by uniting entities VENDOR RECEIPT and CUSTOMER RECEIPT and by uniting both relationships CONTAINS.
But for 1 occurrence of RECEIPT —> 0 or 1 value of Reference;
—> 0 or 1 value of Credit note.
—> Source entities RECEIPT must be reverse joined;
—> Some cardinalities must be changed.

Figure 3-43 Union and reverse join.

3.5 Representation

Objects which are part of a sub-model, a partial model, or which are to be joined, grouped, merged or united may be distinguished with an outline around them.

A non-normal object may be represented as a box with thicker lines.

Derived objects and properties may be marked with an asterisk.

Chapter 4

Conceptual Modeling

> Thus one of the main functions of the concept network is to allow early wrong ideas to be modified slightly, to slip into variations which may be correct.
>
> (D. Hofstadter, *Gödel, Escher, Bach*)

This chapter shows how a conceptual model is developed. An approach is presented, together with three versions of the model, corresponding to three typical systems development stages (Chap. 1). The reader is familiar by now with the example – the same one we have examined from the outset. Consequently, we are in a position to compare various models, to judge their respective correspondence with the 'real world' and to assess the efforts which would be required to complete the final version.

The chapter also gives an example of progression from one version to the next. It demonstrates the practical situations a modeler faces: choices of representations, model transformations (Chap. 3), adjustments to the conceptual model when developing the logical model, etc. By studying it, the reader will be better able to understand how data modeling techniques presented in previous chapters can be put to use when dealing with a real-world case.

4.1 Approach

The purpose of conceptual modeling is to rapidly arrive at well-structured applications which conform to a common architecture. This book proposes an approach (Fig. 1-3) whereby the conceptual model is refined by stages, becoming more detailed and complete as the systems development life cycle progresses.

The overall *corporate conceptual model* (Fig. 4-5) is succeeded by domain specific *general conceptual models* (Fig. 4-18), which identify objects of each functional domain within the organization, and by *detailed conceptual models* (Fig. 4-21 and 4-22) which contain all the required information.

Each conceptual modeling stage includes information gathering, analysis and design steps, followed by a logical modeling stage which verifies the conceptual models and ensures that they meet information requirements.

4.2 Information Sources

To develop a conceptual model, one must look for information which identifies and describes the model's objects, its properties and its business rules.

Managers within the target sector are the primary source of information and it is relatively easy to develop a preliminary draft of the conceptual model by having them describe the purpose of their activities. Key words and statements from these descriptions will generally correspond to entities and relationships between entities.

However, in order to refine the conceptual model, especially with respect to cardinalities and properties, formal documentary sources must often be examined in detail.

Policy statements, government rulings, laws, etc. for a given sector reflect the major rules and regulations governing this sector. So these sources are useful for deducing the main entities in the sector, the most important relationships, and the principal business rules which must be considered. At times they may clearly define certain entities, relationships and even properties.

Data capture or data recording documents, such as forms, manual files and other documents containing detailed information, are especially useful. Any such document is often associated with an entity or relationship, the name for which may be inferred from the document title. The layout of the various parts of the document provides clues concerning the possible existence of other entities connected to the main one, and also concerning the cardinalities involved. Document contents make it possible to list related properties and occasionally business rules. The document view is close to the conceptual model, and indeed is derived from it with a minimum of transformations.

Data processing specifications, such as file design, database design or transaction design, play the same part as forms: they make it possible to identify related entities, relationships, and properties, as well as cardinalities. However, one must be careful in the conceptual model not to include all physical elements found in this way. Some data elements are there only to make processing easier; cardinalities implicit in the physical structure of data might be the result of constraints pertaining to the software being used.

Descriptive systems documentation, such as procedures manuals, user guides and system specifications, contain detailed information on the data and on the applicable business rules which are handled by systems. They are useful for refining and perfecting business rules and the definition of properties.

Lastly, *documents produced by existing systems*, both manual and automated, such as lists, reports, statements and other documents containing summarized information, may be useful to verify the conceptual model. These documents often correspond to views of the model, having undergone one or more transformations.

Information sources, written and oral, sometimes use less than precise and inconsistent terminology. The same concepts are often expressed by different terms, while the same term might designate different concepts. Sometimes essential concepts do not even have a name. It becomes the modeler's task to make the organization's vocabulary more precise, by selecting appropriate terms to name and describe entities, relationships and properties.

4.3 Information Analysis and Model Design

4.3.1 Corporate conceptual model

The *corporate conceptual model* is developed as part of the organization's systems strategic plan.

This summary version of the conceptual model shows the main entities and relationships of interest to the organization, thus displaying the scope of corporate activities. On a logical level, it will also help to identify and relate each management domain within the organization to each other, as views of the model.

The corporate conceptual model is restricted to a high level entity-relationship diagram, without properties, cardinalities or business rules (Fig. 4-5). Objects are inferred from a cursory analysis of the general information available, supplemented by interviews with senior management (Fig. 4-1). Using this information, the analyst identifies entities which are most representative of the activities under consideration (Fig. 4-2); indicates the main relationships which connect them (Fig. 4-3 and 4-4); maintains a high level of generality, to keep the model simple; and summarily describes the model and its entities.

GATHERING INFORMATION FOR THE CORPORATE MODEL

INTERVIEW	COMMENT
SALES MANAGER	"Basically, Mentor is a distributor: we buy school supplies from a variety of vendors and we sell them to customers all over the country"
	"Products are stored at Mentor's branch"
	"Customers are assigned sales representatives on a sector-by-sector basis. Sales reps take orders from them and are paid a commission"
PERSONNEL MANAGER	"At Mentor, we insist that all employees have a recognized position within the organization"
FINANCE MANAGER	"What we do is keeping track of sales and purchases, cashing checks, paying invoices, preparing the payroll, balancing the ledgers"
	"We prepare monthly financial statements and we compare sales and expenses with budgets"

Figure 4-1 Developing the corporate conceptual model: gathering information.

FINDING CORPORATE MODEL ENTITIES

NOUN	ENTITY	NOUN	ENTITY
Distributor		Position	POSITION
School supplies	PRODUCT	Employees	EMPLOYEE
Vendors	VENDOR	Organization	
Customers	CUSTOMER	Sales	SALE
Country		Purchases	PURCHASE
Products	PRODUCT	Checks	TRANSACTION
Branch		Invoices	TRANSACTION
Sales reps	EMPLOYEE	Payroll	PAY
Sector	CUSTOMER	Ledgers	ACCOUNT
Orders	SALE	Statements	
Commission	PAY	Budgets	BUDGET

In statements about the business, nouns indicate entities:
- Plural nouns: vendors, customers;
- Singular nouns with a meaningful plural in the domain's context: sector;
- Nouns which denote collections: payroll —> pay, ledgers —> accounts.

Some entities do not need to be represented in the model:
- Entities with a unique occurrence: distributor, country;
- Entities on which there is no need to keep information: statements.

At the corporate level, some entities may be united or grouped with others:
- Near synonyms: school supplies —> products, orders —> sales;
- Sub-type with super-type: sales reps —> employees, commission —> pay;
- Sub-types with common super-type: checks, invoices —> transactions;
- Non-essential entities with related entities: sector —> customers.

Figure 4-2 Developing the corporate conceptual model: entities.

FINDING CORPORATE MODEL RELATIONSHIPS

ENTITY	VE	PU	PR	SA	CU	EM	PO	PA	TR	AC	BU
VENDOR		√	√						√	√	
PURCHASE			√						√	√	√
PRODUCT				√	√				√		
SALE					√	√			√	√	√
CUSTOMER						√			√	√	
EMPLOYEE							√	√	√		
POSITION								√			
PAY									√		√
TRANSACTION										√	√
ACCOUNT											√
BUDGET											

Relationships are found by examining entities in pairs and deciding which ones are related to each other in the business being studied.
This is done based on previously gathered information and common knowledge about the domains of interest.

Figure 4-3 Developing the corporate conceptual model: relationships.

DRAFTING THE CORPORATE MODEL

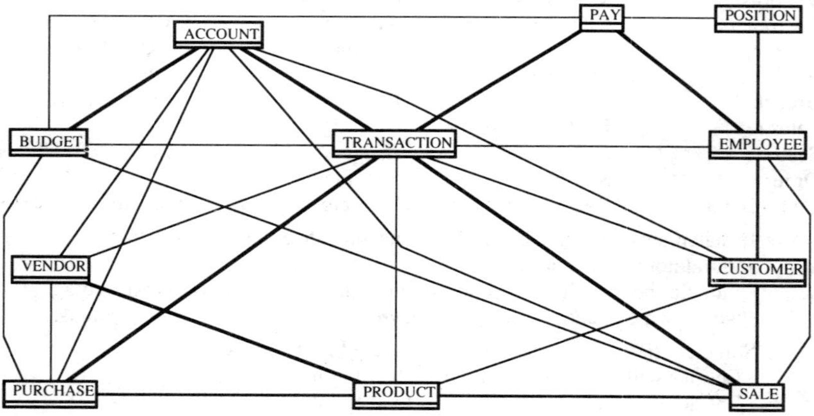

The preliminary draft shows entities and relationships previously found.

At the corporate level, it may be simplified by keeping only the strongest relationships (thick lines). Most others may be considered derived, e.g.:

- The relationship between a customer and a product is through a sale;
- The relationship between a sale and a budget is through a transaction and an account.

Figure 4-4 Developing the corporate conceptual model: draft.

FINALIZING THE CORPORATE MODEL

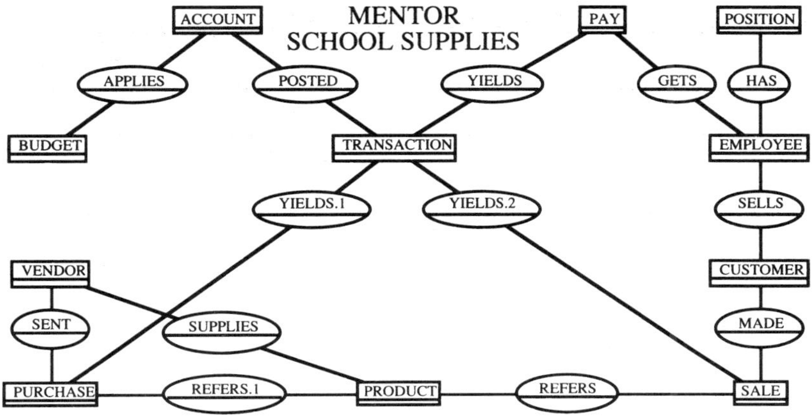

The corporate model is finalized by giving meaningful names to relationships.

Each object of the corporate model represents an unanalyzed view of data which are of interest to the organization.

At this level, the model cannot be normal or complete.

Figure 4-5 Developing the corporate conceptual model: final version.

4.3.2 General conceptual model of a domain

General conceptual models of each domain – or *subject* as domains are sometimes called – are preferably developed simultaneously, during the corporate systems architecture stage; alternatively, they may be developed separately, during the preliminary study of each domain.

These models represent the fundamental structure of each domain. On a logical level, the conceptual model of a domain will help to relate the processes of systems within the domain to each other: these processes will appear as views of the model.

Similarly, conceptual models of neighboring domains highlight shared objects: often an object will be managed by processes in one domain and used for query in several other domains. Indeed, domains are views of the corporate conceptual model.

The general conceptual model of a domain (Fig. 4-18) contains most entities and relationships of the domain, all corresponding cardinalities, and the principal properties and identifiers. It provides narrative descriptions for the domain, its entities, its relationships and its most significant business rules. It shows generalized and specialized entities. Finally, it may indicate which entities are shared with other domains.

The general conceptual model of a domain is built from the corporate model and from the general and detailed information available on the domain. One may use the following approach:

1. *Analysis of the domain*

   (a) Start by showing the domain as a view on the corporate conceptual model (Fig. 4-6). Normally, such a view is a result of the corporate logical modeling stage. It can also be directly developed by identifying entities and relationships of interest for managing the domain.

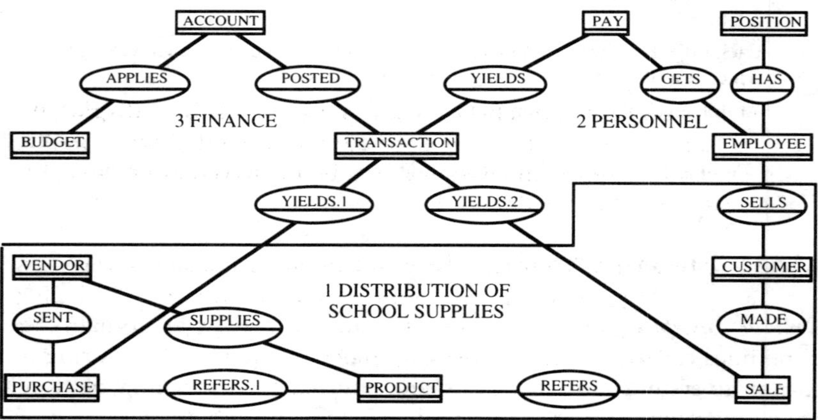

The model of the Distribution of School Supplies domain starts as a view on the corporate model.

Figure 4-6 Developing the general conceptual model of a domain: initial version.

   (b) Put manual documents and data processing specifications into groups which more or less correspond to domain entities shown on the corporate model (Fig. 4-7). Documents which relate two or more entities may be grouped in more than one way. Obtain help from managers who have responsibilities in the domain.

GATHERING INFORMATION FOR THE DOMAIN MODEL

ENTITY	DOCUMENT	DESCRIPTION
VENDOR	Vendor file	Contains basic information on vendors.
	Vendor catalogs	Relate products to vendors.
PURCHASE	Article P.O. form	Used to order articles from vendors.
	Manual P.O. form	Used to order manuals from vendors.
	Receipt form	Records products received from vendors.
PRODUCT	Inventory card	Keeps track of stock on hand.
	Inventory list	Lists products and available quantities.
SALE	Order form	Records customer orders.
	Shipment form	Records products shipped to customers.
	Sales report	Summarizes sales by sales representative.
CUSTOMER	Customer file	Contains basic information on customers.

Figure 4-7 Developing the general conceptual model of a domain: gathering information.

2. *Analysis of each major 'entity'*

   (a) In each group, choose documents which best display the structure of data. As previously mentioned, data recording documents or file design are to be preferred to reports. Examine them in detail.

   (b) For each of these documents, develop a normal view by analyzing properties, cardinalities and identifiers which they contain, and by combining reverse grouping, reverse join and reduction transformations.

   (c) Integrate the various views belonging to the same group by using merge and union transformations; consult with managers to resolve inconsistencies affecting names, meanings, cardinalities, identifiers or existence rules. The resulting integrated view refines the structure of the corresponding 'entity' in the corporate model (Fig. 4-8 to 4-14).

3. *Integration within the domain*

   (a) Integrate views corresponding to each group, following the overall corporate model and using merge and reunion transformations (Fig. 4-15 to 4-18). Resolve inconsistencies by consulting with managers.

INTEGRATING VENDOR VIEWS

VENDOR FILE

CODE	MAN-US-11
NAME	KEMPF
ADDRESS	125 5TH ST. NEW YORK
CATEGORY	MANUFACT.

KEMPF CATALOG

ARTICLE	DESCRIPTION	UNIT	PRICE
342-D12	PAINTBRUSH	DOZEN	$21.00
709-X60	MODELING CLAY	BX OF 60	$17.00
124-X50	CHALK	BX OF 50	$11.00

VENDOR
Code
Name
Address
Category

VENDOR
Name
1,n
SUPPLIES
1,1
ARTICLE
Vend. ref.
Vend. descr.
Vend. unit
Vend. price

Vendor File:
• All properties directly relate to a vendor. As a result, the vendor file yields the single entity VENDOR.

Vendor Catalog :
• For a given vendor, the article properties are repetitive. As a result, vendor catalogs yield two entities, VENDOR and ARTICLE, connected by a relationship (reverse grouping);
• Every vendor has its own list of articles, hence the identifier dependency in SUPPLIES.

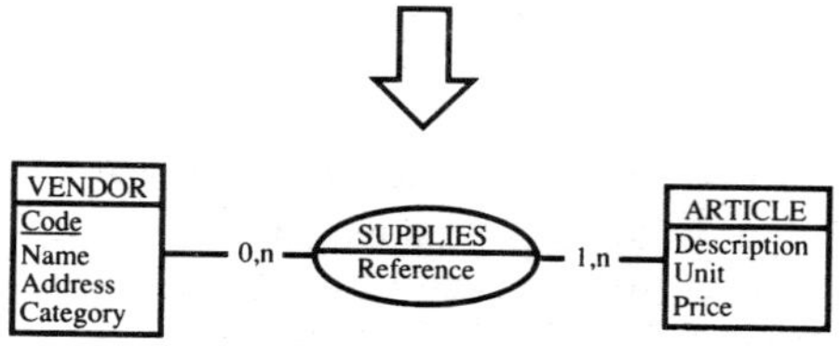

Integration:
• The two incarnations of the VENDOR entity are merged;
• Identical occurrences of the ARTICLE entity supplied by different vendors are united, resulting in 1,*n* instead of 1,1 cardinalities;
• The SUPPLIES relationship is restricted to approved article vendors. Accordingly, the VENDOR cardinalities are changed to 0,*n* to accommodate vendors without approved articles;
• Reference, a vendor dependent article property, is moved to relationship SUPPLIES. Other vendor dependent article properties which do not interest Mentor management are dropped;
• Equivalent Mentor properties unique to each ARTICLE occurrence are assigned. The ARTICLE identifier is not assigned yet.

Figure 4-8 Developing the general conceptual model of a domain: integrating vendor views.

INTEGRATING PURCHASE VIEWS

PURCHASE ORDER

TO: KEMPF — JULY 15, 1993
125 5TH ST — # 4767
NEW YORK — MAN-US-11

ARTICLE	YOUR REF	DESCRIPTION	UNIT	QTY
69415	342-D12	PAINTBRUSH	DOZ	100
70248	122-K60	WAX	CAN	20
63511	683-A00	PAINTBOX	EA	50

RECEIPT

FROM: KEMPF — JULY 29, 1993
CODE: MAN-US-11 — # R903
VENDOR REF.: 72-061

ARTICLE	DESCRIPTION	UNIT	QTY
69415	PAINTBRUSH	DOZ	80
70248	WAX	CAN	20

PURCH. ORDER (Number, Date, Vendor number, Vendor name, Vendor address) — 1,n — INCLUDES — 1,1 — ARTICLE (Article, Vendor ref., Description, Unit, Quantity)

RECEIPT (Number, Date, Vendor code, Vendor name, Vendor reference) — 1,n — INCLUDES — 1,1 — ARTICLE (Article, Description, Unit, Quantity)

Purchase Order:

• For a given P.O., the article properties are repetitive. The P.O. yields two entities, PURCH. ORDER and ARTICLE, connected by a relationship (reverse grouping);

• Every P.O. has its own list of articles, hence the identifier dependency in INCLUDES.

Receipt:

• The Receipt form is analyzed in the same manner as the P. O., yielding two entities connected by a relationship.

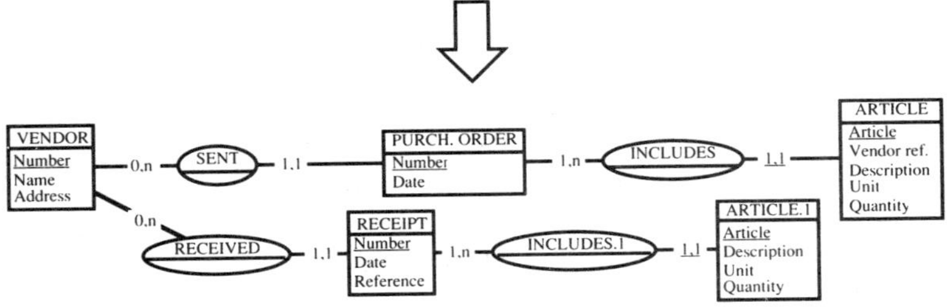

Integration – VENDOR entity:

• The vendor properties of the PURCH. ORDER and RECEIPT entities are dependent on the Vendor code – or Vendor number – property. They are reverse joined from these entities and merged, yielding the VENDOR entity and the SENT and RECEIVED relationships;

• Other properties directly dependent on the purchase order or receipt stay in place.

(Note the difference between the Receipt vendor reference and the Article vendor reference.)

Figure 4-9 Developing the general conceptual model of a domain: integrating purchase views.

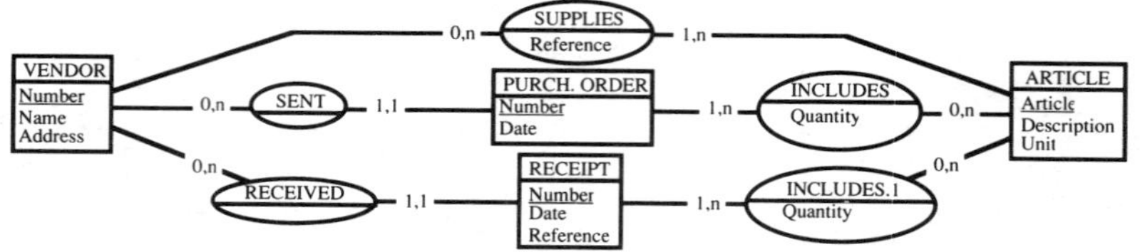

Integration – ARTICLE entity:
• The Description and Unit properties of the ARTICLE entities (Fig. 4-9) are dependent on the Article number. They are reverse joined and merged, yielding the ARTICLE entity. Accordingly, the 1,1 cardinalities of the INCLUDES relationships are changed to 0,*n*;
• Properties which depend on the P.O. article – or the receipt article – combination, are reassigned to the INCLUDES relationships;
(Note that Receipt article quantity ≠ P. O. article quantity.)
• Article vendor reference depends on the vendor article combination but not on the P.O.; it is reassigned to the SUPPLIES relationship.

Figure 4-10 Developing the general conceptual model of a domain: integrating purchase views (continuation).

DEVELOPING A PRODUCT VIEW

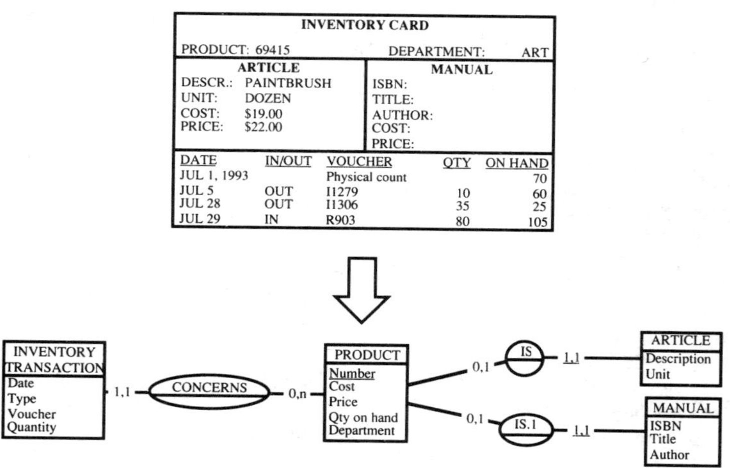

INVENTORY CARD

PRODUCT: 69415 DEPARTMENT: ART

ARTICLE		MANUAL
DESCR.:	PAINTBRUSH	ISBN:
UNIT:	DOZEN	TITLE:
COST:	$19.00	AUTHOR:
PRICE:	$22.00	COST:
		PRICE:

DATE	IN/OUT	VOUCHER	QTY	ON HAND
JUL 1, 1993		Physical count		70
JUL 5	OUT	I1279	10	60
JUL 28	OUT	I1306	35	25
JUL 29	IN	R903	80	105

Inventory Card:
• Mutually exclusive article and manual properties yield separate entities;
• Repetitive transaction properties yield a separate entity;
• Only the last Qty on hand, dependent on product, interests management.

Figure 4-11 Developing the general conceptual model of a domain: product view.

INTEGRATING SALE VIEWS

SALES ORDER

SHIP TO: ALGONQUIN SCHOOL — JULY 29, 1993
101 COLUMBIA DR. — # 1527
PRESTON — 702

#	DESCR./TITLE	UNIT/AUTH.	QTY	PRICE	AMT
57875	DRAWING	SMITH	40	$21.00	840.00
57892	PAINTING	ZONG	40	$15.00	600.00
					1 440.00

SHIPMENT SLIP

SHIP TO: ALGONQUIN SCHOOL — AUGUST 1, 1993
101 COLUMBIA DR. — # 11250
PRESTON — 702
ORDER: 1527

#	DESCR./TITLE	UNIT/AUTH.	QTY	PRICE	AMT
57875	DRAWING	SMITH	30	$22.00	660.00
57892	PAINTING	ZONG	40	$15.00	600.00
					1 260.00
				DISC.:	126.00
				NET:	1 134.00

ORDER: Number, Date, Cust. number, Cust. name, Cust. address, Total amount — 1,n — INCLUDES — 1,1 — PRODUCT: Number, Description, Title, Unit, Author, Quantity, Price, Amount

SHIPMENT: Invoice number, Date, Cust. number, Cust. name, Cust. address, Gross amount, Discount, Net amount, Order number — 1,n — INCLUDES — 1,1 — PRODUCT: Number, Description, Title, Unit, Author, Quantity, Price, Amount

Sales Order and Shipment Slip:
- Views are derived in the same manner as views for purchases (Fig. 4-9);
- Note that the PRODUCT entities are not normalized with respect to properties Description, Title, Unit, Author.

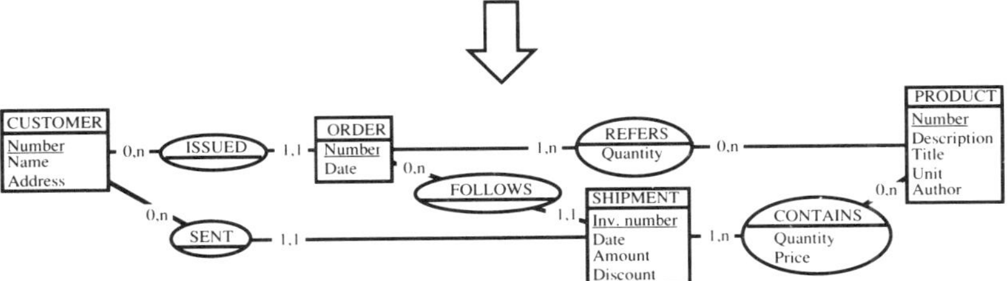

Integration:
- Integration is carried out similarly as for purchases (Fig. 4-9 and 4-10);
- Customer properties of ORDER and SHIPMENT are reverse joined from these entities and merged, yielding the CUSTOMER entity and the ISSUED and SENT relationships;
- Product properties of the PRODUCT entities are dealt with similarly; the INCLUDES relationships are renamed REFERS and CONTAINS;
- Other properties stay in place or are reassigned according to their dependencies. Shipment prices and amounts, which are binding on Mentor, are kept; order prices, which are not, are dropped;
- The FOLLOWS relationship is introduced, as indicated by the Order number in the Shipment Slip, making the SENT relationship redundant.

Figure 4-12 Developing the general conceptual model of a domain: integrating sale views.

SALES REPORT

REP.: MARTHA — JULY 1993

NUMBER: 333

DEPT	DESCRIPTION	REGION	NAME	TARGET	TO DATE
ART	ART	R1	WEST	100 000	55 500
		R4	EAST	70 000	23 000
LIT	LITTERATURE	R1	WEST	20 000	5 000
		R3	MIDWEST	15 000	6 000
	TOTAL			205 000	89 500

SALES REP.
Number
Name

DEPARTMENT
Code
Description

1,n
1,n

SELLS
Target
To date

1,n

REGION
Code
Name

Sales Report:

• Target and To date possibly depend on four identifiers: Sales rep. number, Department code, Region code and Month. But sales targets are set for the whole year; and only the latest sales to date figures are of use. Thus Month may be dropped. Hence the three-way relationship SELLS;

• Other properties are assigned according to their dependencies. Derived properties Total target and Total sales to date are dropped;

• At this stage of modeling, there is no straightforward way to integrate this view with the preceding view (Fig. 4-12).

Figure 4-13 Developing the general conceptual model of a domain: integrating sale views (continuation).

DEVELOPING A CUSTOMER VIEW

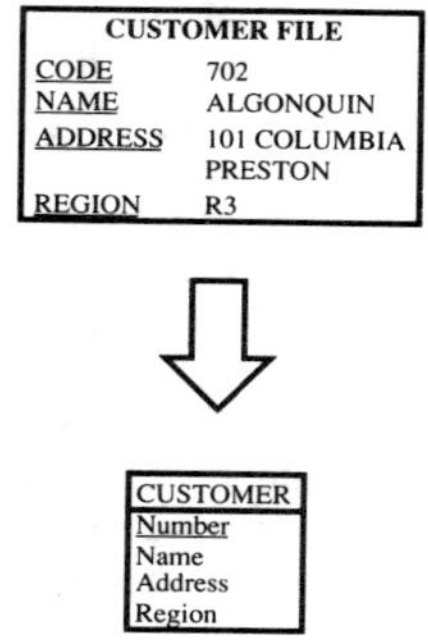

CUSTOMER FILE

CODE	702
NAME	ALGONQUIN
ADDRESS	101 COLUMBIA PRESTON
REGION	R3

Customer File:

• Deriving this view is straightforward.

Figure 4-14 Developing the general conceptual model of a domain: customer view.

ASSEMBLING GROUP VIEWS

VENDOR

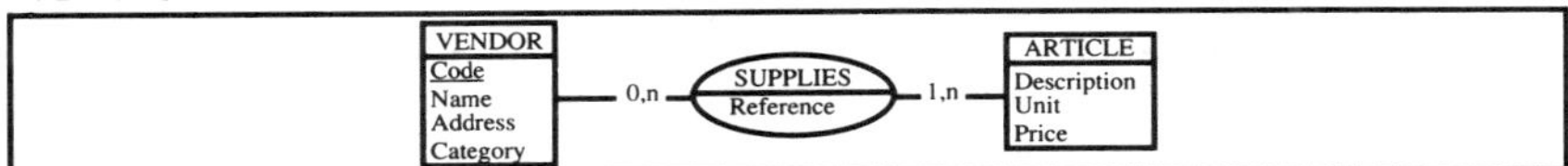

PURCHASE

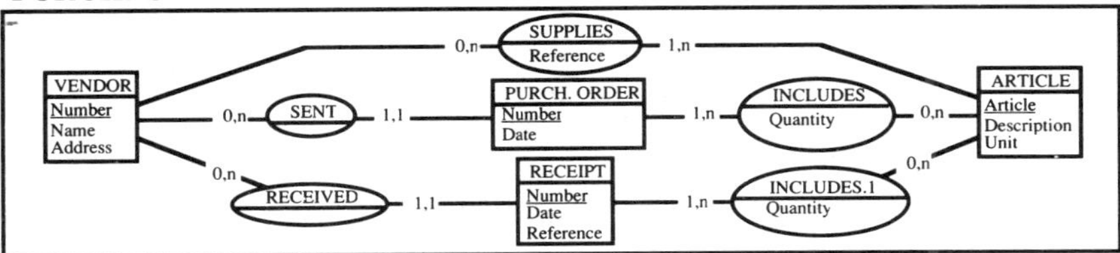

PRODUCT

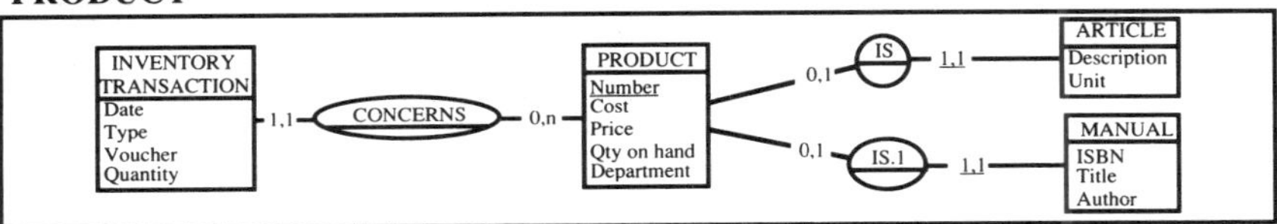

SALE

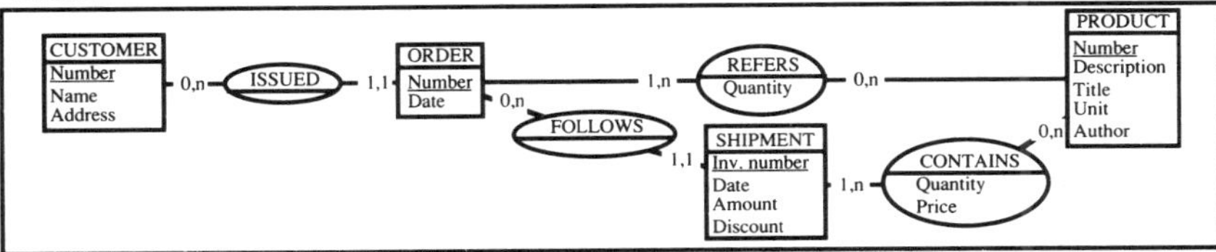

SALE.1

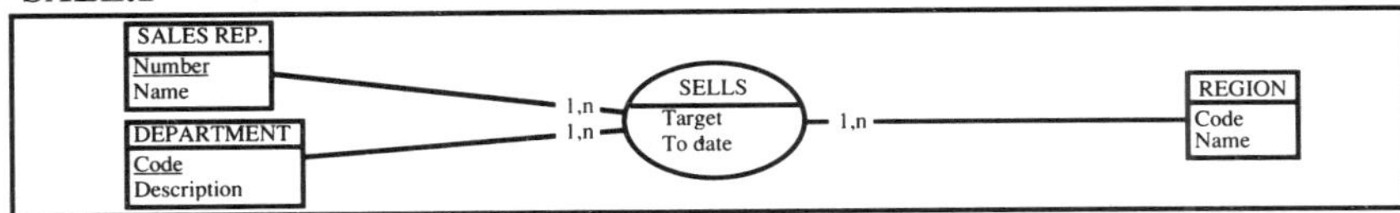

CUSTOMER

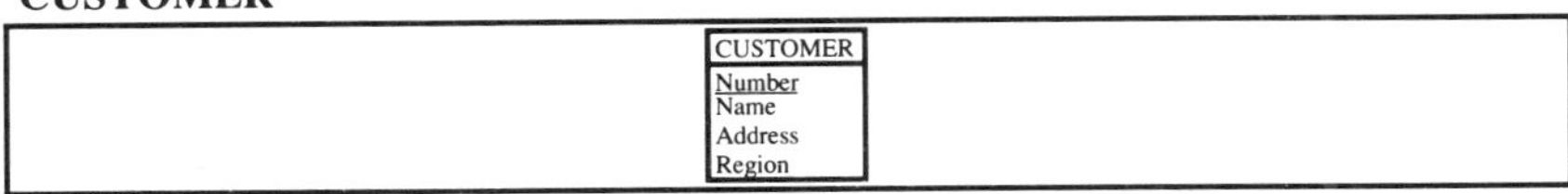

- Views obtained for each group of documents are assembled and examined;
- The corporate conceptual model suggests integrating Vendor with Purchase, Purchase with Product, Product with Sale, and Sale with Customer.

Figure 4-15 Developing the general conceptual model of a domain: assembling group views.

INTEGRATING GROUP VIEWS

VENDOR + PURCHASE

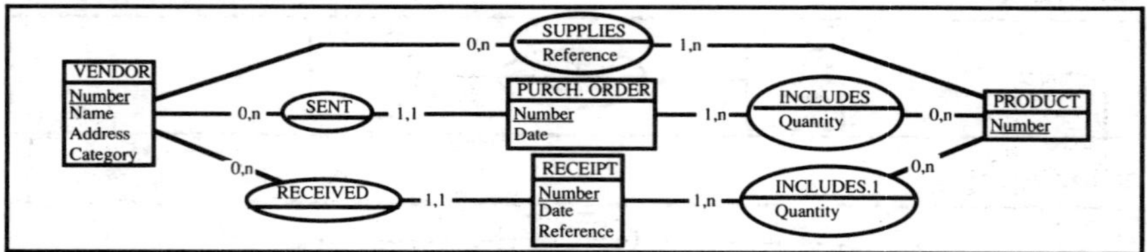

• Vendor view objects are merged with similar objects of the Purchase view;
• The ARTICLE entity is replaced by the more general PRODUCT entity, after checking that all ARTICLE properties are found in the Product view and that all ARTICLE relationships hold for PRODUCT (i.e. MANUAL).

PRODUCT

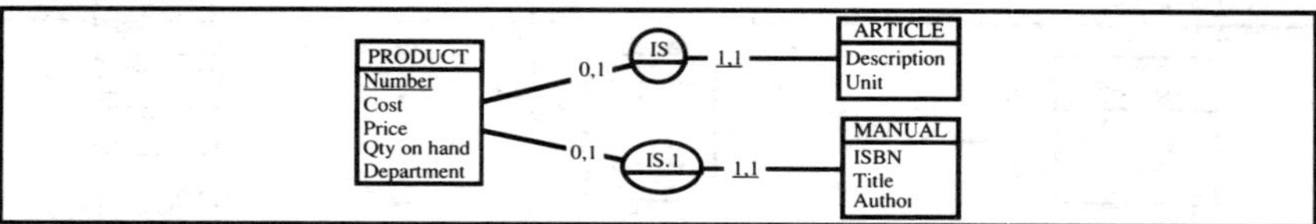

• The INVENTORY TRANSACTION entity is dropped from this view after realizing that a transaction is a receipt item or a shipment item. Those more specialized entities are part of other views and contain all required properties.

SALE + CUSTOMER

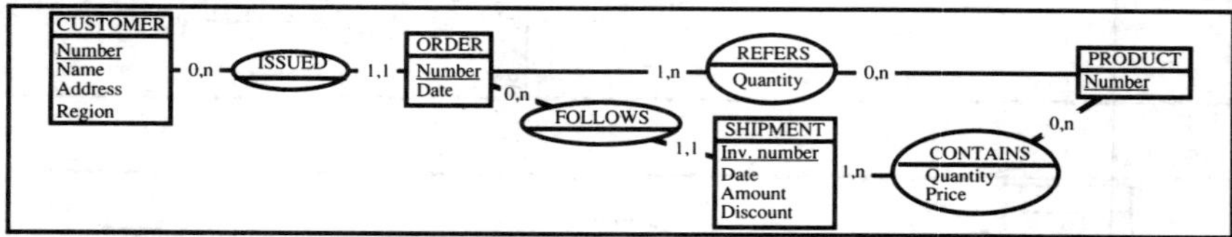

• The CUSTOMER entity is merged with the similar entity of the Sale view;
• The PRODUCT entity is reduced to its identifier after checking that all PRODUCT properties are found in the Product view.

SALE.1

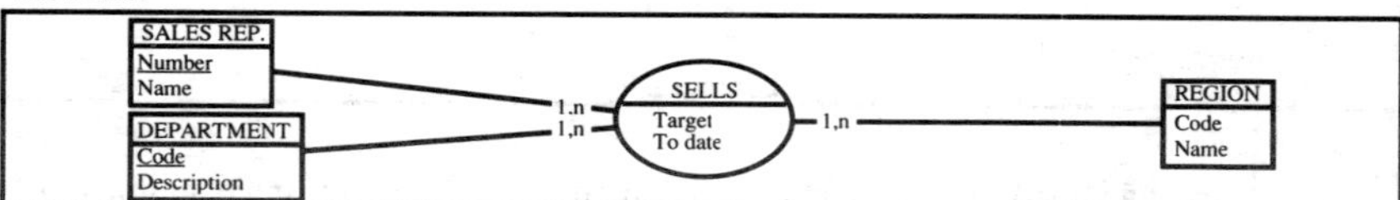

• This view is not integrated for the time being.

Figure 4-16 Developing the general conceptual model of a domain: integrating group views.

INTEGRATING GROUP VIEWS (CONTINUATION)

VENDOR + PURCHASE + PRODUCT + SALE + CUSTOMER + SALE.1

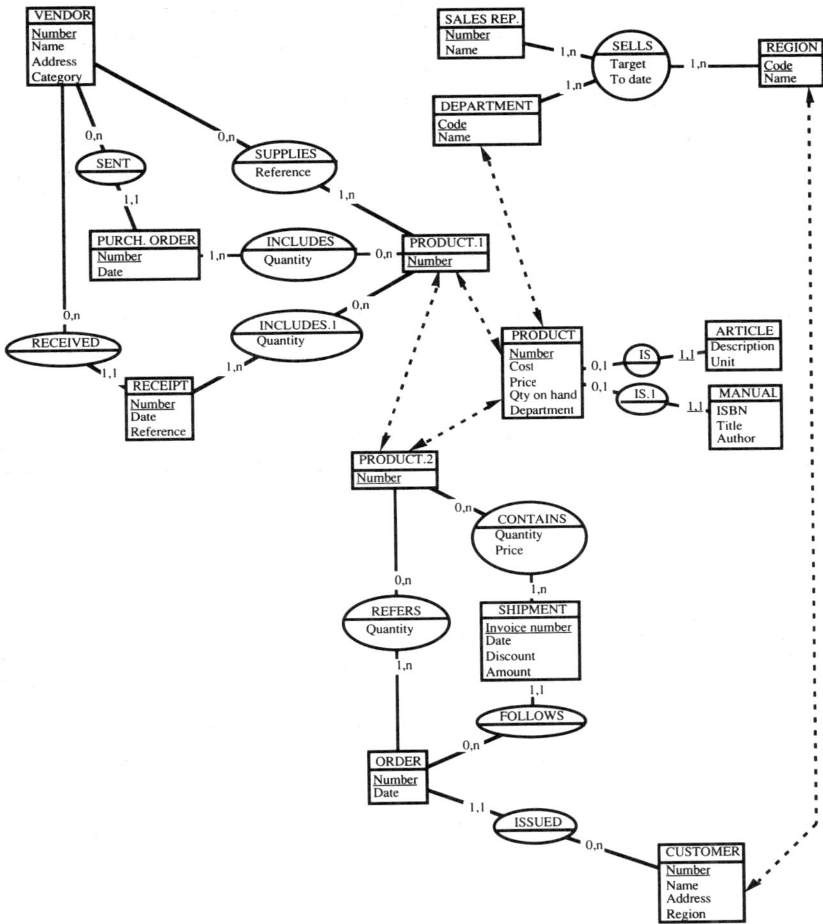

Integration:

- The three views involving products are integrated by merging the PRODUCT entity;
- The Sale.1 view is integrated with the resulting view by recognizing relationships between DEPARTMENT and PRODUCT, and between REGION and CUSTOMER.

Figure 4-17 Developing the general conceptual model of a domain: integrating group views (continuation).

4. *Validations of the domain*

(a) Perform a preliminary validation of the model (Fig. 4-18), ensuring that views contained in outside documents and specifications can be derived from the model.

(b) Verify the general domain model by integrating it with models of other domains. Refine the common entities. Resolve inconsistencies.

(c) Document the general domain's model by defining entities; by explaining relationships and cardinalities which require it; and by noting populations.

(d) Verify the model and its documentation with the domain managers.

Numerous variations of this approach are possible. When the scope of the domain is wide, it may be useful to break it into sub-domains and to integrate each sub-domain first. Then models for sub-domains may be integrated.

One may also progressively develop the model, starting with a nucleus built around a few major entities, and continuing by successively integrating views corresponding to other entities.

4.3.3 Detailed conceptual model of a domain

The *detailed conceptual model* of a domain is developed as part of the systems architecture of the domain.

The model will make it possible to accurately identify all the logical components of systems in the domain by representing them as model views. This will permit specifying them during subsequent stages.

Therefore, it is essential that the model contains all the relevant information, including properties, their descriptions, identifiers, business rules.

The detailed conceptual model (Fig. 4-21) is obtained by refining the general conceptual model in all its details. A possible approach for preparing it is as follows:

1. *Discussing the general conceptual model with users*
Explain the conceptual model to domain users. Discuss special cases and exceptions; check cardinalities. Look for opportunities

FINALIZING THE GENERAL CONCEPTUAL MODEL

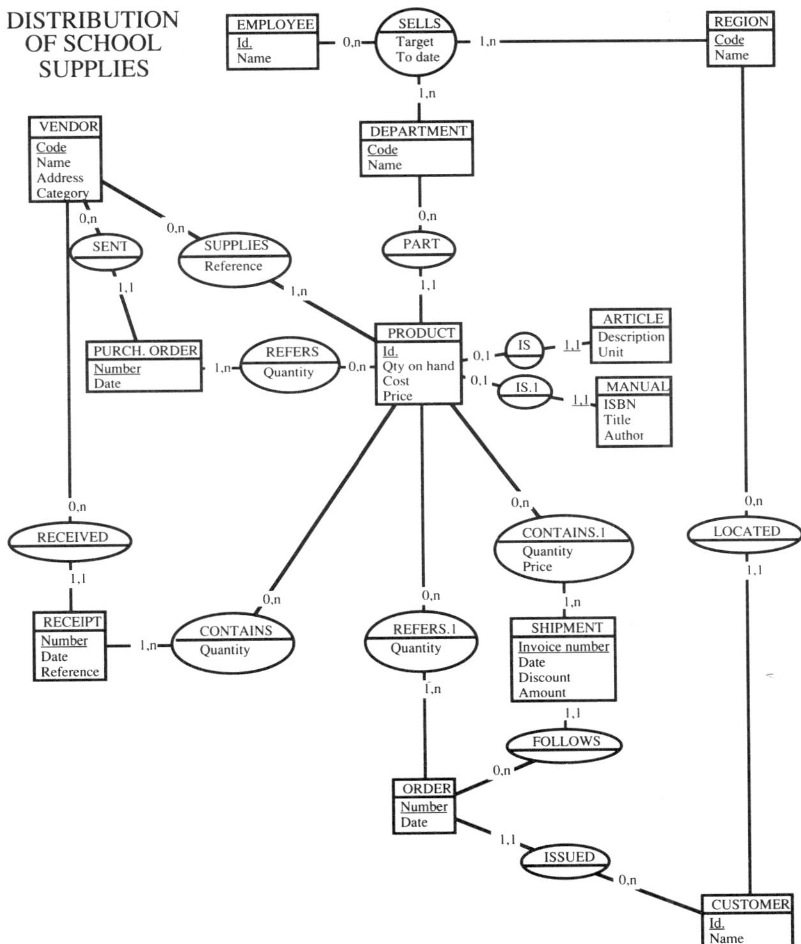

Finalization:

- The SALES REP. entity is generalized into the EMPLOYEE entity from the Human Resources model. SELLS cardinalities are changed accordingly;
- Some objects and properties are renamed to ensure better consistency.

Note: The general model is a refinement of the corporate model and it contains most objects of the detailed model to come. But some less significant objects and properties may still be missing.

Figure 4-18 Developing the general conceptual model of a domain: final version.

to further normalize the model. Uncover overlooked facts and integrate them with the model (Fig. 4-19 to 4-21).

FINDING CONCEPTUAL MODEL REFINEMENTS

	REFINEMENT	OBJECTS
1	Vendors are identified through their category and country.	VENDOR
2	Mentor wants to keep track of which products are manufactured by their vendors.	VENDOR, PRODUCT
3	Some vendors have price discount scales for large quantity purchases.	VENDOR, PRODUCT
4	Sometimes vendor receipts include more than one order. Mentor decides how received quantities relate to ordered quantities.	RECEIPT, REFERS
5	Price of received merchandize must be recorded.	CONTAINS
6	Receipt forms are used to record customer return and corresponding credit note number.	RECEIPT, CUSTOMER
7	Some products have replacements, which are proposed to customers should there be an inventory shortage.	PRODUCT
8	When a product is not immediately available, a special purchase order is sometimes issued in connection with the customer order.	ORDER, PURCHASE ORDER
9	In the future, customer orders will be assigned a target delivery date. Their status with respect to completion will be closely monitored.	ORDER
10	There are discount rates for sales. The discount to a customer is based on the total value of last year's sales to that customer.	CUSTOMER
11	Sales are analyzed by regions, areas and sectors.	REGION
12	Each department-region combination is assigned to a unique sales representative.	EMPLOYEE, REGION, DEPARTMENT
13	One must keep track of employee positions.	EMPLOYEE

Refinements:
• They are found by discussing the general conceptual model correctness with users, by identifying new requirements and by examining available documents;
• Integration starts by determining model objects related to each refinement.

Figure 4-19 Developing the detailed conceptual model of a domain: finding conceptual model refinements.

2. *Determining properties*
Systematically list all primary properties, using documents which have been gathered and user requirements. Merge them with

objects of the model. Create new objects through reverse joins and reverse groupings as required.

LOCATING CONCEPTUAL MODEL REFINEMENTS

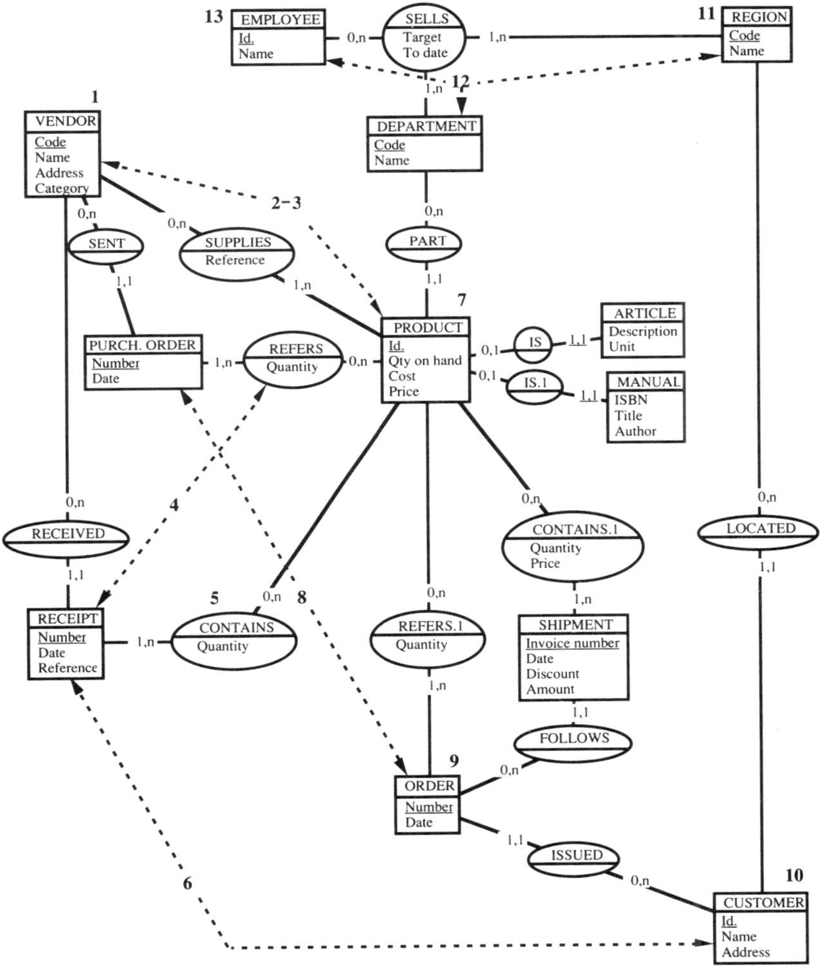

Integration:
• Refinements to the conceptual model are located on the diagram using related objects as a guide (Fig. 4-19);
• They are integrated one after the other using Chap. 3 transformations.

Figure 4-20 Developing the detailed conceptual model of a domain: locating refinements.

3. *Determining identifiers*
   Establish all identifiers based upon those currently used, or by grouping properties or using identifier dependencies.

4. *Determining business rules*
   Define all properties of the model, by using narrative descriptions and specifying the business rules that apply, that is, rules of domain, integrity, calculation and existence (Fig. 4-22).

It is best to ensure that the conceptual model will be able to accommodate information requirements which have not yet been identified. A useful validation consists of ensuring that all current notions pertaining to the domain can be found in the model, or can be inferred from it using the appropriate definitions (Fig. 4-23).

Later stages may result in some additional refinement of the model. Indeed, specifying system components calls for checking that the model actually meets all the requirements for data access and processing. This may help uncover missing – or unnecessary – objects or properties and verify identifiers and cardinalities.

4.4 Validation with Users

Conceptual models developed at the various stages must be verified to ensure that they accurately represent the activity sectors under analysis with their respective rules, such as interpreted by the managers and users of the domain – and analysts familiar with the situation – or by senior management.

These validations take place throughout model development. They are all the more necessary since frequently, written information is not sufficiently precise and uniform to make it possible to choose between variations of the underlying conceptual model. They are also beneficial in that they encourage user participation in developing the model and promote better understanding of the model. Lastly, they require the model designer to use the terms and concepts familiar to the users, thereby making the model more intelligible and useful.

Typically, a validation consists of presenting a graphic or narrative version of the model and interpreting it in everyday language, in terms of entities, relationships, properties, cardinalities, business rules and the related consequences thereof. The model may be changed as a result of comments brought up by the participants in the validation. In practice, it is preferable to proceed with partial validations. As a result

FINALIZING THE DETAILED CONCEPTUAL MODEL

DISTRIBUTION OF SCHOOL SUPPLIES

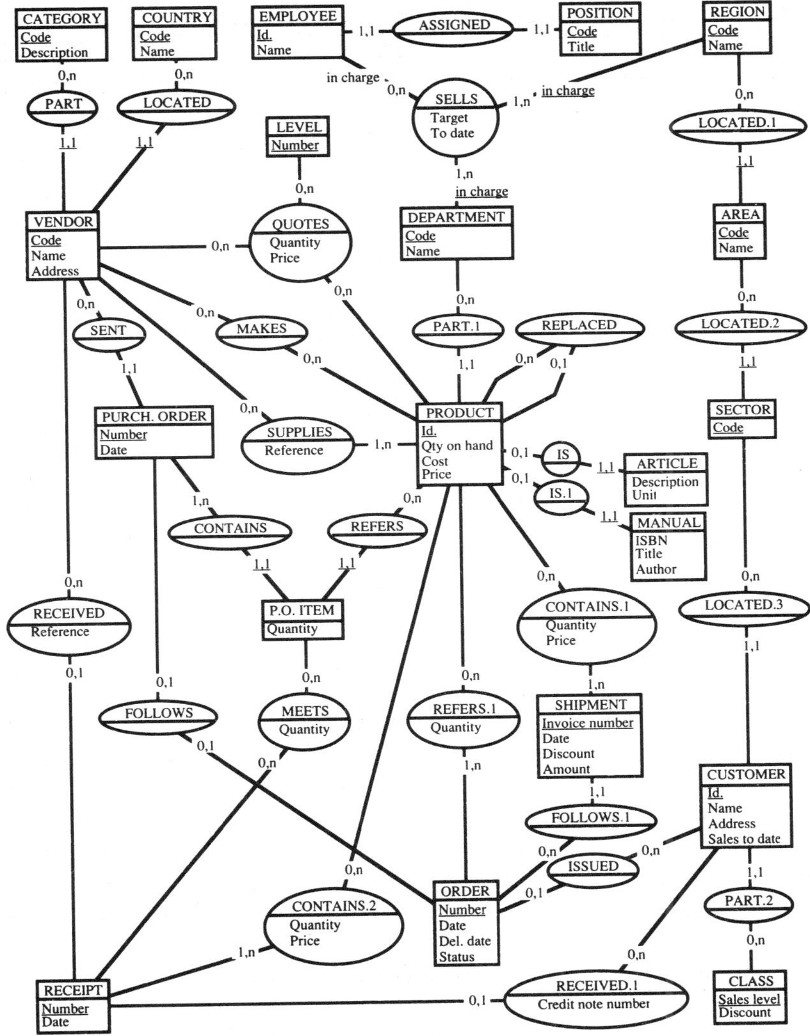

Finalization:

- The detailed conceptual model contains all the relevant information required for logical modeling;
- It may be somewhat refined during logical modeling.

Figure 4-21 Developing the detailed conceptual model of a domain: final version.

of their own specialization, users tend to focus solely on areas of the model which relate to their own responsibilities. With their emphasis on the use of views, the guidelines presented in this chapter lend themselves well to this kind of validation.

DETERMINING BUSINESS RULES

DISTRIBUTION OF SCHOOL SUPPLIES

OBJECT	PROPERTY	BUSINESS RULE
...	...	...
CONTAINS.1	Quantity	= Max (Old Quantity on hand, REFERS.1.Quantity for ORDER - Sum of CONTAINS.1.Quantities for SHIPMENTS FOLLOWING ORDER)
	Price	= PRODUCT.Price (at time of shipping)
PRODUCT	Quantity on hand	= Old Qty on hand - CONTAINS.1.Quantity
and SHIPMENT	Amount	= Sum of (Qties x Prices) for SHIPMENT
(when preparing a shipment)	Discount	= CLASS.Discount for CUSTOMER CLASS
REPLACED (when entering an order)		PRODUCT.Qty on hand = 0 => A Replacement PRODUCT is proposed to the customer, if possible
ETC...		

Business rules are found by examining every object and property in the model (Fig. 4-21).

Figure 4-22 Developing the detailed conceptual model of a domain: business rules.

VERIFYING MODEL COMPLETENESS

CONCEPT	DEFINITION
Over the counter order	= ORDER not ISSUED by an identified CUSTOMER
Order to follow	= ORDER resulting into a PURCHASE ORDER (through relationship FOLLOWS)
Shipment region	= REGION of CUSTOMER who ISSUED the ORDER resulting in the SHIPMENT
Publisher	= VENDOR with the 'PUBLISHER' Category
Return	= RECEIPT RECEIVED from a CUSTOMER
Sales variance	= To date sales - Prorated Target (for a department region combination)
Sales territory	= List of AREAS and SECTORS in a REGION
Etc...	

Figure 4-23 Verification of the detailed conceptual model completeness.

4.5 Modeling in Practice

To develop a conceptual model, the analyst must overcome two types of difficulty.

The first challenge is technical: one has to choose, among the concepts analyzed, those which will become entities, relationships, properties or business rules. The approach proposed in this chapter is only a guide. With experience, the analyst builds a portfolio of more or less standard models, representing patterns that will recur in varying guises; they will increasingly facilitate identification of the models inherent in new situations.

The second challenge is related to the particular culture of the organization being investigated. A conceptual model not only translates tangible facts about the domains being examined, but also the manner in which the organization perceives and relates these facts. If, from the outset, the concepts and rules to be incorporated in the model are clearly defined, familiar and accepted by all parties, then modeling is that much easier. On the other hand, if some of these conditions are missing, and different users insist on the uniqueness of their point of view, it may be difficult to develop a conceptual model consisting of objects acceptable to all parties. It may then become necessary within the model to retain specialized objects which have been adapted to each group of users. The resulting model will be more redundant and less normal, but it will be more consistent with perceptions of the parties concerned.

PART III

Building on the Foundation

Part III shows how the conceptual model can be used as a foundation to develop information systems. It presents other types of models which may be used for this purpose, and shows how they relate to the conceptual model. Chapter 5 deals with the logical model, which abstracts the resources used, while Chapter 7 presents the physical model, which takes these resources into account. Chapter 6, an intermediate chapter, briefly discusses the relational model, and provides a bridge between the conceptual model and relational development tools available on the market.

Chapter 5

The Logical Model

> Another question which comes up in the representation of knowledge is its modularity. How easy is it to insert new knowledge? How easy is it to revise old knowledge?
>
> (D. Hofstadter, *Gödel, Escher, Bach*)

This chapter introduces the logical model of an information system. Terminology and concepts are those of *Structured System Analysis* and the diagramming technique is Gane and Sarson's. In addition, conceptual model views are used to specify logical model components, including processes, through the use of access diagrams and action tables.

The interest of diagramming techniques such as this one lies in their capacity to depict the components of a logical – or physical – model and their interrelationships; and to provide a consistent way to do so at various levels of refinement required for system design.

The primary purpose of this presentation is to show how naturally logical model components can be described using the conceptual model as a starting point and to outline a logical modeling approach which takes advantage of it.

5.1 Components

5.1.1 Logical data flow diagrams

A *logical data flow diagram* or DFD shows the interrelationships between the components of a system: processes, data stores and data flows, as well as with the outside environment: *external entities* or external processes. DFDs are prepared at various levels of detail. The highest level DFD is often called the system *context diagram* (Fig. 5-1). Processes in the context diagram may be repetitively broken down into sub-processes shown in lower level diagrams. Low level diagrams can be used to show *processing units* (Fig. 5-2), that is, basic services provided by the system, as well as processing unit *modules* (Fig. 5-3) and *sub-modules.*

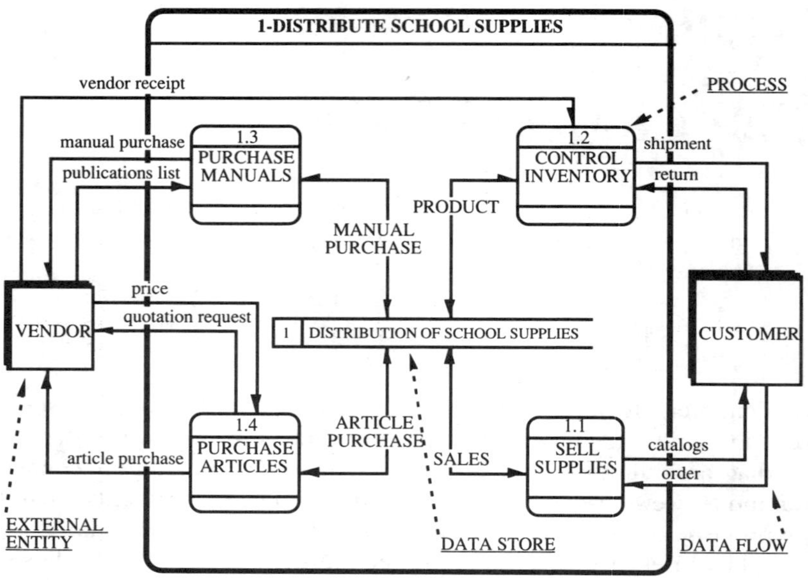

Figure 5-1 Logical DFD: context diagram of Process 1: Distribute School Supplies.

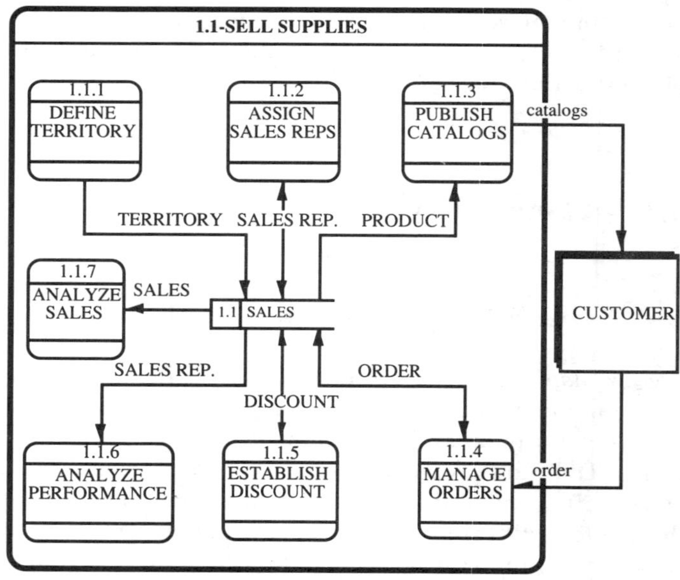

Figure 5-2 Logical DFD: lower level diagram showing processing units of Process 1.1: Sell Supplies.

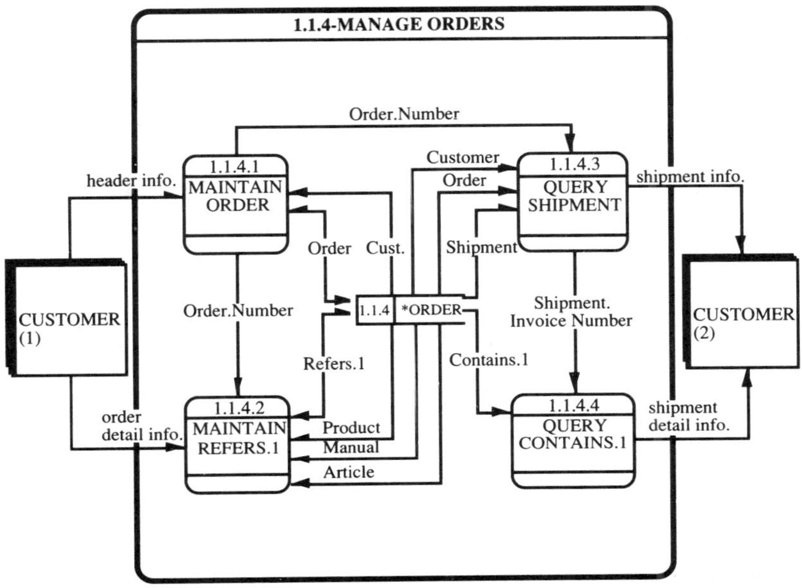

Figure 5-3 Logical DFD: diagram showing first level modules of Processing Unit 1.1.4: Manage Orders.

5.1.2 Data stores and logical views

A *data store* is a set of data at rest – usually connected – used or changed by a set of processes.

The contents of a data store are defined by a view of the conceptual model of the domain, that is, by a sub-model (Fig. 5-4) or, more generally, by a model derived from the conceptual model (Fig. 5-5 and 5-6).

The view of a data store consists of objects which may be used or changed by processes of a system. Occurrences of those objects are considered as recorded in advance and thus immediately available to the processes which use them.

A *logical view* on a data store is a view derived from the stored data (Fig. 5-7 and 5-8). In a data flow diagram, a logical view may be used and represented in the same fashion as a data store (Fig. 5-4), but its data are considered generated on demand each time a process uses the logical view.

To emphasize the existence of those preliminary transformations, the name of the logical view is marked with an asterisk in the logical data flow diagrams.

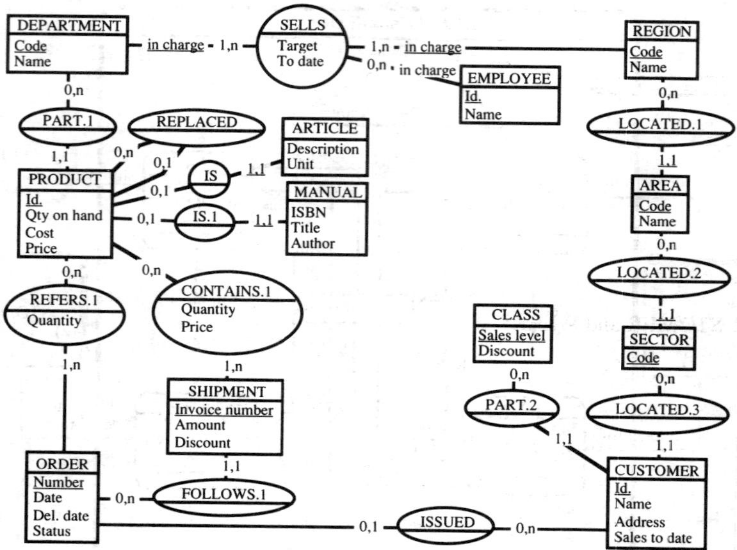

RULES: This is a projection of the conceptual model.

Figure 5-4 Contents of Data Store 1.1: Sales.

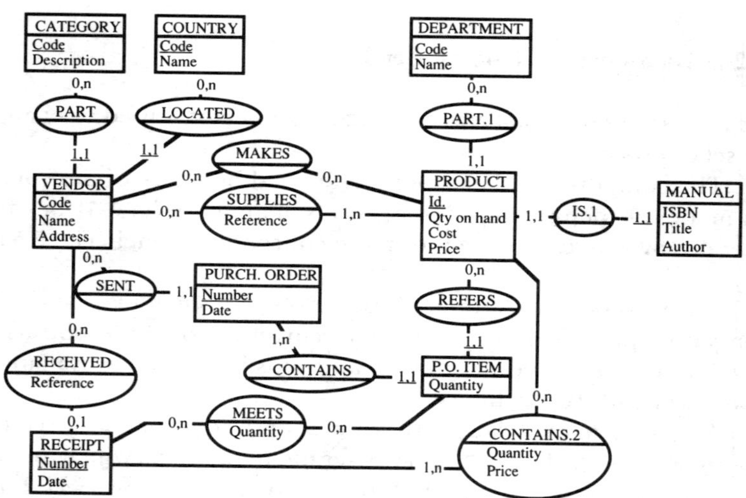

RULES: This is a combined projection/selection with criteria such as:
• a VENDOR with Category = 'DIS' or 'PUB';
• a PRODUCT which IS a MANUAL – notice 1,1–1,1 cardinalities.

Figure 5-5 Contents of Data Store 1.3: Manual Purchase.

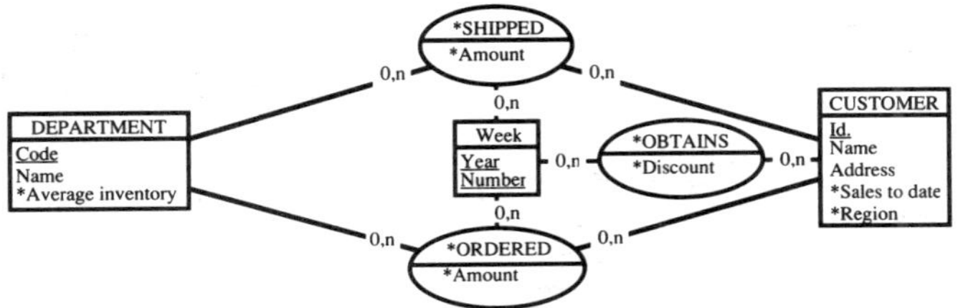

RULES: This is an augmentation of the conceptual model followed by a projection of the augmented objects; derived properties are:

- ORDERED.Amount = Total Amount of ORDERS by DEPARTMENT, CUSTOMER and WEEK;
- Average inventory = Average value of DEPARTMENT Quantities on hand for current year;
- Discount = Total Discounts by CUSTOMER, by WEEK of SHIPMENT;

Etc.

Summarized data in Data Store 4.1 support executive information queries.

Figure 5-6 Contents of Data Store 4.1: Sales Summary.

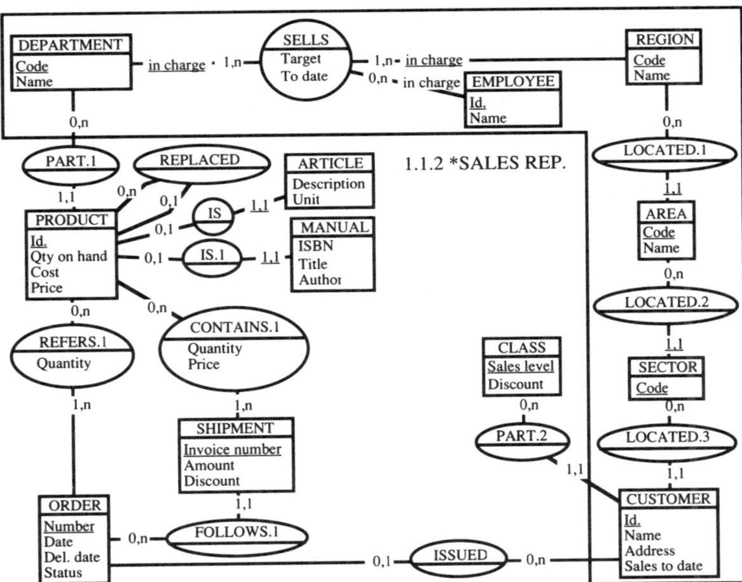

RULES: This is a projection of the conceptual model.

Logical View 1.1.2 supports Processes 1.1.2: Assign Sales Reps and 1.1.6: Analyze Performance.

Figure 5-7 Logical View 1.1.2: *Sales Rep. on Data Store 1.1: Sales.

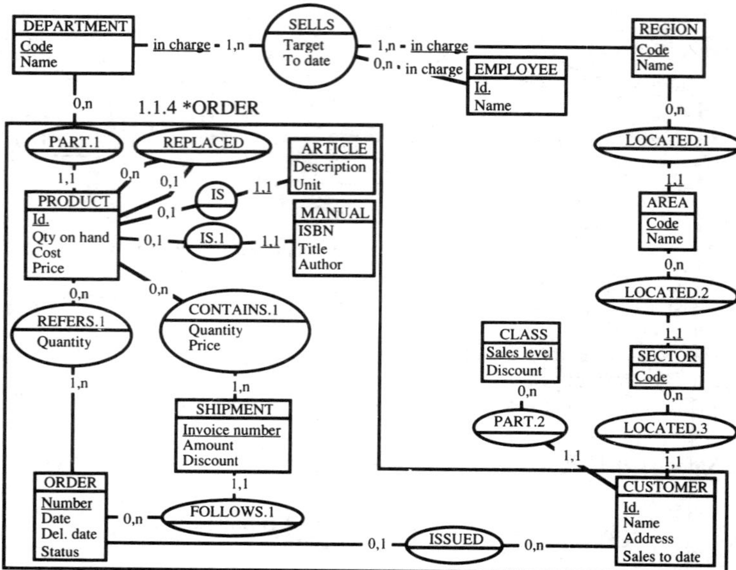

RULES: This is a selection of the conceptual model.

Logical View 1.1.4 supports Process 1.1.4: Manage Orders.

Figure 5-8 Logical View 1.1.4: *Order on Data Store 1.1: Sales.

5.1.3 Data flows

A *data flow* is a set of data in motion – usually connected – exchanged between a process and a data store, an external entity, another process or another system.

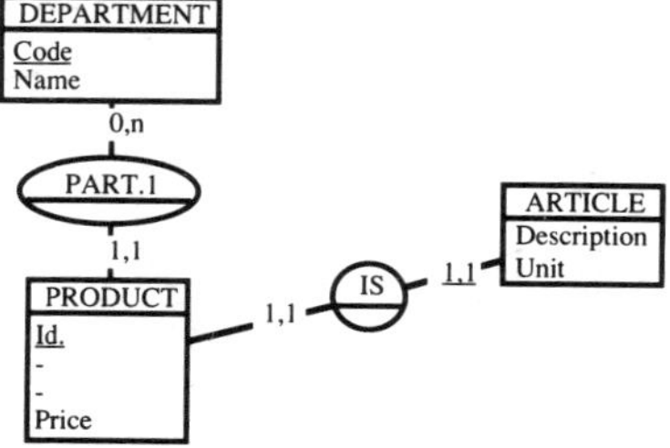

RULE: The PRODUCT must BE an ARTICLE.

This is an output flow from Process 1.1.3: Publish Catalogs.

Figure 5-9 Contents of Data Flow: Catalog of Articles.

The contents of a data flow are defined by a view of the conceptual model of the domain (Fig. 5-9 to 5-11), which includes objects and properties carried by the data flow. The view of a data flow is a submodel or, more generally, a model derived from the conceptual model. In practice, the view of a data flow can be conveniently defined only if it is a low level data flow.

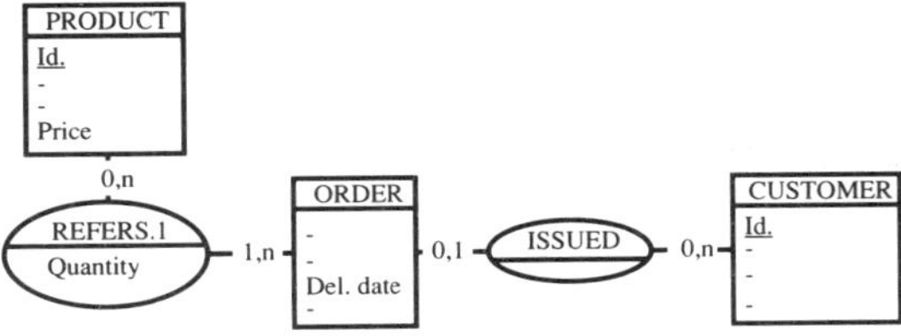

This is an input flow to Process 1.1.4: Manage Orders.

Figure 5-10 Contents of Data Flow: Order.

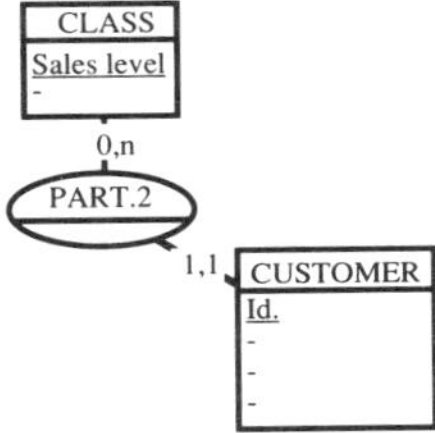

This is an output flow from Process 1.1.5: Establish Discount.

Figure 5-11 Contents of Data Flow: Discount.

5.1.4 Processes

Definitions

A *logical process* is a set of data transformations which produce output flows from input flows and which may also use or change the contents of data stores, directly or through logical views.

Higher level processes are best described by DFDs showing subprocesses, internal data flows and data stores.

But lower level processes, that is, processing units and processing unit modules, are best described in terms of access diagrams, showing the objects of the conceptual model which they manipulate; and action tables, showing the sequence and conditions under which those object manipulations are executed.

It is convenient to distinguish various *module types,* according to their main purpose. The basic module categories are access modules and procedures.

Access modules interact with data stores and consist of two sub-types. *Query* modules input the contents of data stores without changing them and produce output flows, possibly directed toward other modules. *Maintenance* modules change the contents of data stores through inserts, updates or deletes. They obtain data from input flows, possibly supplied by other modules (Fig. 5-3).

Procedures do not act directly on data stores but are part of other modules or communicate with them. They perform calculations on input data and deliver output data or perform choices.

Elementary modules are those access modules or procedures which are not broken down further because they interact with a single object or they perform a single calculation or choice.

Access diagrams

For processing units and their modules, it is possible to identify *control flows,* that is, flows which activate processes (Fig. 5-12). Most often such flows also supply processes with parameter values, such as values of selection criteria or of coefficients for calculations. Control flows may be seen as *events* or stimuli which trigger a reaction from the system.

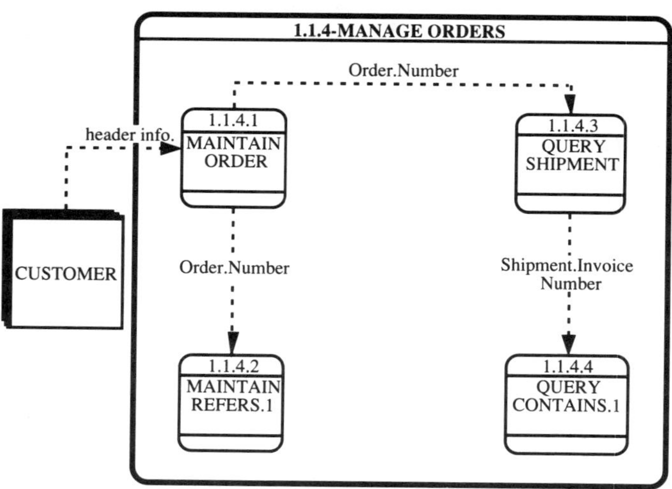

Figure 5-12 Control flows between first level modules of Processing Unit 1.1.4: Manage Orders.

The *access diagram* (Fig. 5-13 and 5-14) of a process consists of the view of the associated data store on which an access path to view objects is superimposed with descriptions of types of accesses to each object.

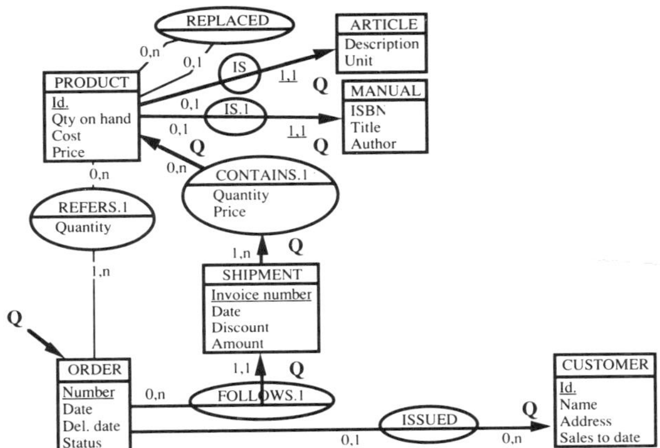

In Processing Unit 1.1.4, shipment queries are carried out as follows:
- **Q**uery of ORDER – entry point – and related CUSTOMER;
- **Q**ueries of related SHIPMENT;
- **Q**ueries of related CONTAINS.1, PROD., ARTICLE and MANUAL.

Figure 5-13 Access diagram for a query process.

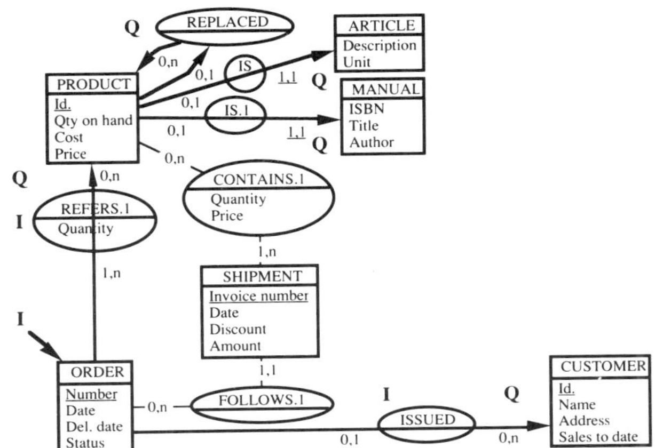

In Processing Unit 1.1.4, order entry is carried out by queries and inserts:
- **I**nsert of ORDER – entry point – and ISSUED based on **Q**uery of CUST.;
- **I**nsert of REFERS.1 based on **Q**uery of PROD., ART. and MANUAL.

Figure 5-14 Access diagram for a maintenance process.

An *access path* maps control flows within a process to the stored objects. Some flows point directly to an object: access is obtained through the identifier or some combination of properties and a selection criterion. Other flows lead from one object to the next, on the basis of relationship roles: again, access is usually obtained through identifiers, supplemented, as appropriate, by selection criteria.

Action tables

A process *action table* (Fig. 5-15 and 5-16) shows its hierarchy of access modules and sub-modules, the objects on which they act, the predecessor modules, the access types, the properties and procedures used, and the cardinalities of each step. Action tables are based on access diagrams and provide a blueprint for further development.

MODULE	PRED.	ACC.	PROPERTY	PROCEDURE	CARD.
1 Order		Q	Number Date Delivery date Status	If = Specified Number	0,1
1.1 Customer		Q	Id. Name Address	If ORDER ISSUED by CUSTOMER	0,1
3 Shipment	1	Q	Invoice number Date Amount Discount	If SHIPMENT FOLLOWS ORDER	0,*n*
4 Contains.1	3	Q	(Product.Id.) Quantity Price	If SHIPMENT CONTAINS PROD.	1,*n*
4.1 Product		Q	Id. Price	If SHIPMENT CONTAINS PROD.	1,1
4.2 Article		Q	Description Unit	If PRODUCT IS ARTICLE	0,1
4.3 Manual		Q	ISBN Title Author	If PRODUCT IS MANUAL	0,1

In Processing Unit 1.1.4, shipment queries are carried out as follows:

- Module 1 is entered directly and **Q**ueries 0,1 ORDER;
- Module 3 is entered from Module 1 and **Q**ueries 0,*n* SHIPMENTS;
- Module 4 is entered from Module 3 and **Q**ueries 1,*n* CONTAINS.1;
- Sub-modules carry out auxiliary **Q**ueries after the main module access.

Figure 5-15 Action table for a query process.

Access modules query (Q), update (U), insert (I) or delete (D) some occurrences of an object in the conceptual model.

Procedures prepare selection criteria, apply business rules or perform auxiliary functions such as input, output or sorts, usually as part of access modules.

Access modules select entity or relationship occurrences using rules which specify which values some properties must have or which relationships must hold. The permissible numbers of occurrences at each step are called the cardinalities of the access, in a way similar to roles in relationships.

MODULE	PRED.	ACC.	PROPERTY	PROCEDURE	CARD.
1 Order		I	Number	= Last Number + 1	1,1
			Date	= Date of day	
			Delivery date	If ≥ Date of day + 2	
			Status	= 'New'	
				If REFERS.1 > 0 occ.	
1.1 Customer		Q	Id.	If = Specified Id.	0,1
			Name		
			Address		
1.2 Issued		I		ORDER ISSUED by CUSTOMER	1,1
2 Refers.1	1	I		ORDER REFERS.1 to PRODUCT	1,*n*
			Quantity	If > 0 and ≤ Qty on hd	
2.1 Product		Q	Id.	If = Specified Id.	0,1
			Price		
			Qty on hand		
2.2 Article		Q	Description	If PRODUCT IS ARTICLE	0,1
			Unit		
2.3 Manual		Q	Title	If PRODUCT IS MANUAL	0,1
			Author		
2.4 Replaced		Q		If Qty > Qty on hand	0,1
			(Replacement Product.Id.)	If PRODUCT is REPLACED by PRODUCT	

In Processing Unit 1.1.4, order entry is carried out by queries and inserts:
- Module 1 is entered directly and **I**nserts 1,1 ORDER;
- Module 2 is entered from Module 1 and **I**nserts 1,*n* REFERS.1;
- Sub-modules carry out auxiliary **Q**ueries and **I**nserts, before or after the main module access.

Figure 5-16 Action table for a maintenance process.

5.1.5 Activity levels

Activity levels measure the number of accesses to be performed in a given time period.

The *activity level of a process* on a logical view or a data store is characterized by the number of accesses of each type to each object in a given time period (Fig. 5-17).

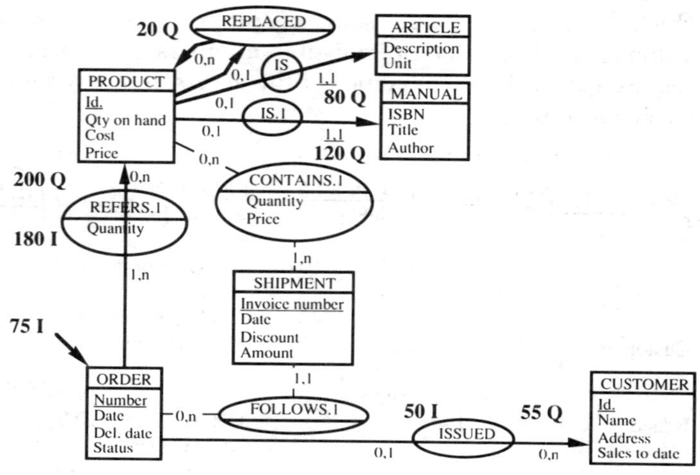

OBJECT	QUERY	UPDATE	INSERT	DELETE
CUSTOMER	55			
ORDER			75	
SHIPMENT				
PRODUCT				
directly	200			
thru REPLACED	20			
ARTICLE	80			
MANUAL	120			
ISSUED			50	
thru CUSTOMER				
thru ORDER				
REFERS.1			180	
thru ORDER				
thru PRODUCT				

These charts show peak hour activity – accesses per hour – for the order entry process, a part of Processing Unit 1.1.4: Manage Orders.

Figure 5-17 Activity level of a process.

The *activity level of a logical view* or *of a data store* is the aggregate of the activity levels of all processes which use it in a given time period.

The *activity level of a logical model* is the aggregate of the activity levels of all data stores in the model in a given time period.

High activity levels with complex processes are a warning of potential performance problems. Data stores may have to be modified prior to the physical modeling phase to avoid them (Fig. 5-18).

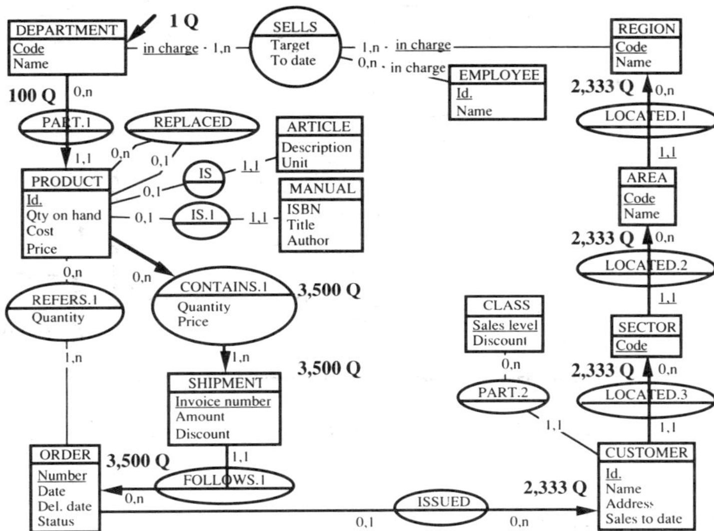

Each query of Data Store 1.1: Sales for a DEPT Sales to date by REGIONS may generate the following activity – based on average cardinalities:

- 1 **Q**uery of DEPARTMENT;
- 1 x 2,000 / 20 = 100 **Q**ueries of PRODUCT;
- 100 x 70,000 / 2,000 = 3,500 **Q**ueries of CONTAINS.1;
- 3,500 x 1 = 3,500 **Q**ueries each of SHIPMENT and ORDER;
- 3,500 x 10,000 / 15,000 = 2,333 **Q**ueries of CUSTOMER;
- 2,333 x 1 = 2,333 Queries each of SECTOR, AREA and REGION.

Maintaining the SELLS.*To date derived property as part of Process 1.2: Manage Inventory will reduce this activity level.

Figure 5-18 Augmentation of a data store to improve performance.

5.2 Observations

5.2.1 Logical data flow diagrams

(a) Logical DFDs are based on a top-down partitioning of processes (Fig. 5-19, 5-20, 5-1 to 5-3).

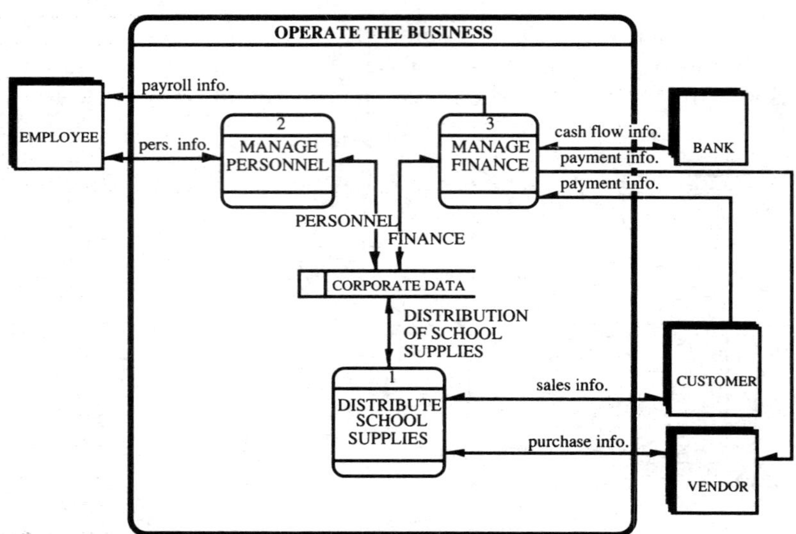

Figure 5-19 Logical DFD: corporate context diagram.

LEVEL	PROCESS	VIEW
DOMAIN	**1-DISTR. SCHOOL SUPPLIES**	**DISTRIBUTION**
PROCESS	1.1 SELL SUPPLIES	SALES
Proc. Unit	1.1.1 Define Territory	Territory
Proc. Unit	1.1.2 Assign Sales Reps	Sales Rep.
Proc. Unit	1.1.3 Publish Catalogs	Product
Proc. Unit	1.1.4 Manage Orders	Order
Proc. Unit	1.1.5 Establish Discount	Discount
Proc. Unit	1.1.6 Analyze Performance	Sales Rep.
Proc. Unit	1.1.7 Analyze Sales	Sales
PROCESS	1.2 CONTROL INVENTORY	PRODUCT
PROCESS	1.3 PURCHASE MANUALS	MANUAL PURCH.
PROCESS	1.4 PURCHASE ARTICLES	ARTICLE PURCH.
DOMAIN	**2-MANAGE PERSONNEL**	**PERSONNEL**
PROCESS	2.1 MANAGE POSITIONS	POSITION
DOMAIN	**3-MANAGE FINANCE**	**FINANCE**
PROCESS	3.1 MANAGE ACCOUNTS	ACCOUNT

Figure 5-20 Top-down partitioning of processes.

(b) The partitioning into processes shown in logical DFDs is mirrored in the conceptual model by a hierarchy of partially overlapping views (Fig. 5-20, 5-4 to 5-8).

5.2.2 Data stores and logical views

(a) In a logical model, a unique high level data store which contains the complete conceptual model and is directly accessed by all processes is always an initial possibility (Fig. 5-19).

(b) For practical reasons, it is often necessary to replace this unique data store by a set of data stores each dedicated to a high level process. The most useful transformation is *domain partitioning* using sub-models (Fig. 5-4) and partial models (Fig. 5-5). It keeps together objects which are usually accessed simultaneously and separates objects which are not.

(c) Additional data stores, containing *summary views* (Fig. 5-6), may be required in order to facilitate high activity queries such as executive information queries.

(d) When data stores are partitioned, some entities are replicated in order to preserve all relationships in the model. This replication may be partial but it involves at least the entity identifier. The additional processes which are required to maintain the consistency between data stores are included in the logical model.

(e) When a data store is used by many processes, it may be useful to define logical views common to several processes (Fig. 5-8, 5-13 and 5-14). In addition, separate logical views often share objects (Fig. 5-7 and 5-8).

(f) Data stores often use *augmented views* (Fig. 5-18) to improve the performance of particular processes, adding derived properties which they may access rather than calculate.

5.2.3 Data flows

Data flows and logical views associated with a given process must be compatible: output views must be derivable from the set of input views (Fig. 5-14 vs. Fig. 5-10).

5.2.4 Processes

Processing units

(a) Processing units usually focus on a limited number of neighboring objects (Fig. 5-3 and 5-8), possibly a single one. However, it is often required to query related, sometimes remote, neighbors to access additional information.

(b) Maintenance processing units may process a limited number of occurrences, possibly a single one, at a time. They may group query, update, insert and delete modules when they are needed in similar circumstances (Fig. 5-21).

MAIN OBJECT	PRED.	MODULE	OBJECT	ACC.
1 ORDER		QUERY	1 Order	Q
			1.1 Issued	Q
			1.2 Customer	Q
		UPDATE	1 Order	U
			1.1 Customer	Q
			1.2 Issued	D
			1.3 Issued	I
		INSERT	1 Order	I
			1.1 Customer	Q
			1.2 Issued	I
		DELETE	1 Order	D
			1.2 Issued	D
			1.3 Refers.1	D
2 REFERS.1	1	QUERY	2 Refers.1	Q
			2.1 Product	Q
			2.2 Article	Q
			2.3 Manual	Q
		UPDATE	2 Refers.1	U
		INSERT	2 Refers.1	I
			2.1 Product	Q
			2.2 Article	Q
			2.3 Manual	Q
			2.4 Replaced	Q
		DELETE	2 Refers.1	D

Processing Unit 1.1.4 groups all modules required for order maintenance.

Figure 5-21 Processing unit with grouped query, update, insert and delete modules.

(c) Processing units may group processes which are used in similar circumstances and access some of the same objects (Fig. 5-22).

MAIN OBJECT	PRED.	MODULE	OBJECT	ACC.
1 ORDER		QUERY UPDATE INSERT DELETE	1 Order etc.	Q etc.
2 REFERS.1	1	QUERY UPDATE INSERT DELETE		
3 SHIPMENT	1	QUERY		
4 CONTAINS.1	3	QUERY		

Processing Unit 1.1.4 groups modules for order entry and shipment query.

Figure 5-22 Processing unit with grouped processes.

(d) Maintenance processing units may process a large number of occurrences, possibly all, at a time. They usually implement an update, insert or delete capability (Fig. 5-23).

MODULE	PRED.	ACC.	PROPERTY	PROCEDURE	CARD.
1 Customer		Q	Id. Sales to date	If stated selection criterion is met	0,*n*
1.1 Part.2		D		If CUSTOMER is PART of CLASS	1,1
1.2 Class		Q	Sales level Discount	If S. Level ≤ Sales to date < Next S. Level	1,1
1.3 Part.2		I		CUSTOMER is PART of CLASS	1,1

Processing Unit 1.1.5 updates discount classes for selected customers.

Figure 5-23 Update processing unit.

(e) In addition to the basic processing units required to maintain the conceptual model, the logical model may include many queries processing any number of occurrences at a time (Fig. 5-24).

MODULE	PRED. ACC.	PROPERTY	PROCEDURE	CARD.
1 Product	Q	Id. Price	If stated selection criterion is met	0,n
1.1 Article	Q	Description Unit	If PRODUCT IS ARTICLE	0,1
1.2 Manual	Q	ISBN Title Author	If PRODUCT IS MANUAL	0,1
1.3 Department	Q	Code Name	If PRODUCT is PART of DEPT	1,1

Processing Unit 1.1.3 produces a catalog of selected products.

Figure 5-24 Query processing unit.

Access diagrams

(a) Within a processing unit, the access diagram of a process usually contains a single entry point, which is an entity or a relationship of interest for the process (Fig. 5-13 and 5-14).

(b) The entry point of an access diagram may be followed by a number of paths leading to additional objects with an interest for the process. Paths may branch out at the entry point or at any object located downstream (Fig. 5-13 and 5-14).

(c) An object may sometimes be reached by more than one path in the same access diagram. This object, and the downstream objects, are replicated in the access diagram (Fig. 5-25) for clarity.

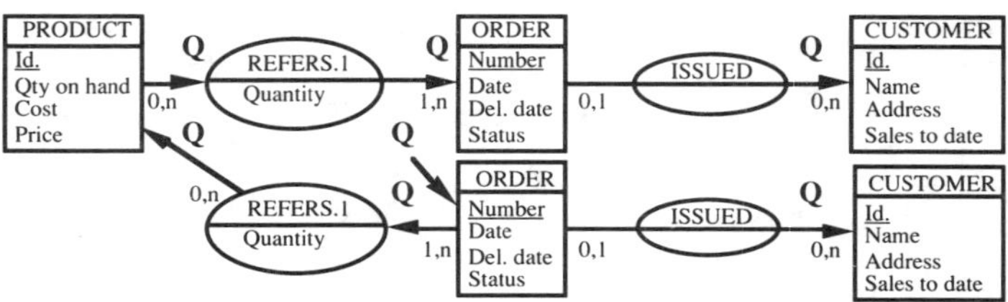

This processing unit queries orders which refer to some of the same products as a selected order.

Figure 5-25 Access diagram with replicated objects.

(d) Access to the entry object is usually *free*: it has 0,1 cardinalities if the selection is done through the identifier, 0,n cardinalities otherwise. Accesses required to prepare an insert are also usually free and have 0,1 or 0,n cardinalities (Fig. 5-26).

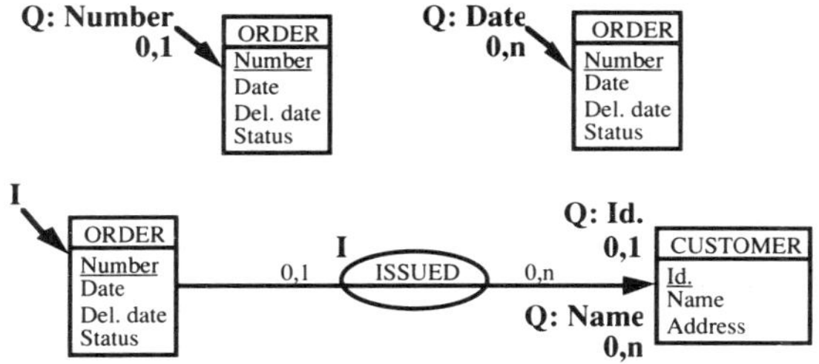

Access to entry object ORDER through Number has 0,1 cardinalities.
Access through Date has 0,n cardinalities.
Access to CUSTOMER required to prepare ORDER and ISSUED inserts may be performed thru Id. with 0,1 cardinalities or Name with 0,n cardinalities.

Figure 5-26 Free accesses.

(e) Access from an entity to a relationship – or between entities through a relationship – is usually *constrained* by the relationship: it has the cardinalities of the entering connector. Access from a relationship to a neighbor entity is also constrained and has 1,1 cardinalities (Fig. 5-27). These accesses are used for queries, updates or deletes. In each case, the path must start with an actual entity or relationship occurrence.

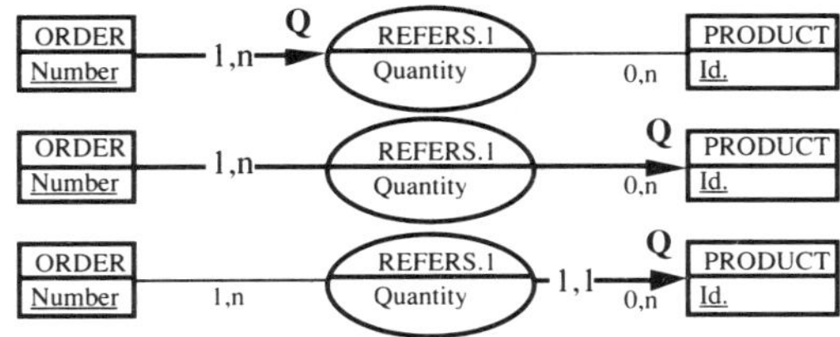

Accesses from ORDER to REFERS.1 and to PRODUCT through REFERS.1 have the entering connector cardinalities: 1,n.
Access from REFERS.1 to PRODUCT has 1,1 cardinalities no matter what the connector cardinalities are.

Figure 5-27 Constrained accesses.

(f) Processes accessing the same objects with different paths may have similar results but are not necessarily equivalent (Fig. 5-28).

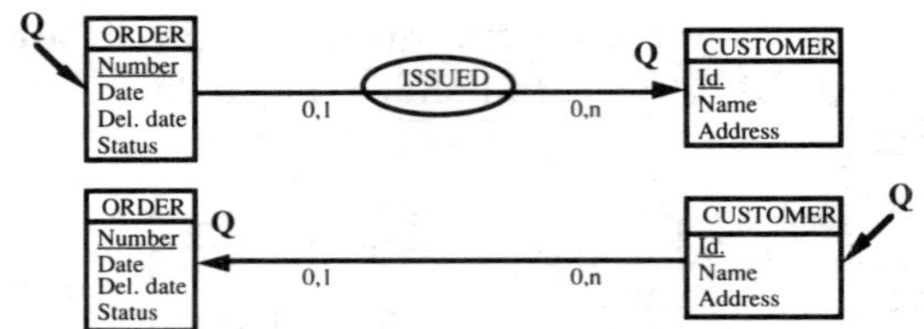

Path entering through ORDER can access all ORDERS and related CUSTOMERS but not CUSTOMERS without ORDERS.
Path entering through CUSTOMER can access all CUSTOMERS and related ORDERS but not ORDERS without an identified CUSTOMER.

Figure 5-28 Access paths with different results.

Action tables

(a) The action table of a process consists of a list of modules and sub-modules (Fig. 5-15 and 5-16), which implements the paths in its access diagram (Fig. 5-13 and 5-14).

(b) Modules usually correspond to the entry object and to objects accessed by entering through 0,*n* or 1,*n* cardinalities in the model. Other path objects give rise to sub-modules (Fig. 5-29 and 5-30).

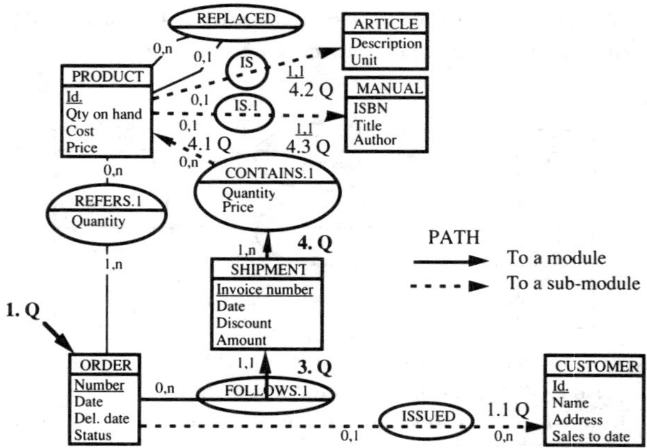

In Processing Unit 1.1.4, shipment queries are carried out by:
- Mod. 1 corresponding to the ORDER entry object;
- Mod. 3 corresp. to SHIPMENT, accessed through 0,*n* cardinalities;
- Mod. 4 corresp. to CONTAINS.1, accessed through 1,*n* cardinalities.
- Related sub-modules corresponding to other objects in the access path.

Figure 5-29 Modules and sub-modules of a query process.

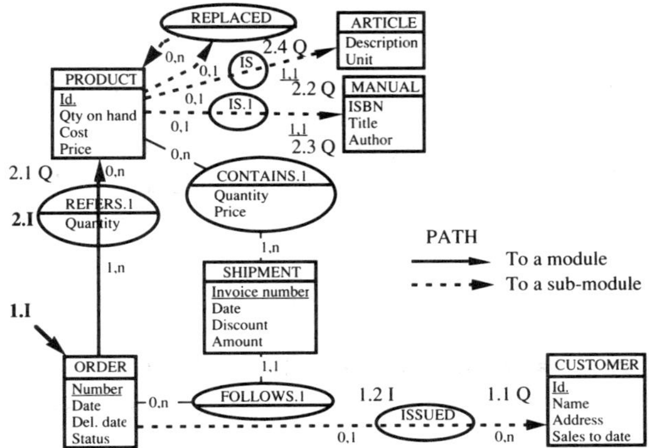

In Processing Unit 1.1.4, order entry is carried out by:

- Mod. 1 corresponding to the ORDER entry object;
- Mod. 2 corresp. to REFERS.1, accessed through 1,*n* cardinalities;
- Related sub-modules corresponding to other objects in the access path.

Figure 5-30 Modules and sub-modules of a maintenance process.

(c) Modules and sub-modules include the procedures required to implement applicable selection criteria and business rules, that is: free and constrained accesses, validations and calculations for derived objects and properties (Fig. 5-15, 5-16, 5-23 and 5-24).

(d) Each object in the conceptual model usually gives rise to at least one access module or sub-module of each type in some processing unit.

(e) Each business rule in the conceptual model usually gives rise to at least one procedure in some processing unit.

5.3 Representation

5.3.1 Logical data flow diagrams

Logical DFDs may be drawn using a diagramming technique such as Gane and Sarson's, that is, a flat rectangular box open on one side for a data store or a logical view, a rectangular box with rounded corners for a process, a square box for an external entity and an arrow line for a data flow.

A data flow diagram may show a central data store or logical view corresponding to its view on the conceptual model. In the data flow diagram, each data flow between a process and this central data store may be named for its own view on the conceptual model (Fig. 5-1 and 5-2). At lower levels, these data flows may reduce to objects or properties (Fig. 5-3).

Diagrams are supplemented by narrative descriptions (Fig. 5-31).

PROCESS 1.1.4: MANAGE ORDERS

PURPOSE	To maintain orders and to follow up orders and related shipments.
DESCRIPTION	Incoming orders are entered taking product availability and replacement products into account. Existing orders may be changed or cancelled. Orders may also be queried with respect to their status, which reflects the progress of shipments. In addition, related shipments may be queried individually.
VIEW	1.1.4: *Order.
DATA FLOW	Order.
BUSINESS RULES	Orders are numbered in sequence as they are entered. Delivery lead time is at least 2 days. Etc.

Figure 5-31 Summary description of a process.

5.3.2 Data stores and logical views

In DFDs, data stores and logical views are represented in the same way, but the name of a logical view is marked by an asterisk. The contents of data stores and logical views are represented as views on the conceptual model (Fig. 5-4 to 5-8).

LOGICAL VIEW 1.1.4: *ORDER

PURPOSE	To support order maintenance and related shipment queries.
DESCRIPTION	Includes orders and order details, customer information, related shipment and shipment details and related product information.

Figure 5-32 Summary description of a logical view.

Data stores and logical views may be named according to the principal objects they contain. They are supplemented by narrative descriptions (Fig. 5-32).

5.3.3 Data flows

A data flow (Fig. 5-33) may always be described in a free-format narrative. An elementary data flow may be represented more accurately as a view on the conceptual model (Fig. 5-9 to 5-11).

DATA FLOW: ORDER

CONNECTION	From Customer to Process 1.1.4: Manage Orders.
PURPOSE	To allow the customer to specify which products are required in which quantities.
DESCRIPTION	Identifies customer, delivery date, products and quantities required.

Figure 5-33 Summary description of a data flow.

5.3.4 Processes

Processing units
Any process (Fig. 5-31) may always be described in a free-format narrative. A processing unit may also be described more accurately as an access diagram (Fig. 5-13) or an action table (Fig. 5-15).

Access diagrams
An access diagram may be represented as a view to which arrows are added to show required accesses and access paths (Fig. 5-13). Symbols for access types are shown near the objects accessed. Return control flows are usually assumed and not shown. Objects in the access diagram may have to be replicated (Fig. 5-25), if they are accessed through different paths or selection criteria.

An access diagram is normally named for the process which it represents.

Action tables
An action table may be represented as a table which lists modules and sub-modules, predecessor modules, access types, properties used, applicable procedures and access cardinalities (Fig. 5-15).

Modules and sub-modules may be named according to their type: query, update, insert or delete, and according to the object which they access. Modules and sub-modules are listed in a sequence which reflect the sequence of accesses in the access diagram.

Procedures may be named for the business rules which they implement or spelled out in full. They are entered next to the modules or properties to which they apply.

5.4 Approach

5.4.1 Overview

The approach for logical modeling proposed in this book (Fig. 1-3) consists of refining the logical model by stages, so that it becomes progressively more detailed and complete (Fig. 5-20).

The *corporate logical model* (Fig. 5-34 and 5-35) is succeeded by *domain specific general logical models* (Fig. 5-36 and 5-37), by *detailed logical models* (Fig. 5-38 to 5-40) and finally by *detailed logical specifications* of releases (Fig. 5-13 to 5-16).

Each logical modeling stage follows a conceptual modeling stage and includes information gathering, analysis and design steps.

This approach also offers an opportunity to further circumscribe, validate and refine the conceptual model, in order to ensure that it conforms to the real-world situation it represents and that it will support the information requirements of users of the future system.

In addition, in later stages, the detailed logical model itself may be physically validated through development and testing of prototypes.

5.4.2 Information sources

Information sources already studied in order to develop the conceptual model are also useful for developing the logical model of a system.

Policy statements, government rulings, laws, etc. often specify roles and responsibilities and how communications are to be carried out with external entities.

Data capture or data recording documents carry data flows and suggest input processes.

Systems documentation and *data processing specifications* provide additional information on data flows, both manual and automated.

However, this information must be put in perspective through interviews with management and users. Developing higher levels of the logical model requires an ability to conceptualize business operations. Designing lower levels benefits most from knowing the existing system but must take into account new information requirements, thus suggesting new processes.

5.4.3 Corporate logical model

The *corporate logical model* consists of the corporate context diagram (Fig. 5-34) and descriptions of its components. It is put together as part of the corporate systems strategic plan. The purpose of this modeling stage is to provide a high level perspective on corporate activities.

The corporate context diagram is developed by stages. The principal external entities or external systems and related data flows are identified through a preliminary analysis of information obtained as part of the initial collection. Processes may be determined using a product/resource or a life cycle based partition approach. External data flows are connected to specific processes. Data stores and related data flows must be analyzed in connection with the conceptual model.

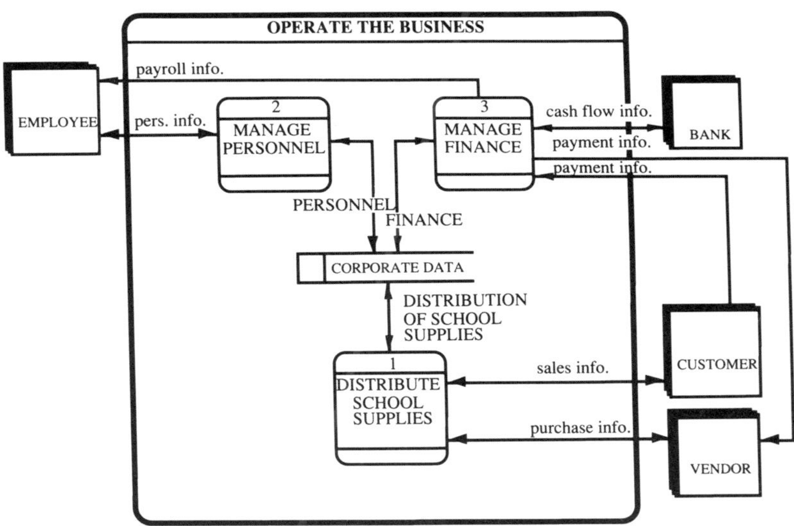

This DFD may be developed by progressively including:

- External entities Employee, Bank, Customer and Vendor and related data flows;
- Processes related to School Supplies, Personnel and Finance resources;
- Assignment of external data flows to individual processes;
- 'Corporate Data' data store and related flows based on the conceptual model.

Figure 5-34 Logical DFD: developing the corporate context diagram.

The analysis of data store and data flows is carried out by establishing views of corporate processes on the corporate conceptual model (Fig. 5-35). Each view may be restricted to objects maintained by the process, which usually results in non-overlapping domains.

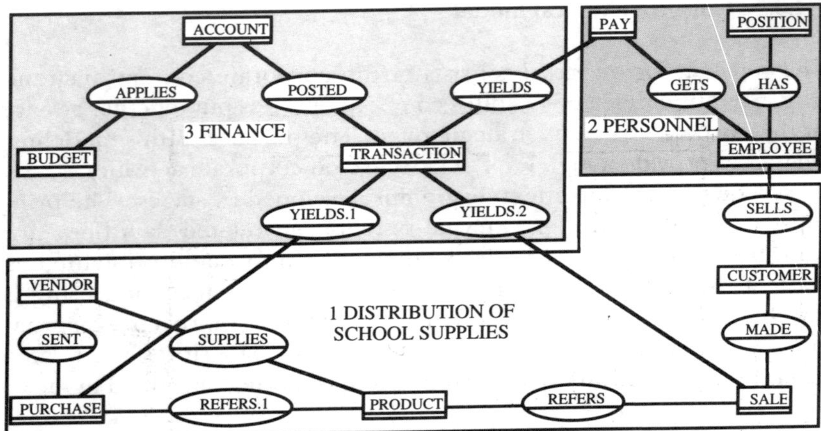

Views in this model are developed by deciding which objects of the conceptual model are maintained by each corporate process (Fig. 5-34).

Figure 5-35 Developing the views of corporate processes.

The corporate logical model is supplemented by narrative descriptions of its processes, data flows, data stores and external entities.

5.4.4 General logical model of a domain

The *general logical model* of a domain consists of the domain context diagram (Fig. 5-36) and descriptions of its components. It is developed after the domain general conceptual model, during the corporate systems architecture stage or, failing this, during the domain preliminary study.

The purpose of this modeling stage is to identify and summarily describe processes and data stores of systems in the domain and associated data flows with their sources and destinations. By providing a process-oriented view of the domain, this stage also makes it possible to double-check the conceptual model of the domain and ensure that important objects have not been overlooked or misunderstood.

The general logical model of a domain uses the corporate logical model as a starting point, and specific documentation on the domain.

The domain context diagram is initiated by copying the related corporate process, data flows and external entities from the corporate context diagram. Domain processes may then be determined using a product/resource or life cycle based partition approach. External entities and data flows may have to be refined so that they can be connected to specific processes. Data store and related data flows must be analyzed in connection with the conceptual model.

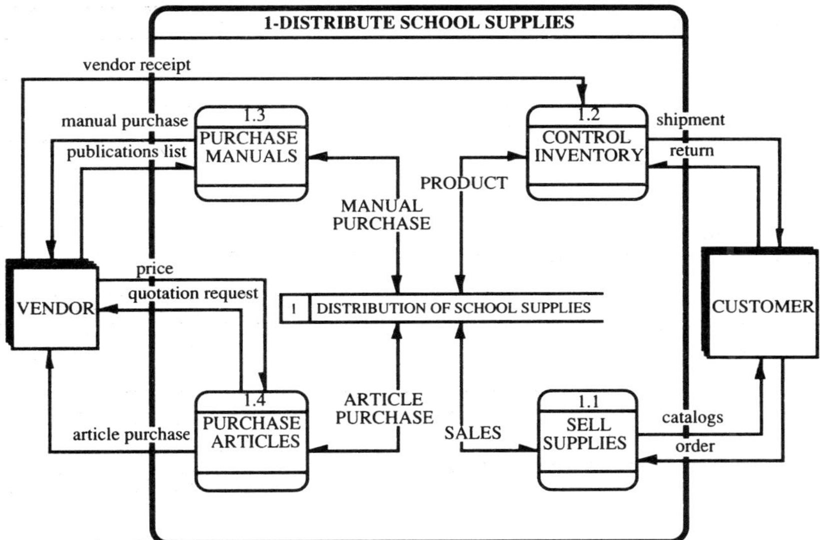

This DFD is developed by refining the parent DFD (Fig. 5-34):

- Customer and Vendor external entities connected to Process 1 are included;
- Process 1 is sub-divided based on life cycle and manual vs article distinctions;
- External data flows are refined and assigned to individual processes;
- Domain data store and related data flows are based on the conceptual model.

Figure 5-36 Logical DFD: developing a domain context diagram.

The analysis of data store and data flows is carried out by establishing views of domain processes on the domain general conceptual model (Fig. 5-37). For convenience, views may be restricted to objects maintained by each process.

The domain general logical model is supplemented by narrative descriptions of its processes, data flows and data stores.

Having developed the domain general logical model, it may become necessary to revise the corporate logical model to take into account more detailed knowledge gained at this stage.

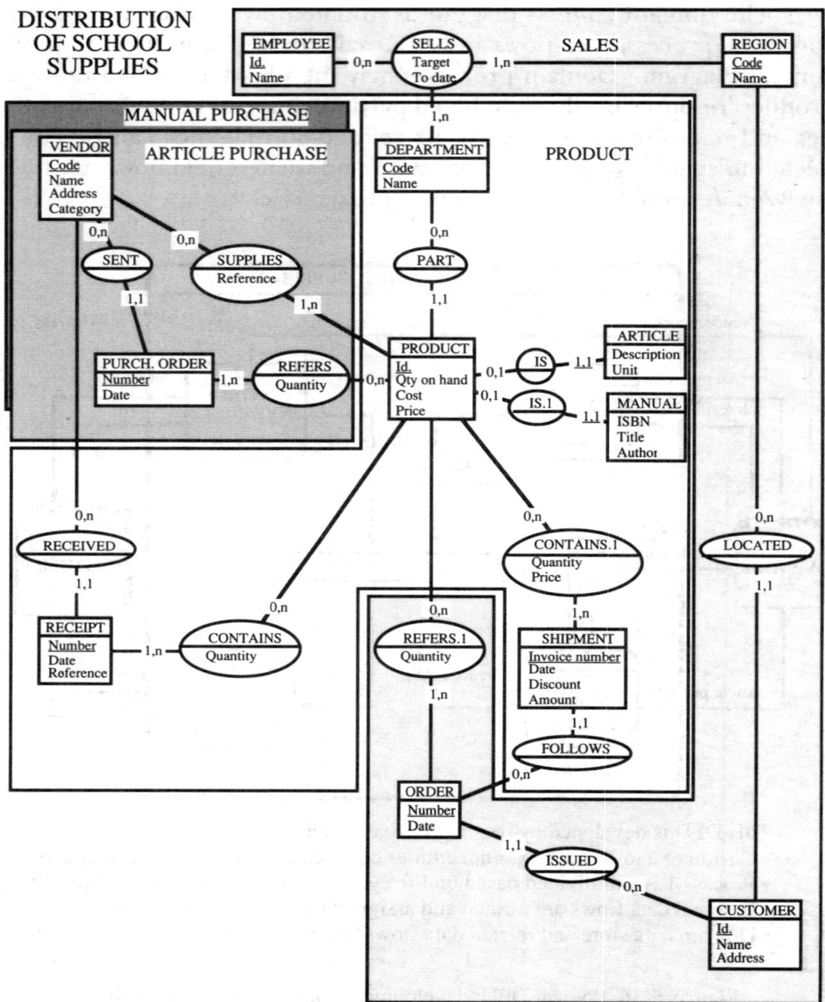

Views in this model are developed by determining which domain objects are maintained by each domain process (Fig. 5-36):
• Sales view includes objects maintained by 1.1: Sell Supplies. It also includes entity EMPLOYEE – from the Personnel domain – which is queried in connection with relationship SELLS;
• Product view includes objects maintained by 1.2: Manage Inventory;
• Manual Purchase and Article Purchase views include objects maintained by 1.3: Purchase Manuals and 1.4: Purchase Articles. Views overlap but object selection criteria are different.

Figure 5-37 Developing the views of processes on a domain general conceptual model.

5.4.5 Detailed logical model of a domain

The *detailed logical model* of a domain is a refinement of the general logical model of the domain and consists of the domain context diagram (Fig. 5-36), its subordinate DFDs down to the level of processing units (Fig. 5-38) and descriptions of their components. It is developed as part of the systems architecture of the domain.

The purpose of this modeling stage is to precisely identify the logical components of domain systems, without having to specify them.

The detailed logical model is obtained by carrying through to the level of processing units the approach started with the domain general logical model. Processing units may be identified through a life cycle approach and an analysis of the existing system. In addition, maintenance processing units are recognized through the need to maintain all objects in the conceptual model; query processing units result mostly from requirements stated by users.

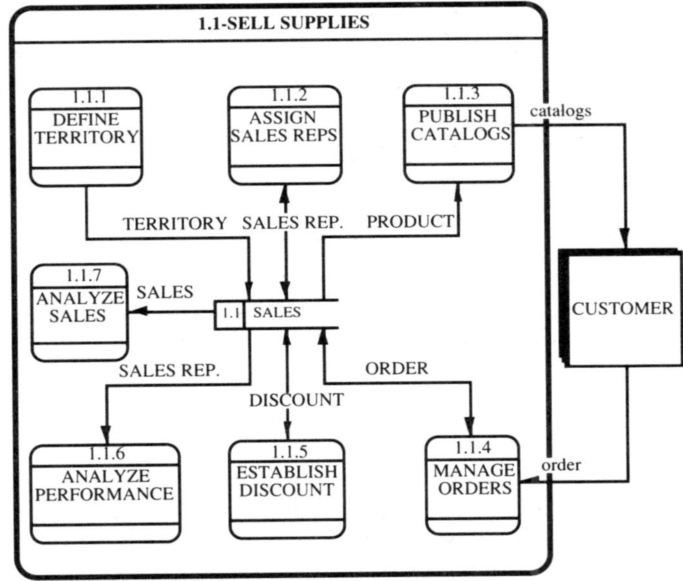

This DFD is developed by refining the parent DFD (Fig. 5-36):

- Customer external entity connected to Process 1.1 is included;
- Process 1.1 is sub-divided into processing units based on life cycle;
- External data flows are assigned to individual processes;
- Data store and related data flows are based on the conceptual model.

Figure 5-38 Developing a domain detailed logical model.

The analysis of data stores (Fig. 5-39), logical views (Fig. 5-40) and associated data flows is carried out by establishing views of processing units on the domain detailed conceptual model, based on their information requirements.

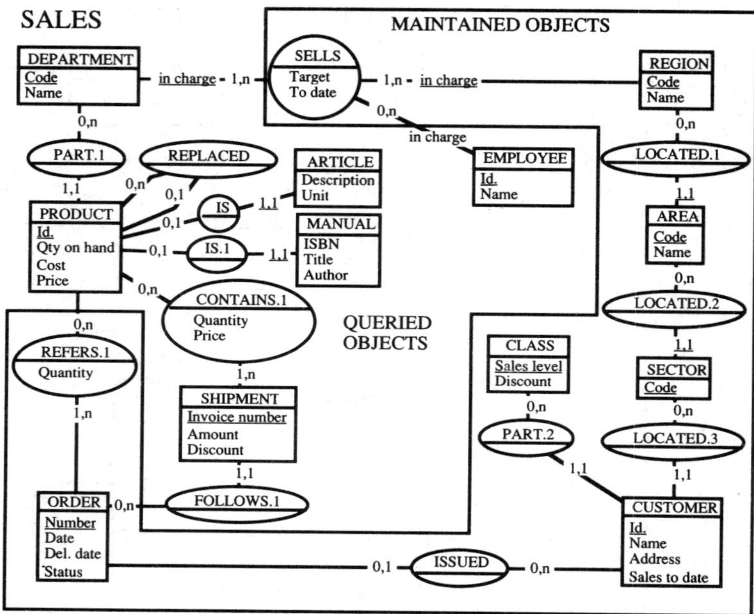

Data Store 1.1 Sales must contain:
- All objects in outline, maintained by Process 1.1: Sell Supplies;
- Additional objects maintained by other processes, required for queries.

Figure 5-39 Analysis of a data store.

The domain detailed logical model is supplemented by narrative descriptions of processing units, data flows, stores and logical views.

After having developed the domain detailed logical model, it may become necessary to revise its general logical model to take into account more detailed knowledge gained at this stage.

5.4.6 Detailed logical specifications of a release

Detailed logical specifications complement the detailed logical model by providing a precise description of processing units included in a specific release. Preparing them is the first step in its implementation.

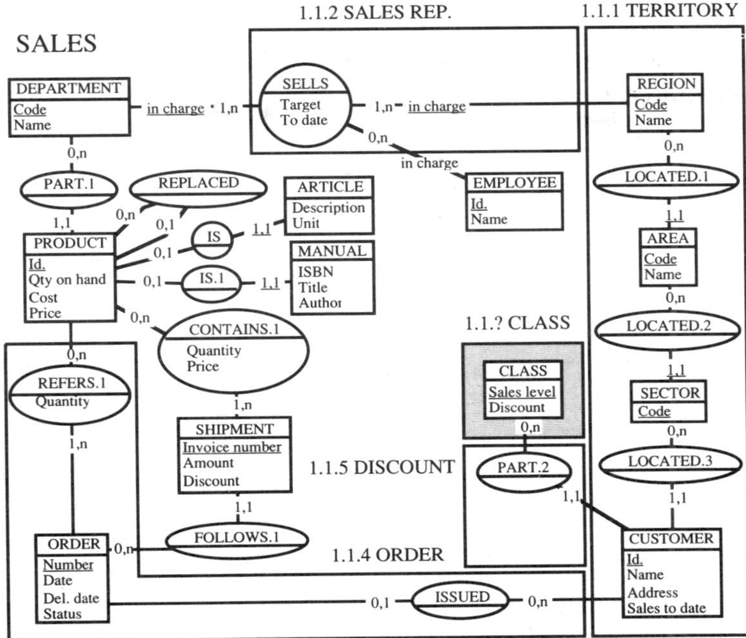

Views on Data Store 1.1 Sales are developed by determining which objects are maintained by each processing unit (Fig. 5-38):

- Most objects to be maintained have a processing unit to do so;
- The processing unit to maintain the CLASS entity is missing;
- The CUSTOMER entity, maintained as part of Territory, might need a distinct processing unit;
- Objects such as ORDER, CUSTOMER and SELLS which include derived properties Status, Sales to date and SELLS.To date, will require additional updates as part of other processing units.

Figure 5-40 Analysis of maintenance process views on a data store.

Detailed logical specifications of a release may be provided in the form of access diagrams (Fig. 5-13 and 5-14) and action tables (Fig. 5-15 and 5-16).

Access diagrams are developed from processing unit views by deciding which particular path should be used to access relevant objects. An object which is the main focus of a processing unit may be used as the entry point, unless a preliminary selection based on properties of other objects is required (Fig. 5-41). The access path is then extended to related objects providing additional information.

Action tables are developed from access diagrams on the basis of an analysis of cardinalities along the path (Fig. 5-29 and 5-30).

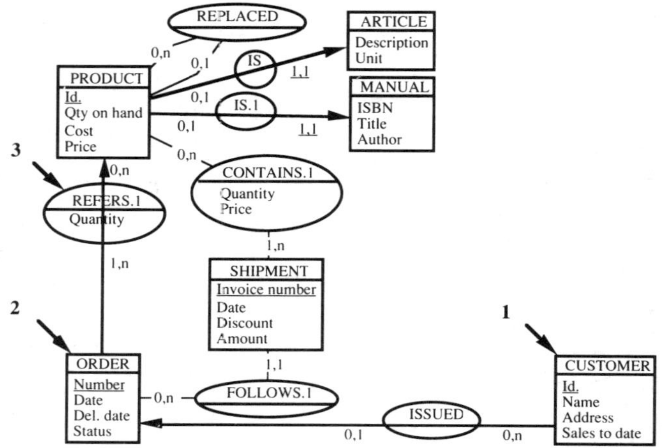

A processing unit focusing on orders may have access paths with various entry points:

- Entry Point 1 is useful for selections based on CUSTOMER properties;
- Entry Point 2 on ORDER is the normal entry point;
- Entry Point 3 is useful when processing all occurrences of REFERS.1.

From the chosen entry point, the access path may be extended backward toward CUSTOMER and forward toward MANUAL and ARTICLE.

Figure 5-41 Analysis of possible access paths.

Data flows may also be described by narratives (Fig. 5-33) or specified by views on the conceptual model (Fig. 5-9 to 5-11).

Developing logical specifications is conducive to additional verifications that the logical model is consistent with the conceptual model in its finest details, and that processes, data stores and data flows are consistent with one another. During this stage, the conceptual model may have to be extended to include objects and properties which are specifically required for the logical description of the system.

Chapter 6

The Relational Model

> My roads will not exactly be the same as yours, but, with our separate maps, we can each get from a particular point of the country to another.
>
> (D. Hofstadter, *Gödel, Escher, Bach*)

A book which deals with a data driven approach must refer to the relational model. Indeed, this model provides a very sound theoretical foundation; furthermore, it is the basis for numerous software tools: relational databases and languages that are more or less consistent with the approach it advocates to the structure and use of data.

In a book such as this one, this topic can only be broached, without an in-depth examination. Fortunately there is a similarity between the concepts of the relational and entity-relationship approaches. This chapter is intended to demonstrate that similarity and to show that relational diagrams may be derived from entity-relationship diagrams in a straightforward manner.

The diagramming technique proposed here may be used on the conceptual and logical levels. But, in this book, it will be mostly used to express the physical model of a system. This chapter may thus be considered a transition from the logical model of a system to its physical model.

6.1 Components

6.1.1 Relational diagrams

A *relational diagram* consists of a set of tables (Fig. 6-1) connected by links, and a set of explicit constraints (Fig. 6-2). Tables represent system data, while links and explicit constraints represent the conditions with which they must comply.

A relational diagram may be normal: this has the same meaning as for a conceptual model or a view.

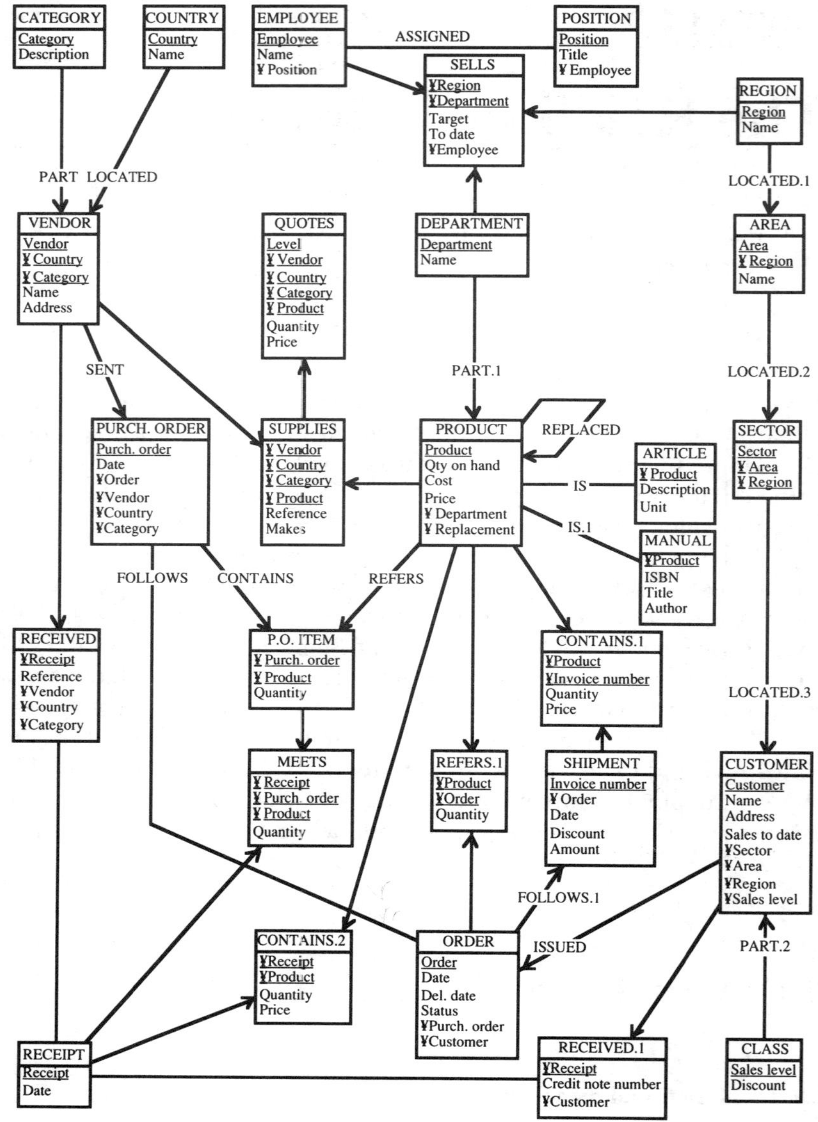

This relational diagram is derived and adapted from the Distribution of School Supplies entity-relationship diagram (Fig. 4-21).

Note: Identifiers are renamed to avoid synonyms, for instance: PRODUCT.Id. —> Product.

Figure 6-1 Relational diagram: tables and links.

TABLE	PROPERTY	CONSTRAINT
PRODUCT	Product	5 digit number (Domain)
	Price	≥ Cost x (1 + Profit rate) (Calculation)
PRODUCT and SHIPMENT (when preparing a shipment)	Quantity on hand	= Old Qty on hand - CONTAINS.1.Quantity
	Amount	= Sum of (Qties x Prices) for SHIPMENT
	Discount	= Amount x CLASS.Discount for CUSTOMER CLASS (Calculation)
PRODUCT		A PRODUCT IS either an ARTICLE or a MANUAL (Exclusion)
QUOTES	Quantity	Increases with Level
	Price	Decreases with Level for a Product.Vendor combination (Integrity)
ETC...		

Figure 6-2 Relational diagram: constraints.

When implemented in a relational environment, a relational diagram and its data may be manipulated using a small number of fundamental primitives which constitute a *relational language.*

Some of these primitives produce new tables which are called *relational views,* which are normal or not normal, as the case may be.

6.1.2 Tables

A *table* consists of a list of data elements. A table may have a *fixed structure,* consisting of a fixed number of unique and mandatory data elements (Fig. 6-3). In a normal relational diagram, this is the case for all tables. Such a structure is very simple; however, it makes it possible to represent all the data of a system and, with a proper relational language, to define most required processes.

The VENDOR table contains only mandatory unique elements.

Figure 6-3 Fixed-structure table.

A table may also possess a *variable structure,* consisting of a variable number of data element groups with a fixed structure, *optional* or *mandatory, unique* or *multiple* (Fig. 6-4 and 6-5). The number of occurrences allowed in a table group are called *cardinalities of the group.* This structure results from the diagram being 'de-normalized' using groupings or other transformations. It is used to address performance considerations or physical limitations of the software. But, as a result of its complexity, manipulating this structure only with relational primitives may become impossible.

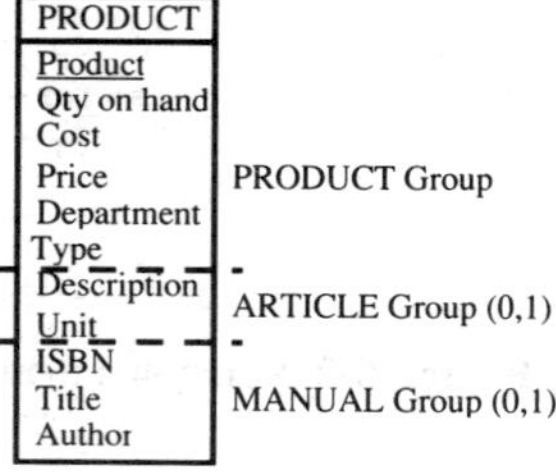

CONSTRAINT: Depending on the value of Type, either the ARTICLE Group is present or the MANUAL Group is present.

The PRODUCT table contains optional unique groups: all their elements are simultaneously present or null.

Figure 6-4 Variable-structure table: optional unique groups.

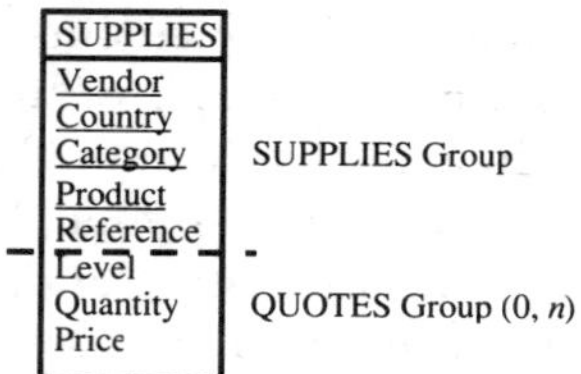

CONSTR.: Price decreases with Level for any given VENDOR.PRODUCT.

The SUPPLIES table contains an optional multiple group, that is, a number of group occurrences equal to the group maximal cardinality.
All elements of a group occurrence are simultaneously present or null.

Figure 6-5 Variable-structure table: optional multiple group.

A table possesses a variable number of occurrences. Each table occurrence may possess a specific number of occurrences of each data element group. Each occurrence of a group possesses specific values for each data element.

6.1.3 Constraints

A *constraint* is a rule with which occurrences of some tables and values of some data elements must comply, in order to ensure the consistency of data represented by the diagram.

While some constraints may be represented as links – and cardinalities – on the diagram, other constraints are *explicit*, in that they must be stated separately (Fig. 6-2).

6.1.4 Primary keys

In a normal diagram, each table must have a *primary key*, that is, a data element or a group of data elements whose values make it possible to identify table occurrences (Fig. 6-6). A primary key specifies direct access to the unique occurrence to which it points.

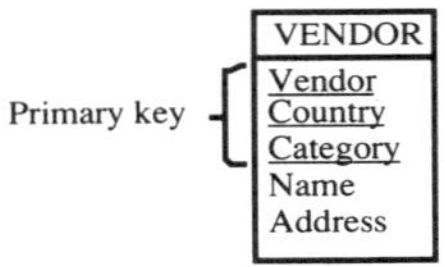

The VENDOR table primary key consists of Vendor, Country and Category. It specifies direct access to a unique occurrence of the VENDOR table.

Figure 6-6 Primary key.

6.1.5 Links and foreign keys

A *referential integrity constraint* between two tables specifies that some data element – or data element group – of the first table refers to a corresponding data element – or data element group – in the second table; values in the first table must be present in the second table. The data element or data element group in the second table is usually its key (Fig. 6-7); the data element or data element group in the first table is thus called a *foreign key*.

Referential integrity constraints may be represented as *links* between tables. They may be expressed more completely by showing cardinalities next to the links (Fig. 6-8).

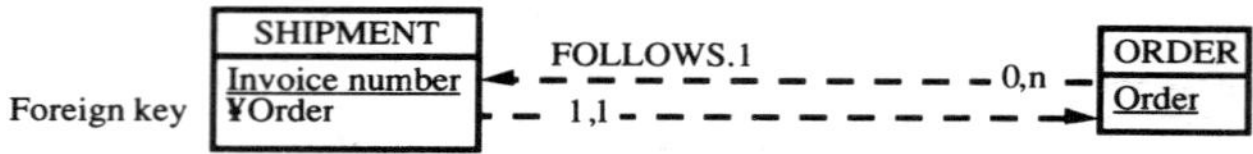

The Order element of the SHIPMENT table is a foreign key (¥ sign); it refers to the Order primary key of the ORDER table:
• For a given SHIPMENT occurrence, it makes it possible to access a unique ORDER occurrence;
• For a given ORDER occurrence, it makes it possible to access, through a selection, the corresponding multiple SHIPMENT occurrences.

Figure 6-7 Foreign key.

The referential integrity constraint on the Order foreign key may be shown as a link between the SHIPMENT and the ORDER tables.

Cardinalities may be shown next to the link to more fully specify the referential integrity constraint.

Figure 6-8 Referential integrity constraint as a link.

Arrowheads may be used to indicate maximum cardinalities of *n* (Fig. 6-9).

An arrowhead is often drawn on the end opposite to 0,*n* or 1,*n* cardinalities. It is a shorthand for the maximum cardinality of *n* and reads:
For one ORDER occurrence, there are multiple SHIPMENT occurrences.

When the arrowhead convention is used, a link without arrowheads is indicative of maximum cardinalities of 1 on both ends.

Figure 6-9 Arrowhead convention for links.

6.1.6 Indexes

In addition to primary keys, a data element or data element group may be specified as an *index* (Fig. 6-10): submitting the value of this element provides direct access to the – possibly multiple – occurrences of the table to which it belongs.

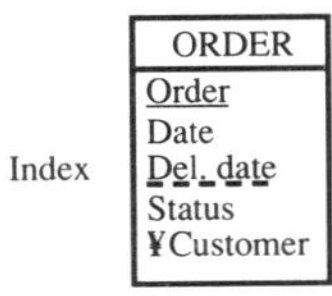

Specifying Delivery date as an index provides direct access to all ORDER occurrences with a given delivery date.

Figure 6-10 Data element specified as an index.

In accordance with their role in navigating between tables, foreign keys are usually specified as indexes (Fig. 6-11).

Specifying the Vendor.Country.Category foreign key as an index provides direct access to all PURCH. ORDER occurrences with a given VENDOR.

Figure 6-11 Foreign key specified as an index.

6.1.7 Relational language

Several languages have been defined to make it possible to define relational tables and to manipulate their contents. The *Structured Query Language (SQL)* developed by IBM researchers is a popular example of such a language. With an extension (Fig. 6-12), it might be feasible to define constraints associated with tables, links, views with multiple tables and links, and to manipulate data accordingly.

A powerful feature of relational languages is that their primitives are set-oriented: all occurrences complying with stated selection criteria are processed at once. This results in very concise programming, which would otherwise require 'procedural' logic with loops.

SUBJECT	COMMAND	FUNCTION
DEFINITION		
TABLE	Create Table	Specifies a table, its data elements and related constraints.
	Alter Table	Modifies table specifications by adding or modifying elements and constraints.
INDEX	Create Index On	Specifies an index for a table.
PRIMARY KEY	Create Key On	Specifies a primary key for a table.
LINK	Create Link On	Specifies a link between tables.
VIEW	Create View	Specifies a multi-table view as a function of actual tables and links.
CANCELLA-TION	Drop Table, Index, etc	Cancels a previously specified table, index, etc.
MANIPULATION		
QUERY	Select	Identifies tables and links or views to be queried, occurrences selection criteria, queried and derived elements.
UPDATE	Update	Identifies table or link to be updated, occurrences selection criteria, elements and their values.
INSERT	Insert	Identifies table or link where insert is to take place, elements and their values.
DELETE	Delete	Identifies tables and links where delete is to take place and occurrences selection criteria.

Figure 6-12 Overview of an extended relational language.

When a relational diagram is normal, all accesses may be implemented using relational primitives. When it is not normal, additional procedures are required to update, query and delete data element groups embedded in tables.

6.2 Derivation Rules

6.2.1 Relational diagrams

(a) A relational diagram (Fig. 6-1) is derived from a model (Fig. 4-21) or a view by applying specific derivation rules (Fig. 6-13 and 6-25).

6.2.2 Tables and links

Normal derivations

Applying normal derivation rules (Fig. 6-13) to a normal model or a normal view yields a normal relational diagram. This process can be carried out in an automatic way.

ENTITY-RELATIONSHIP DIAGRAM	RELATIONAL DIAGRAM
ENTITY	TABLE
PARENT-CHILD RELATIONSHIP	LINK AND FOREIGN KEY IN CHILD TABLE
NON PARENT-CHILD RELATIONSHIP	TABLE
NON PARENT-CHILD ROLE	LINK AND FOREIGN KEY IN RELATIONSHIP TABLE
CARDINALITIES	CARDINALITIES (AND ARROWHEAD)
PROPERTY	DATA ELEMENT
IDENTIFIER	PRIMARY KEY
IDENTIFIER DEPENDENCY	FOREIGN KEY IN PRIMARY KEY OF CHILD TABLE
DEPENDENCY RULE IN RELATIONSHIP	FOREIGN KEY NOT IN PRIM. KEY OF RELATIONSHIP TABLE
BUSINESS RULE	CONSTRAINT

Figure 6-13 Overview of normal derivation rules for a relational diagram.

(a) An entity becomes a table (Fig. 6-14). Entity properties become data elements of the table. The entity identifier becomes the primary key of the table.

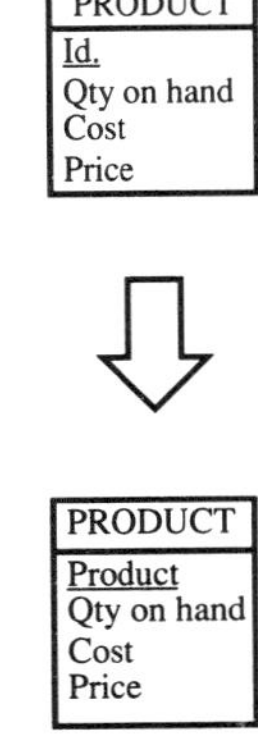

Figure 6-14 Relational diagram: normal derivation of an entity.

(b) A parent-child relationship yields a single link with $0,n$–1,1 or $1,n$–1,1 cardinalities (Fig. 6-15). The parent role yields a foreign key in the child table. If the child entity is identified through the parent entity (Fig. 6-16), this foreign key is also part of the child table primary key.

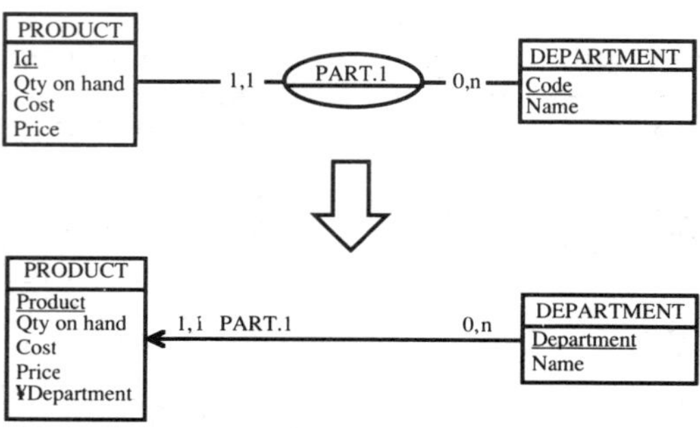

Figure 6-15 Relational diagram: normal derivation of a parent-child relationship.

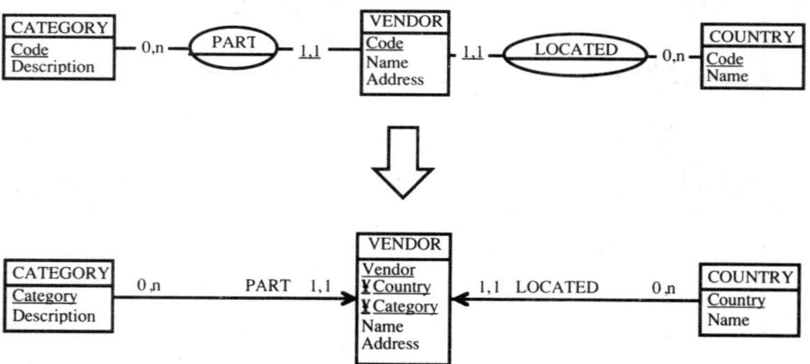

Figure 6-16 Relational diagram: normal derivation of parent-child relationships with identifier dependencies.

(c) A semi-mandatory assignment relationship is a parent-child relationship and is dealt with using Rule (b) above, yielding a single link with 0,1–1,1 cardinalities (Fig. 6-17). Similarly, a mandatory assignment relationship is a double parent-child relationship and yields a single link with 1,1–1,1 cardinalities (Fig. 6-18).

(d) As a consequence of normal derivation rules, a super-entity and its sub-entities yield separate linked tables (Fig. 6-17).

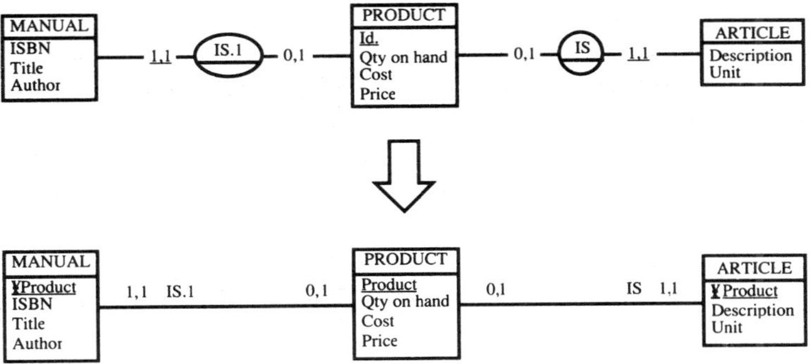

Figure 6-17 Relational diagram: normal derivation of semi-mandatory assignments relationships.

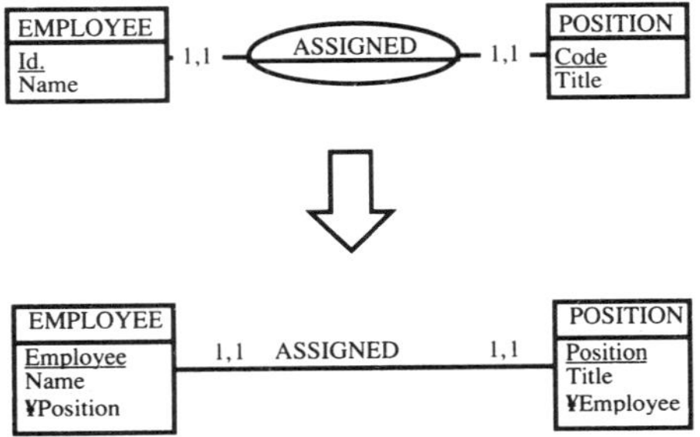

Figure 6-18 Relational diagram: normal derivation of a mandatory assignment relationship.

(e) A regular relationship – in which all cardinalities are $0,n$ or $1,n$ – becomes a table (Fig. 6-19). Relationship properties become data elements of the table. Roles become links with $0,n$–1,1 or $1,n$–1,1 cardinalities and yield foreign keys in the table. The relationship identifier becomes the primary key of the table.

(f) A quasi parent-child relationship is dealt with as a relationship in Rule (e) above, yielding a separate table (Fig. 6-20). The quasi-parent role becomes a link with $0,n$–1,1 or $1,n$–1,1 cardinalities. The quasi-child role becomes a link with 0,1–1,1 cardinalities.

(g) An optional assignment relationship is a quasi parent-child relationship and is dealt with using Rule (e) above, yielding a separate table (Fig. 6-21). Roles become links with 0,1–1,1 cardinalities.

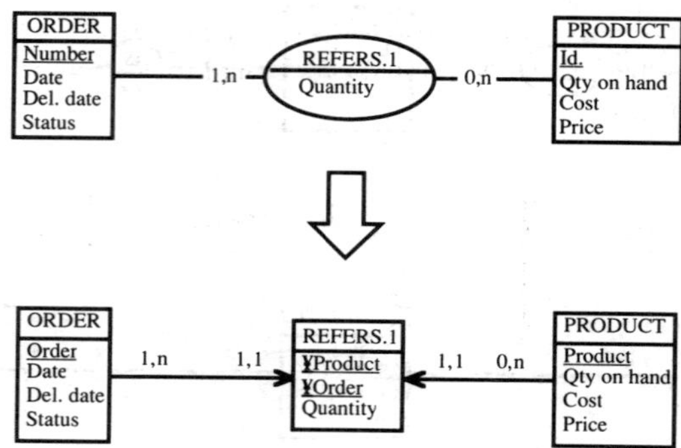

Figure 6-19 Relational diagram: normal derivation of a regular relationship.

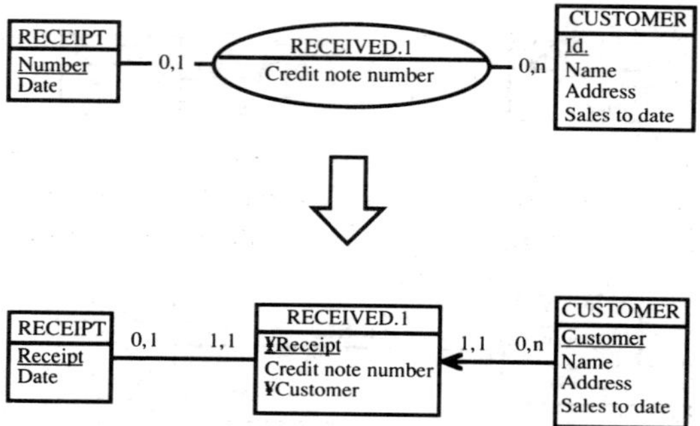

Figure 6-20 Relational diagram: normal derivation of a quasi parent-child relationship.

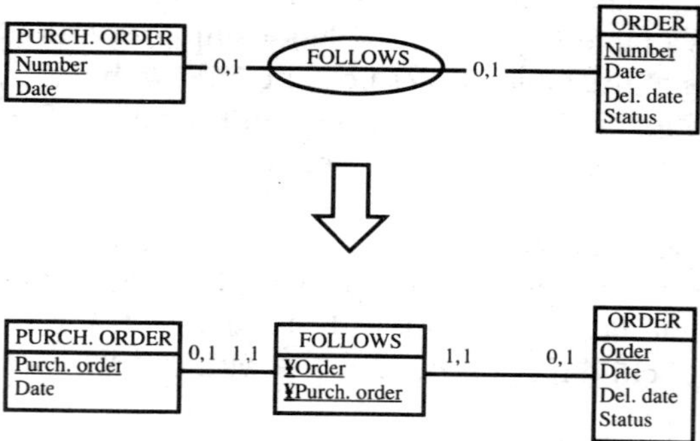

Figure 6-21 Relational diagram: normal derivation of an optional assignment relationship.

(h) Recursive relationships (Fig. 6-22) are dealt with using rules (b) to (g), whichever one applies. Foreign keys are renamed to avoid ambiguity.

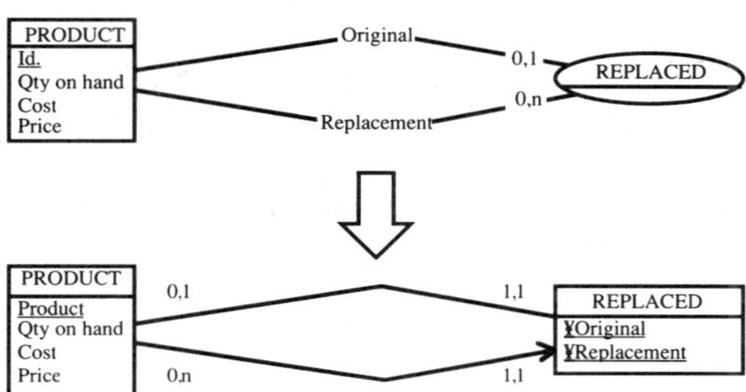

Figure 6-22 Relational diagram: normal derivation of a recursive relationship.

(i) Relationships with a dependency rule (Fig. 6-23) are dealt with using rules (b) to (h), whichever one applies. The foreign key derived from the dependent role is excluded from the primary key for the derived table.

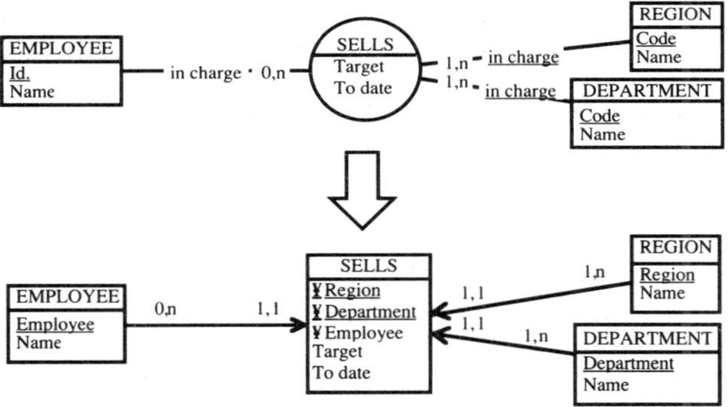

Each role in the SELLS relationship yields a foreign key.
Foreign keys Region and Department are part of the SELLS table primary key.
The 'In charge' dependency rule, with dependent entity EMPLOYEE, causes the Employee foreign key to be excluded from the SELLS table primary key.

Figure 6-23 Relational diagram: normal derivation of a relationship with a dependency rule.

(j) Implication rules may sometimes yield links (Fig. 6-24).

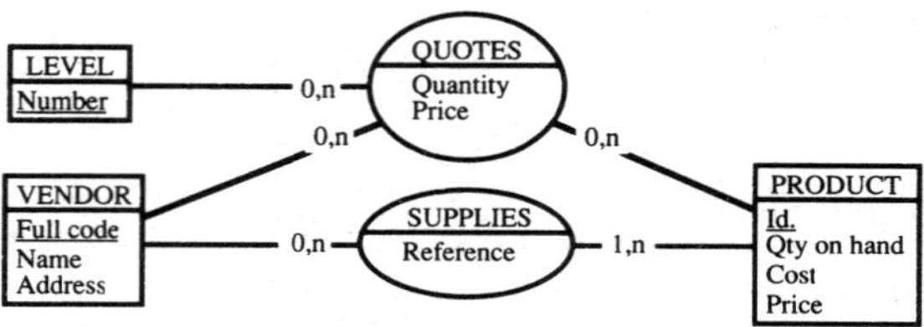

IMPLICATION RULE: A VENDOR who QUOTES a PRODUCT, SUPPLIES the PRODUCT.

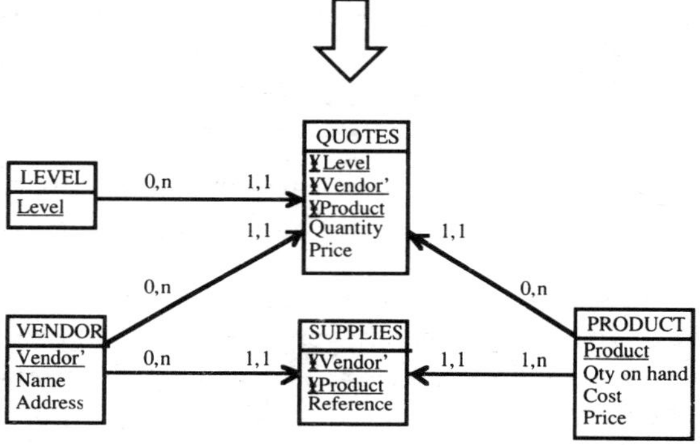

CONSTRAINT: A VENDOR who QUOTES a PRODUCT, SUPPLIES the PRODUCT.

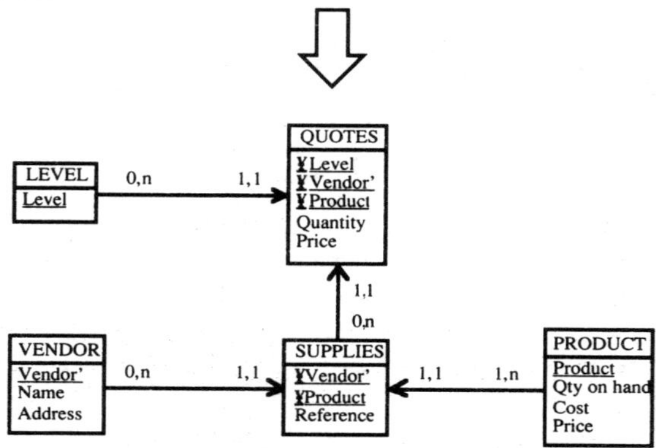

The constraint is replaced by the equivalent 0,*n*–1,1 link between SUPPLIES and QUOTES.
The VENDOR and PRODUCT links with QUOTES become redundant and are deleted.

Figure 6-24 Relational diagram: normal derivation of an implication rule.

Non-normal derivations

Non-normal derivation rules (Fig. 6-25) group objects which are kept separate by normal derivation rules. They result in optional or multiple data elements, thus violating First Normal Form, but may improve processing performance by reducing the number of accesses. Applying non-normal derivation rules to a normal model or a normal view yields a non-normal relational diagram. These rules offer additional design choices and, for the greater part, can be automated.

ENTITY-RELATIONSHIP DIAGRAM	RELATIONAL DIAGRAM
QUASI PARENT-CHILD RELATIONSHIP	LINK AND GROUP IN QUASI-CHILD TABLE
ENTITY	GROUP IN TABLE
SUPER/SUB-ENTITIES	GROUPS IN SUPER/SUB-TABLES
RELATED OBJECTS	GROUPS IN SINGLE TABLE

Figure 6-25 Overview of non-normal derivation rules for a relational diagram.

(a) A quasi parent-child relationship – especially one without explicit properties – may be dealt with as a parent-child relationship, yielding a link and an optional group of data elements including a foreign key (Fig. 6-26) instead of a separate table (Fig. 6-20).

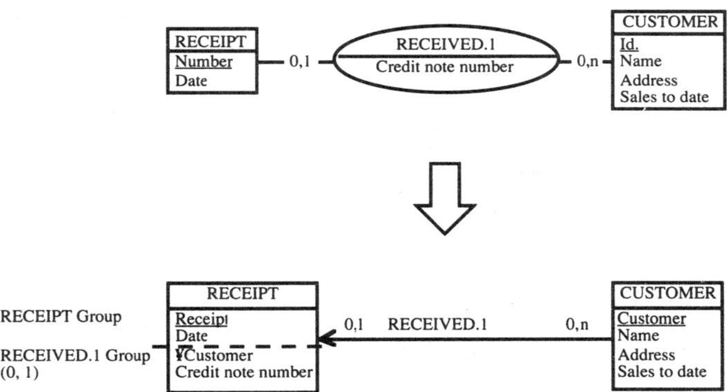

Relationship RECEIVED.1 is grouped into the same table as quasi-child entity RECEIPT.
Foreign key Customer and dependent data element Credit note number are null or simultaneously present.

Figure 6-26 Relational diagram: non-normal derivation of a quasi parent-child relationship.

(b) An optional assignment relationship – especially one without explicit properties – may be dealt with as a parent-child relationship, yielding a link and two optional groups of data elements including a foreign key (Fig. 6-27) instead of a separate table (Fig. 6-21).

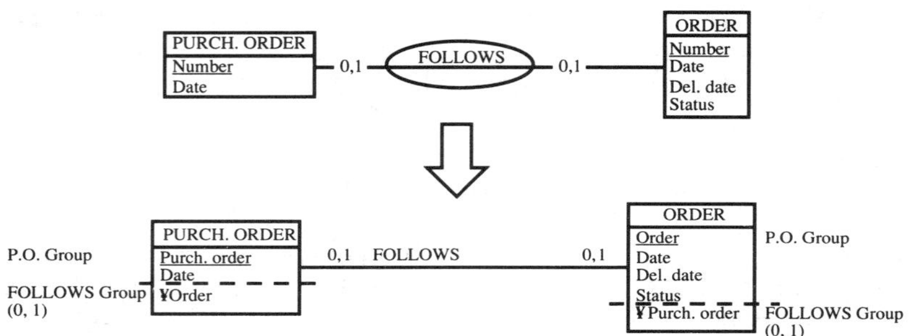

Relationship FOLLOWS is grouped into the same tables as quasi-child entities PURCHASE ORDER and ORDER.
Foreign keys Order and Purchase order are null or simultaneously present.

Figure 6-27 Relational diagram: non-normal derivation of an optional assignment relationship.

(c) A super-entity and its sub-entities may be grouped, for example with the super-entity (Fig. 6-4) or the sub-entity (Fig. 6-28) tables.

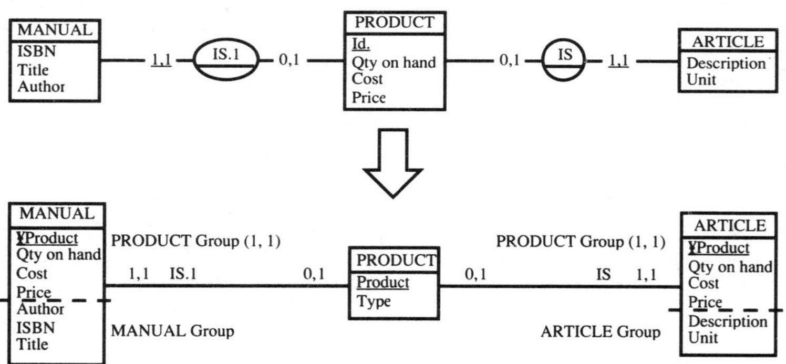

Super-entity PRODUCT is grouped into the same tables as quasi-child entities MANUAL and ARTICLE, to facilitate their independent processing.
A stripped-down PRODUCT table facilitates generic PRODUCT processing.

Figure 6-28 Relational diagram: non-normal derivation of a super-entity and its sub-entities.

(d) Two related objects may be grouped in a single table (Fig. 6-29).

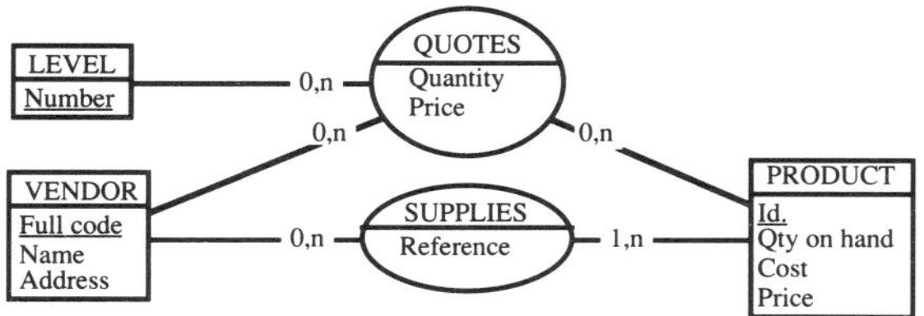

IMPLICATION RULE: A VENDOR who QUOTES a PRODUCT, SUPPLIES the PRODUCT.

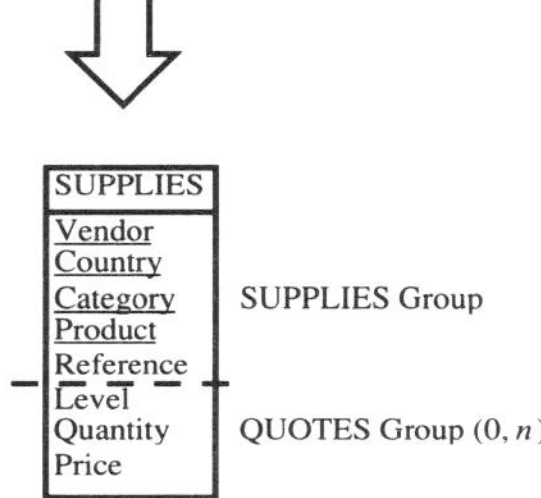

Objects SUPPLIES and QUOTES are related through an implication rule. QUOTES may be grouped in the same table as SUPPLIES.

Figure 6-29 Relational diagram: non-normal derivation of two related objects.

(e) Additional groupings are feasible. Caution must be exercised, since reducing accesses by de-normalizing the model makes it more difficult to use the facilities of relational languages.

6.2.3 Constraints

Explicit business rules of the conceptual model yield constraints of the relational diagram (Fig. 6-2). Cardinality rules yield referential integrity constraints and links (Fig. 6-8).

6.2.4 Primary keys and indexes

Normal derivations

(a) When an object becomes a table, its identifier yields the primary key of the table (Fig. 6-14, 6-19 to 6-23).

(b) A foreign key yields an index (Fig. 6-11 and 6-30), unless it already is the primary key (Fig. 6-31).

Product.Order, the identifier of the REFERS.1 relationship, yields a primary key.
Product, a foreign key in the REFERS.1 table, yields an index.
In the same manner, Order, a foreign key in the REFERS.1 table, yields an index.

Figure 6-30 Relational diagram: primary key and indexes for a table derived from a relationship.

Product, the identifier of the PRODUCT entity, is a foreign key in the MANUAL and ARTICLE tables, due to the IS and IS.1 parent-child relationships.
But it is also the primary key of those entities, due to identifier dependencies:
—> It does not need to be defined as an index.

Figure 6-31 Relational diagram: primary key and indexes for tables derived from entities.

(c) A property or property group which is used as an access criterion yields an index (Fig. 6-10), unless it already is the primary key.

Non-normal derivations

(a) An object which becomes the main group of data elements in a table keeps its primary key and indexes (Fig. 6-32).

(b) An object which becomes an optional group of data elements in a table keeps its indexes; its primary key yields an index (Fig. 6-32).

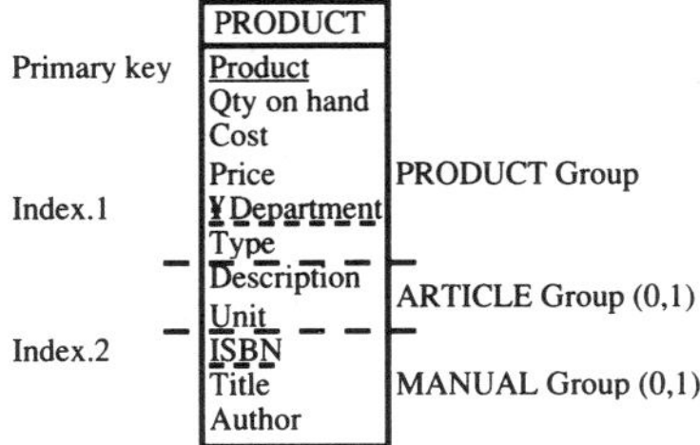

PRODUCT is the main group in the PRODUCT table:
—> It keeps its Product primary key and Department index.

MANUAL is an optional group in the PRODUCT table:
—> Its ISBN primary key becomes an index.

Figure 6-32 Relational diagram: primary key and indexes for main and optional groups in a table.

(c) An object which becomes a multiple group of data elements in a table keeps its indexes; its primary key yields an index. In addition, each index is replicated a number of times equal to the group maximal cardinality (Fig. 6-33). This is not convenient unless the maximal cardinality is small.

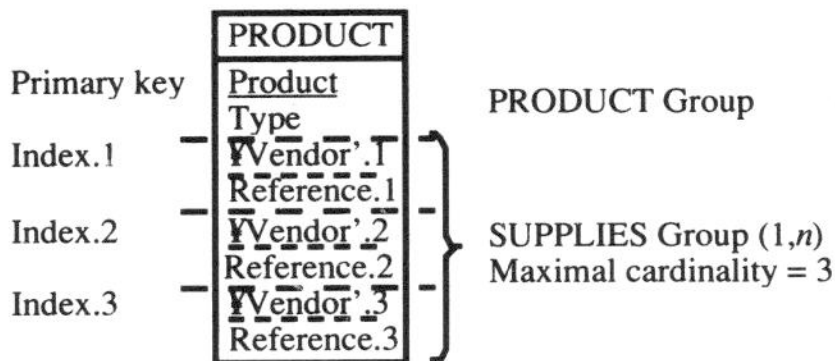

SUPPLIES is a multiple group in the PRODUCT table with a maximal cardinality of three:
—> Its Vendor' index is replicated three times.

Figure 6-33 Relational diagram: indexes for a multiple group in a table.

Elimination of indexes

An index speeds up queries – when the table population is not too small – but penalizes inserts and updates. Indexes may be eliminated to improve data entry performance, when query response time is not critical (Fig. 6-34) or when the object population is small.

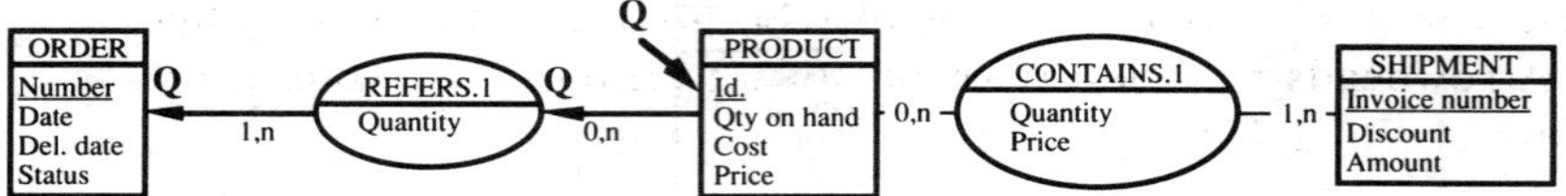

REFERS.1 is frequently queried from PRODUCT to find orders which refer to some selected product.
CONTAINS.1 is never queried from PRODUCT.

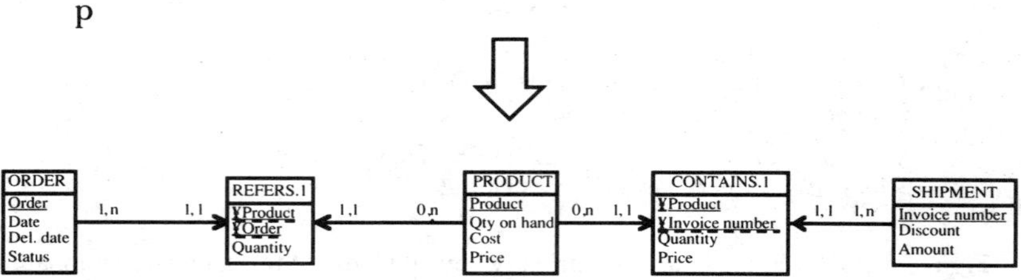

The Product index in REFERS.1 cannot be eliminated without increasing the response time of product-related order queries.
The Product index in CONTAINS.1 may be eliminated without inconvenience to improve shipment data entry.

Figure 6-34 Relational diagram: elimination of an index.

6.2.5 Processes

(a) Processes as well as their access diagrams, access modules and procedures are expressed in the same way using relational diagrams as they are using entity-relationship diagrams. When objects are grouped into tables, access modules must be grouped similarly.

(b) As far as possible, access modules are expressed using relational primitives.

6.3 Representation

A relational diagram is named for the model or view from which it derives. A table – or a group – may be named for the principal object it contains. A group may be outlined and its cardinalities in the table shown next to it. The name of a derived table or group may be marked with an asterisk. Primary keys are underlined. Foreign keys may be marked with a ¥ symbol. Indexes may be underlined with a dashed line. Arrowheads may be drawn on links to indicate maximum cardinalities of *n* (Fig. 6-9).

6.4 Approach

Relational diagrams may be derived from entity-relationship diagrams at any stage in the systems development life cycle. But, in practical terms, this is done toward the later stages, when detailed models are available (Fig. 4-21) and detailed specifications are required. The approach is straightforward (Fig. 6-1, 6-35 to 6-38).

DISTRIBUTION OF SCHOOL SUPPLIES

1. **All entities**

   Apply normal derivation rules.
   (Fig. 6-14)

2. **All parent-child relationships**

   Apply normal derivation rules.
   (Fig. 6-15 to 6-18)

3. **Quasi parent-child relationships FOLLOWS and ISSUED**

   Apply non-normal derivation rule concerning quasi parent-child relationships.
   (Fig. 6-27)

4. **Recursive quasi parent-child relationship REPLACED**

   Apply non-normal derivation rule concerning quasi parent-child relationships.
   (Fig. 6-36)

5. **Relationship SELLS with dependency rule 'in charge'**

   Apply normal derivation rule concerning relationships with dependency rule.
   (Fig. 6-23)

6. **Relationships QUOTES and SUPPLIES**

   Apply normal derivation rule concerning implications between relationships.
   (Fig. 6-24)

   Delete LEVEL table which contains only trivial information.
   (Fig. 6-37)

7. **Relationships MAKES and SUPPLIES**

   Apply normal derivation rule concerning implications between relationships.

   Apply non-normal derivation rule concerning quasi parent-child relationships.
   (Fig. 6-38)

8. **All other relationships**

   Apply normal derivation rules.
   (Fig. 6-19 and 6-20)

9. **Business rules**

   Business rules become constraints.
   (Fig. 6-2)

Figure 6-35 Relational diagram: derivation of a diagram.

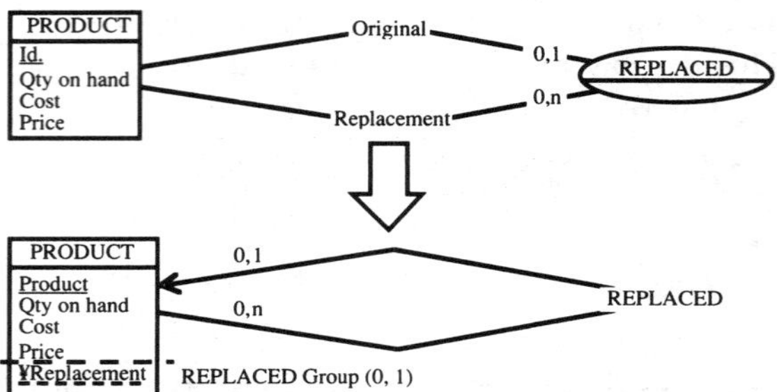

Relationship REPLACED is grouped with quasi-child entity PRODUCT. Foreign key Replacement is optional and points to the PRODUCT table.

Figure 6-36 Relational diagram: non-normal derivation of a recursive relationship.

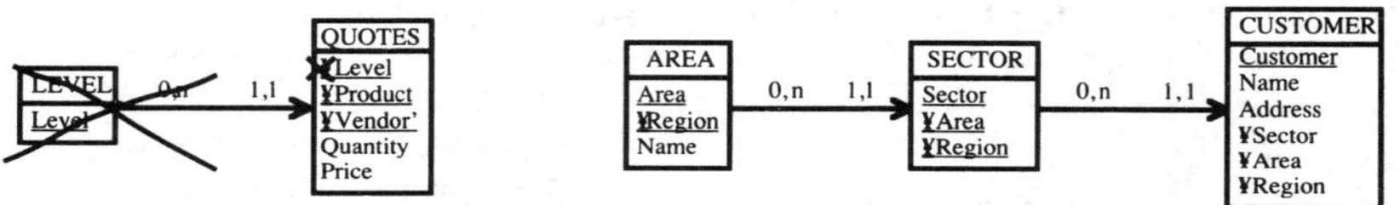

Tables LEVEL and SECTOR contain only primary keys: they are used for enforcing referential integrity constraints with other tables.
But LEVEL is not needed since it contains only a trivial sequence of integers.

Figure 6-37 Relational diagram: deletion of a table.

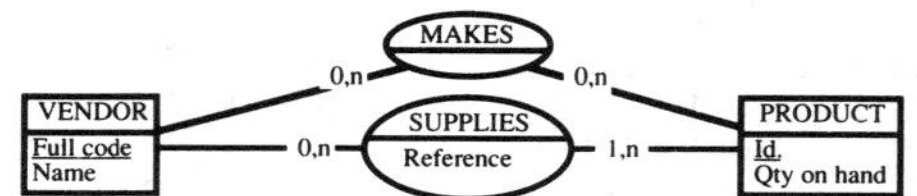

IMPLICATION RULE: A VENDOR who MAKES a PRODUCT, SUPPLIES the PRODUCT. A VENDOR who SUPPLIES the PRODUCT either MAKES it or does not.

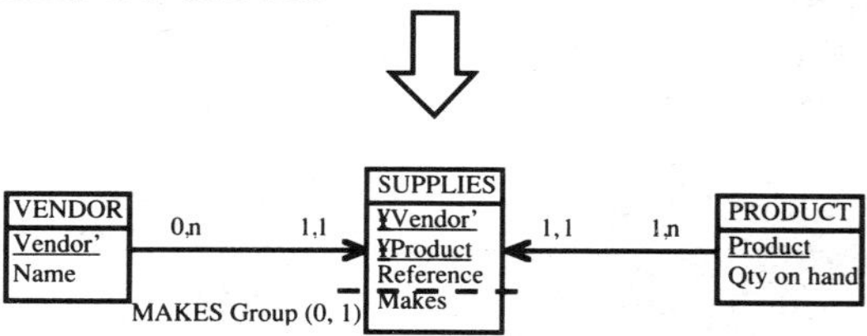

The constraint is replaced by the equivalent 0,1–1,1 link between SUPPLIES and MAKES, then by the non-normal equivalent Makes data element in SUPPLIES. Makes may be optional single-valued or logical.

Figure 6-38 Relational diagram: non-normal derivation of an implication rule.

Chapter 7

The Physical Model

> It goes without saying that *some* knowledge has to be embodied in programs; otherwise one would not have a program at all, but merely an encyclopedia.
>
> (D. Hofstadter, *Gödel, Escher, Bach*)

The purpose of this chapter is to briefly indicate how the concepts presented in this book lead to the implementation of an information system.

The physical model of a system is closely connected with the resources and the technology being used. As a result, this chapter limits itself to high level observations. Examples, which are based on the relational language of the previous chapter, are only outlined.

Relational tools are easy to learn and continue to gain ground, so even outline examples are useful. The reader is encouraged to transpose the proposed approach to other tools.

7.1 Components

7.1.1 Physical data flow diagrams

A *physical data flow diagram* or *DFD* has the same components as a logical DFD: processes, data stores and data flows, external entities and external processes. In addition, it shows resources which are used.

DFDs are prepared at various level of detail, paralleling the breakdown of logical DFDs.

Depending on the point of view, resources displayed on a physical DFD may be technological (Fig. 7-1), geographical (Fig. 7-2) or organizational (Fig. 7-3 and 7-4).

Lower level physical DFDs may be used to distinguish between manual and automated components. For processes and data stores, this must be shown directly (Fig. 7-3 and 7-4). For data flows, it may be usually be inferred from their connections.

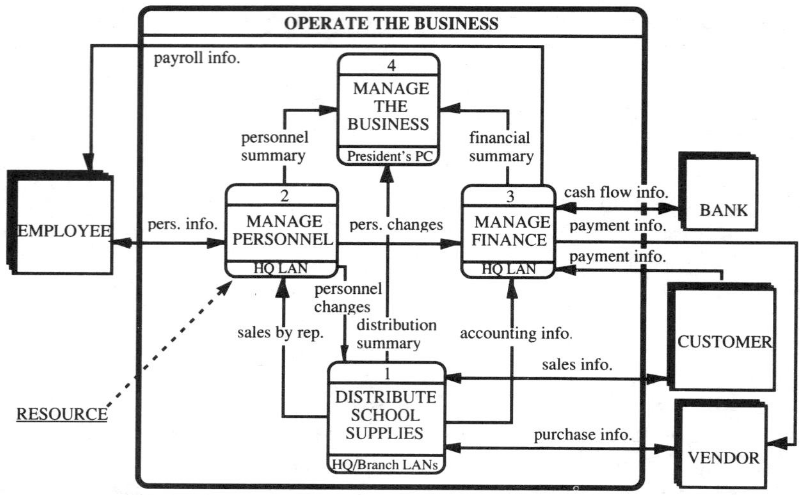

Figure 7-1 Physical DFD: corporate context diagram showing technological resources.

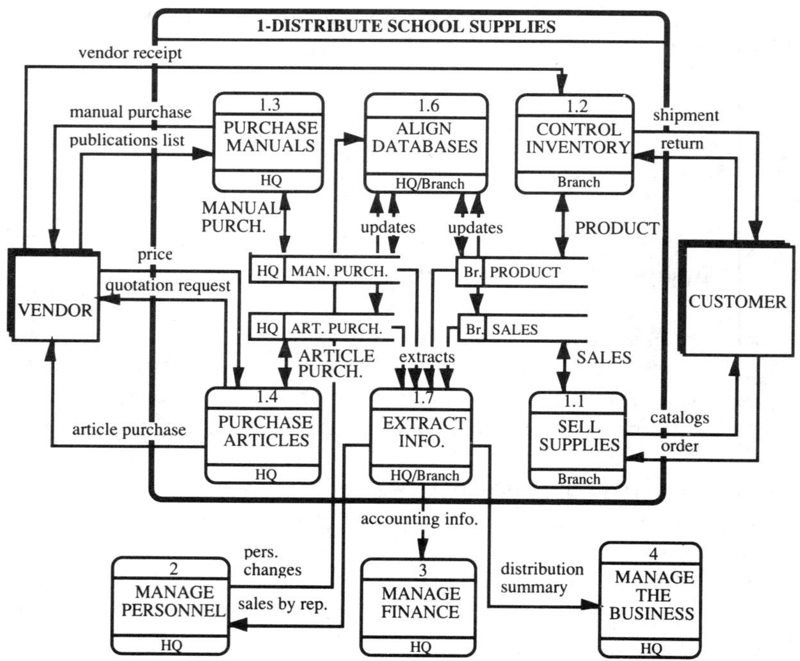

Figure 7-2 Physical DFD: first level diagram showing locations.

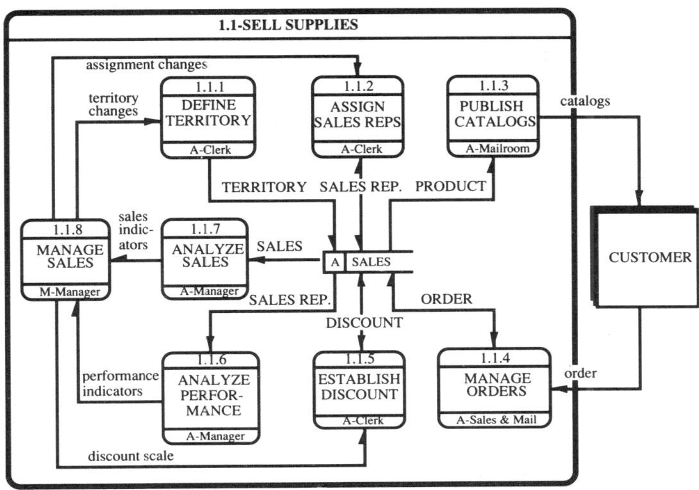

LEGEND: **A** Automated
M Manual

Figure 7-3 Physical DFD: second level diagram showing organizational resources, automated and manual processes.

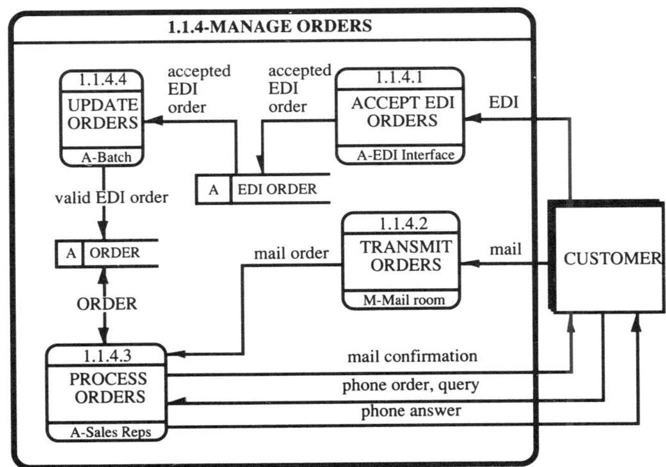

LEGEND: **A** Automated
M Manual

Figure 7-4 Physical DFD: third level diagram showing resources, automated and manual processes.

7.1.2 Automated components

Data stores and views

An *automated physical data store* is a set of conventional files or a database, possibly supporting constraints. Its contents may be specified by a relational diagram (Fig. 7-5) and constraints, and implemented using a relational language (Fig. 7-6).

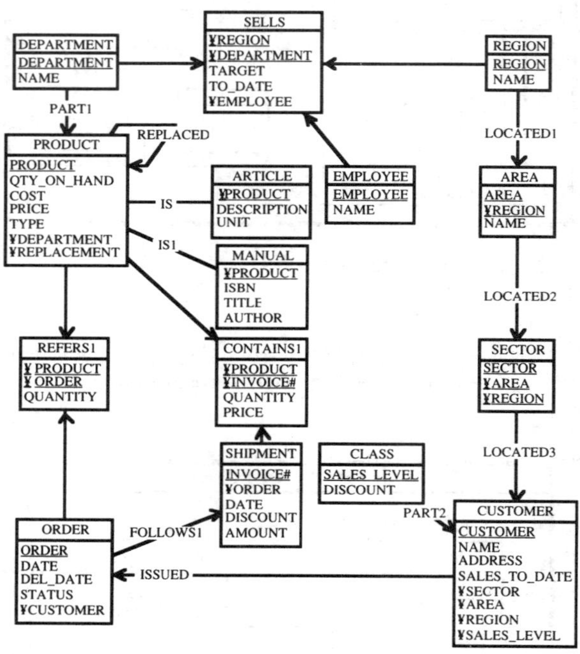

This data store is derived from the Sales logical data store (Fig. 5-4).

Figure 7-5 Preliminary specification of an automated data store.

Create Table	ORDER		
	ORDER	Char (4)	
	DATE	Date	
	DEL_DATE	Date	≥ DATE + 2
	STATUS	Char (10)	= 'New', 'Back order', 'Filled'
	CUSTOMER	Char (3)	Null or in CUSTOMER table
Create Unique Index	ORDER_SEQ	On	ORDER (ORDER)
Create Index	ORDER_CUST	On	ORDER (CUSTOMER)

Figure 7-6 Implementation of a table in an automated data store.

Similarly, an *automated physical view* designates an extract from a database produced on demand by a relational language. Its contents may be a conventional view, consisting of a single table, or a view including multiple tables and links. It may be specified by a relational diagram and constraints which define the view. It may be implemented by a relational language.

Data flows

An *automated data flow* is a query or data entry screen, a document read in or produced in an automated way, or an automated interface.

Its contents may be specified using a relational diagram (Fig. 7-7 and 7-8). A screen or report may be implemented using automated design tools (Fig. 7-9 and 7-10). An interface may be similarly specified.

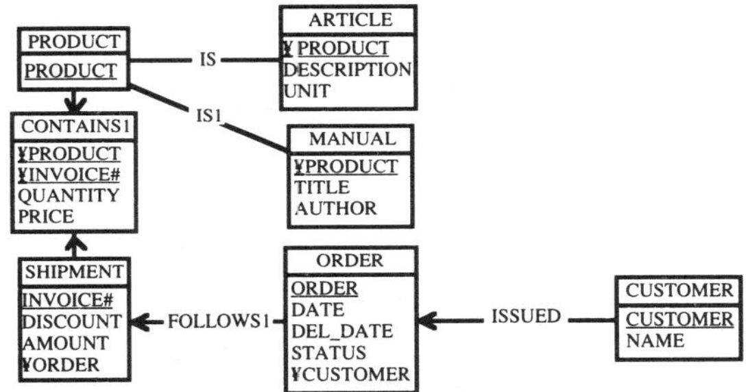

This physical data flow is adapted from an output logical data flow concerning shipments following a given order.

Figure 7-7 Specification of an automated data flow: Shipments By Order.

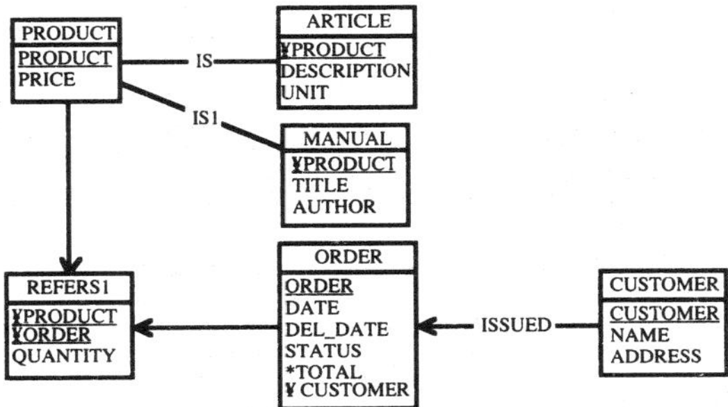

This physical data flow is derived from a set of input and output logical data flows concerning orders.

Figure 7-8 Specification of an automated data flow: Order.

```
                         S H I P M E N T S   B Y   O R D E R
        ORDER
        Order#  ORDE           Customer#  CUS
ORDER   Date    DATE....       Name       NAME................
TITLE   Deliv.  DEL_DATE
        Status  STATUS....

        SHIPMENT
SHIPT   Inv.#   INV.#          Discount   DISCOUNT..              Shipt  Amount $ AMOUNT.....
TITLE
(0,n)   PRODUCTS
        #       Description/Title         Unit/Author             Price    Qty
        PRODU   DESCRIPTION_TITLE...      UNIT_AUTHOR.........    PRICE..  QUANTI

        PRODU   DESCRIPTION_TITLE...      UNIT_AUTHOR.........    PRICE..  QUANTI

SHIPT   PRODU   DESCRIPTION_TITLE...      UNIT_AUTHOR.........    PRICE..  QUANTI
DETAIL
(1,n)   PRODU   DESCRIPTION_TITLE...      UNIT_AUTHOR.........    PRICE..  QUANTI

        PRODU   DESCRIPTION_TITLE...      UNIT_AUTHOR.........    PRICE..  QUANTI

        PRODU   DESCRIPTION_TITLE...      UNIT_AUTHOR.........    PRICE..  QUANTI
```

This screen displays forms ORDER_TITLE, SHIPMENT_TITLE and SHIPMENT_DETAIL.

Figure 7-9 Implementation of an automated data flow: Shipments By Order.

```
                                   O R D E R
        ORDER
        Order#  ORDE           Customer#  CUS                  Address  ADDRESS...........
        Date    DATE....       Name       NAME................          ..................
ORDER   Deliv.  DEL_DATE                                                ..................
HEADER  Status  STATUS....                                     Order Total  $  TOTAL.....


        PRODUCTS
        #       Description/Title         Unit/Author          Price    Qty     $
        PRODU   DESCRIPTION_TITLE...      UNIT_AUTHOR.........  PRICE..  QUANTI  AMOUNT.....

        PRODU   DESCRIPTION_TITLE...      UNIT_AUTHOR.........  PRICE..  QUANTI  AMOUNT.....

        PRODU   DESCRIPTION_TITLE...      UNIT_AUTHOR.........  PRICE..  QUANTI  AMOUNT.....
ORDER
DETAIL  PRODU   DESCRIPTION_TITLE...      UNIT_AUTHOR.........  PRICE..  QUANTI  AMOUNT.....
(1,n)
        PRODU   DESCRIPTION_TITLE...      UNIT_AUTHOR.........  PRICE..  QUANTI  AMOUNT.....

        PRODU   DESCRIPTION_TITLE...      UNIT_AUTHOR.........  PRICE..  QUANTI  AMOUNT.....

        PRODU   DESCRIPTION_TITLE...      UNIT_AUTHOR.........  PRICE..  QUANTI  AMOUNT.....
```

This screen displays forms ORDER_HEADER and ORDER_DETAIL.

Figure 7-10 Implementation of an automated data flow: Order.

Processes

An *automated process* is similar to a process in the logical diagram.

Automated processes may be specified using *physical access diagrams* (Fig. 7-11 and 7-12), similar to logical access diagrams, and *physical action tables,* similar to logical action tables (Fig. 5-15 and 5-16).

An *automated processing unit* is similar to a processing unit in the logical model, in that it should provide a basic service to the user.

However, for reasons of feasibility or convenience, a logical processing unit sometimes gives rise to more than one automated processing unit; conversely, a number of logical processing units are sometimes grouped into a single automated processing unit.

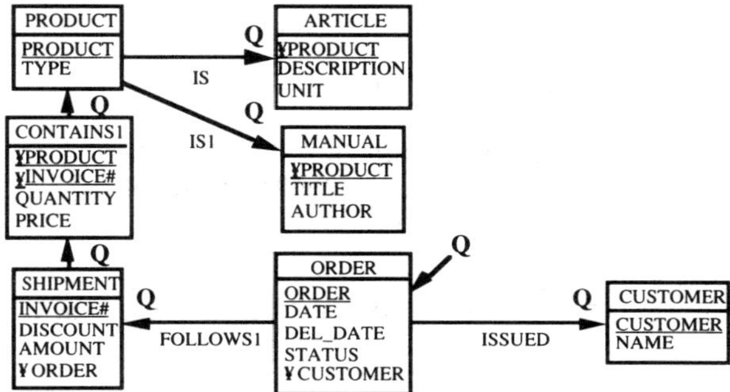

This physical access diagram is adapted from the logical access diagram for shipment queries (Fig. 5-13).

Figure 7-11 Physical access diagram for an automated query process.

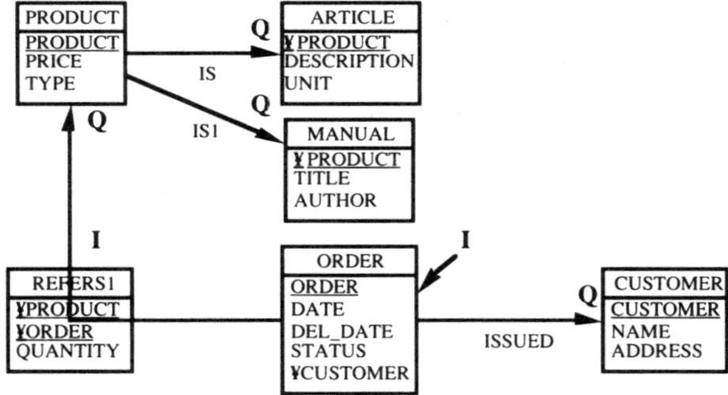

This physical access diagram is adapted from the logical access diagram for order entry (Fig. 5-14).

Figure 7-12 Physical access diagram for an automated maintenance process.

Automated processes may be implemented using a relational language embedded in a procedural language (Fig. 7-13 to 7-16). This consists in writing or generating the detailed logic implied by process specifications (Fig. 7-11 and 7-12).

```
Declare order module and associated screen form
Module          1_ORDER_MODULE_Q
Form            ORDER_TITLE (ORDER, DATE, DEL_DATE, STATUS,
                   CUSTOMER, NAME)
Enter order identifier
Accept From     ORDER_TITLE (ORDER)
         Values (ORDER)
On Query
Query order table
Select          DATE, DEL_DATE, STATUS
           From ORDER
          Where ORDER.ORDER = ORDER_TITLE.ORDER
If customer is specified, get customer information
If              ORDER.CUSTOMER Not Null
Select          NAME
           From CUSTOMER
          Where CUSTOMER.CUSTOMER = ORDER.CUSTOMER
EndIf
Display order title
Display Into    ORDER_TITLE
         Values (ORDER, DATE, DEL_DATE, STATUS, CUSTOMER, NAME)
EndOnQuery
Call shipment module
On Next
Call            3_SHIPMENT_MODULE_Q
EndOnNext
EndModule       1_ORDER_MODULE_Q
Declare shipment module and associated screen form
Module          3_SHIPMENT_MODULE_Q
Form            SHIPMENT_TITLE (INVOICE#, DATE, DISCOUNT, AMOUNT)
Query shipment table
Select          INVOICE#, DATE, DISCOUNT, AMOUNT
           From SHIPMENT
          Where SHIPMENT.ORDER = ORDER_TITLE.ORDER
For Each One
Display shipment title
Display Into    SHIPMENT_TITLE
         Values (INVOICE#, DATE, DISCOUNT, AMOUNT)
Call shipment detail module
On Next
Call            SHIPMENT_DETAIL_MODULE
EndOnNext
EndForEachOne
Return to order module
On Return
         Return
EndOnReturn
EndModule       3_SHIPMENT_MODULE_Q
                (Process continued)
```

Highlights of Modules 1 and 3 of Process QUERY_SHIPMENTS (Fig. 5-15).

Figure 7-13 Implementation of a query processing unit.

(Continuation)

```
Declare shipment detail module and associated screen form
Module          4_CONTAINS1_MODULE_Q
Form            SHIPMENT_DETAIL (PRODUCT, DESCR_TITLE,
                   UNIT_AUTHOR, PRICE, QUANTITY)
Query shipment detail table
Select          PRODUCT, QUANTITY, PRICE
           From CONTAINS1
          Where CONTAINS1.INVOICE# = SHIPMENT_TITLE.INVOICE#
For Each One
Query product table
Select          TYPE
           From PRODUCT
          Where PRODUCT.PRODUCT = CONTAINS1.PRODUCT
If product is an article, get article information and display shipment detail
If              TYPE = 'Article'
Select          DESCRIPTION, UNIT
           From ARTICLE
          Where ARTICLE.PRODUCT = PRODUCT.PRODUCT
Display Into    SHIPMENT_DETAIL
         Values (PRODUCT, DESCRIPTION, UNIT, PRICE, QUANTITY)
EndIf
If product is a manual, get manual information and display shipment detail
If              TYPE = 'Manual'
Select          TITLE, AUTHOR
           From MANUAL
          Where MANUAL.PRODUCT = PRODUCT.PRODUCT
Display Into    SHIPMENT_DETAIL
         Values (PRODUCT, TITLE, AUTHOR, PRICE, QUANTITY)
EndIf
EndForEachOne
Return to shipment module
On Return
          Return
EndOnReturn
EndModule       4_CONTAINS1_MODULE_Q
```

Highlights of Module 4 of Process QUERY_SHIPMENTS (Fig. 5-15).

Figure 7-14 Implementation of a query processing unit (continuation).

7.1.3 Manual components

The manual components of an information system are *manual files* (physical data stores), *manual documents* (physical data flows) and *manual processes* (physical processes).

Manual components may be specified by conventional systems and procedures descriptions.

```
Declare order module and associated screen form
Module          1_ORDER_MODULE_I
Form            ORDER_HEADER (ORDER, DATE, DEL_DATE, STATUS,
                   CUSTOMER, NAME, ADDRESS, TOTAL)
Enter order header
Accept From     ORDER_HEADER (DEL_DATE, CUSTOMER)
         Values (DEL_DATE, CUSTOMER)
On Insert
Compute order identifier and update control table
Select          LAST_ORDER
           From CONTROL
          Where CONTROL = 1
Compute         NEW_ORDER = LAST_ORDER + 1
Update          CONTROL
            Set LAST_ORDER = NEW_ORDER
          Where CONTROL = 1
If customer is specified, get customer information
If              ORDER_HEADER.CUSTOMER Not Null
Select          CUSTOMER, NAME, ADDRESS
           From CUSTOMER
          Where CUSTOMER.CUSTOMER
                = ORDER_HEADER.CUSTOMER
EndIf
Insert order into table – integrity checks assumed
Insert Into     ORDER
         Values (NEW_ORDER, SYSDATE, DEL_DATE, 'New', CUSTOMER)
Display order header
Display Into    ORDER_HEADER
         Values (NEW_ORDER, SYSDATE, DEL_DATE, 'New', CUSTOMER,
                   NAME, ADDRESS, Null)
EndOnInsert
Call order detail module
On Next
Call            2_REFERS1_MODULE_Q
EndOnNext
Compute total amount of order
Compute         TOTAL =
        (Select Sum (QUANTITY * PRODUCT.PRICE)
           From REFERS1, PRODUCT
          Where REFERS1.ORDER = NEW_ORDER
            And REFERS1.PRODUCT = PRODUCT.PRODUCT)
Display total amount of order
Display Into    ORDER_HEADER (TOTAL)
         Values (TOTAL)
EndModule       1_ORDER_MODULE_I

                (Process continued)
```

Highlights of Module 1 of Process INSERT_ORDER (Fig. 5-16).

Figure 7-15 Implementation of a maintenance processing unit.

(Continuation)

```
Declare order detail module and associated screen form
Module          2_REFERS1_MODULE_Q
Form            ORDER_DETAIL (PRODUCT, DESCR_TITLE,
                   UNIT_AUTHOR, PRICE, QUANTITY, AMOUNT)
For Each One
Enter order detail
Accept From     ORDER_DETAIL (PRODUCT, QUANTITY)
        Values  (PRODUCT, QUANTITY)
Insert detail into table – integrity checks assumed
On Insert
Insert Into     REFERS1
        Values  (PRODUCT, NEW_ORDER, QUANTITY)
Query product price
Select          PRICE, TYPE
          From  PRODUCT
         Where  PRODUCT.PRODUCT
                = REFERS1.PRODUCT
Compute amount
Compute         AMOUNT = QUANTITY * PRICE
If product is an article, get article information and display order detail
If              TYPE = 'Article'
Select          DESCRIPTION, UNIT
          From  ARTICLE
         Where  ARTICLE.PRODUCT
                = PRODUCT.PRODUCT
Display Into    ORDER_DETAIL
        Values  (PRODUCT, DESCRIPTION, UNIT, PRICE, QUANTITY,
                   AMOUNT)
EndIf
If product is a manual, get manual information and display order detail
If              TYPE = 'Manual'
Select          TITLE, AUTHOR
          From  MANUAL
         Where  MANUAL.PRODUCT = PRODUCT.PRODUCT
Display Into    ORDER_DETAIL
        Values  (PRODUCT, TITLE, AUTHOR, PRICE, QUANTITY,
                   AMOUNT)
EndIf
EndForEachOne
Return to order module
On Return
         Return
EndOnReturn
EndModule       2_REFERS1_MODULE_Q
EndProcunit     INSERT_ORDER
```

Highlights of Module 2 of Process INSERT_ORDER (Fig. 5-16).

Figure 7-16 Implementation of a maintenance processing unit (continuation).

7.2 Observations

7.2.1 Physical data flow diagrams

(a) Physical data flow diagrams are derived and adapted from logical data flow diagrams by assigning their components to specific resources (Fig. 7-1 to 7-4). Data flow diagrams components which cannot be assigned to a unique resource must be partitioned, either in the same or in lower level data flow diagrams (Fig. 7-3 and 7-4).

(b) A logical model may give rise to a variety of physical models, depending on organization, activity levels and available resources. Alternative physical models must be evaluated and compared with respect to design objectives. Selections between candidate models must be made, starting with higher levels and going on to lower levels.

7.2.2 Physical data stores

(a) Automated data stores are derived and adapted from data stores in the logical model by assigning them to specific servers. In a decentralized design (Fig. 7-2), servers are assigned to users according to their location and responsibility; data stores must be partitioned accordingly, so that data may reside close to their main users, thus minimizing requirements for communications. In a centralized design, data stores are located on a common central server.

(b) When data stores are partitioned, automated processes are required to synchronize their contents (Fig. 7-17). The minimum information to be transferred includes table occurrences which are changed, the type of change: update, insert or delete, and values of new or changed primary data elements. Additional derived information may be transferred in order to eliminate the need for calculating it on the receiving site.

(c) Similarly, users may access remote data stores through communications or make their own copies which they can access locally. In the latter case (Fig. 7-18), they must periodically update this information to keep it current.

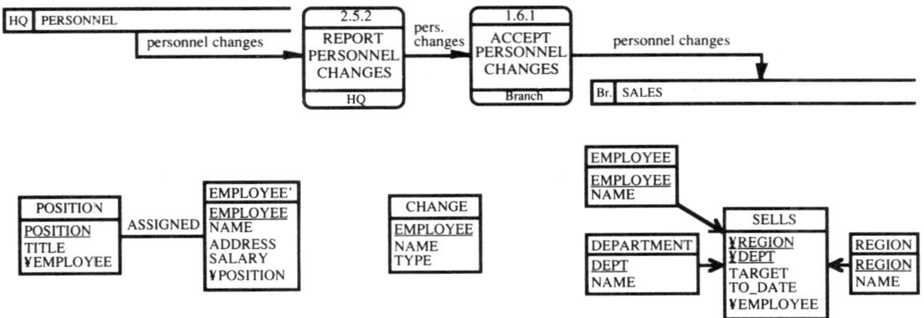

The Sales data store is synchronized with the Personnel data store by:
- Proc. Unit 2.5.2, which detects personnel changes in the Personnel data store;
- Proc. Unit 1.6.1, which accepts changes and updates the Sales data store.

Branch processes requiring the Name data element may find it in the Sales data store since it is part of the data transfer. Otherwise, they would have to obtain it from the remote Personnel data store through communications.

Figure 7-17 Synchronization of automated data stores.

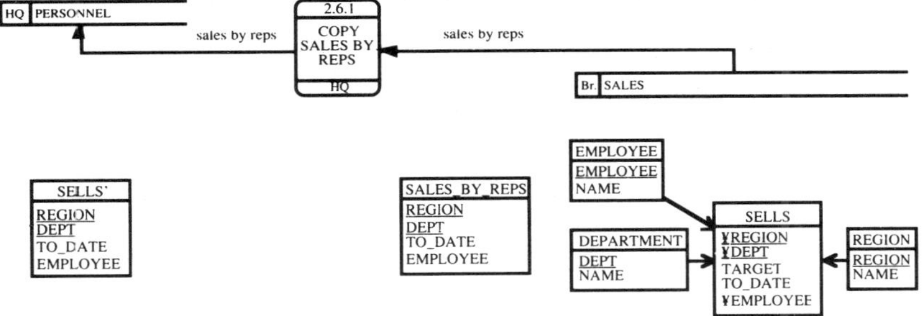

Processing Unit 2.6.1 copies part of the SELLS table from the remote Sales data store into the local Personnel data store.

Headquarter processes requiring this information may find it locally instead of obtaining it through communications. But it must be periodically updated.

Figure 7-18 Local copy from a remote automated data store.

(d) The physical contents of automated data stores (Fig. 7-5) are derived from their logical contents (Fig. 5-4). Then adaptations are made case by case, based on requirements of specific processes (Fig. 7-19 to 7-21). This may involve grouping or adding tables or adding derived, replicated or control data elements.

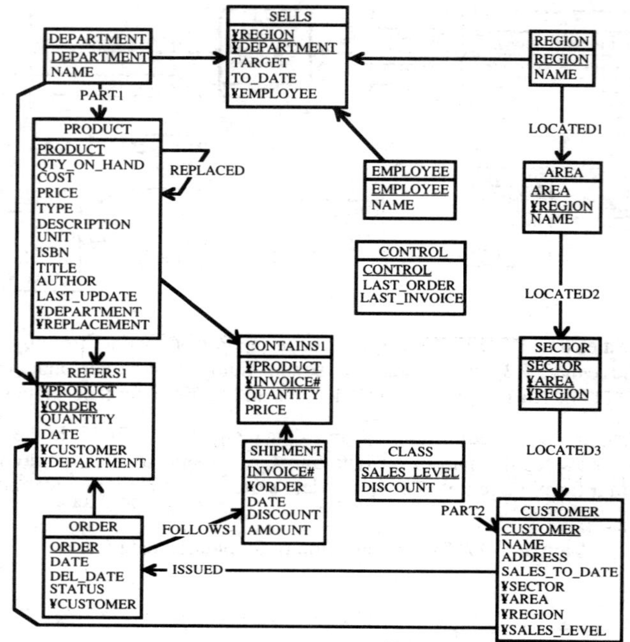

In order to meet performance requirements of specific processes, a degree of 'de-normalization' and redundancy is brought to the model:

- Tables PRODUCT, ARTICLE and MANUAL, which are usually accessed together, are grouped to reduce the number of accesses;
- Derived data element PRODUCT.TYPE eliminates the need to test for the existence of corresponding occurrences in tables ARTICLE and MANUAL;
- Control element PRODUCT.LAST_UPDATE notes last processing date;
- Table CONTROL, with a single occurrence, is added to store single-valued data elements: retrieving the most recent order number from the CONTROL table is more efficient than calculating it from the ORDER table;
- Duplicated foreign keys REFERS1.DEPARTMENT and REFERS1. CUSTOMER create direct (redundant) paths which facilitate order summarization by department and customer;
- Note that foreign key duplication occurs naturally as a result of identifier dependencies, e.g. CUSTOMER.REGION creates a direct path from CUSTOMER to REGION;
- Duplicated element REFERS1.DATE helps summarizing orders by week.

Figure 7-19 Specification of a data store including new tables and data elements.

(e) Implementing a data store based on its specification is straightforward when using relational tools (Fig. 7-6). Tuning it requires setting up appropriate indexes (Fig. 6-30 to 6-34) and is done when processing units are ready to be tested for performance.

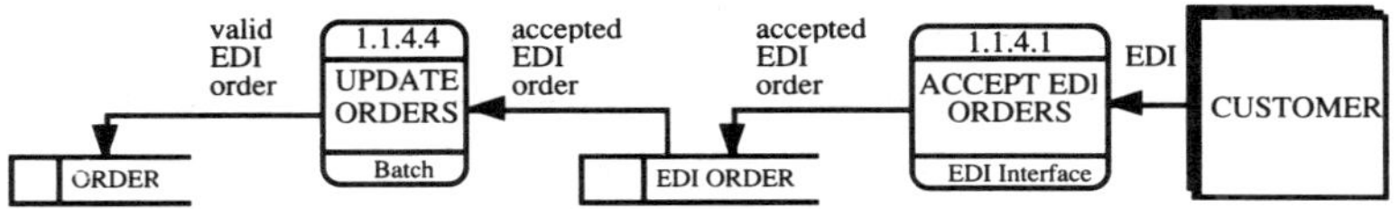

Tables EDI_ORDER and EDI_CONTAINS1 are added to the physical model as part of the EDI Order data store.
They store electronically received orders until they can be processed.

Figure 7-20 Added data entry tables.

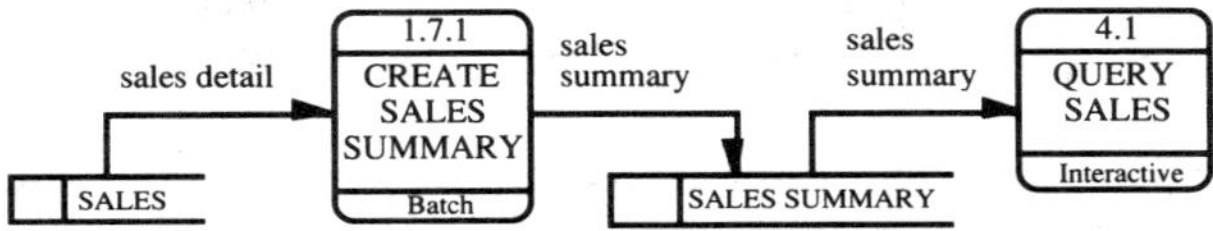

Tables ORDER_SUM, SHIPMENT_SUM and DISCOUNT_SUM are added to the physical model as part of the Sales Summary data store. Querying those derived tables is more efficient than querying and summarizing the source tables whenever it is required.

Figure 7-21 Added query tables.

7.2.3 Physical data flows

Physical data flows are derived and adapted from logical ones by assigning them to specific media and formats. Logical data flows requiring multiple media or formats yield multiple physical data flows, requiring additional processes and data stores (Fig. 7-4).

7.2.4 Physical processes

(a) Physical processes are derived and adapted from logical processes by assigning them to specific resources or resource combinations. Processes for which this cannot be done are partitioned using sequential or parallel sub-processes (Fig. 7-4).

(b) Automated processes are usually assigned to the same servers as the data stores which they access. In a decentralized design, they are executed on the local server or the client workstation. In a centralized design, they are executed on the common server.

(c) For organizational, technical or performance reasons, a data entry process may have to be partitioned into two processing units: one for data entry and the other for batch update (Fig. 7-20). A query process may similarly have to be partitioned into a batch update and an interactive query processing unit (Fig. 7-21).

(d) Processes that share similar components may be combined into the same processing unit. This is the case for interactive data entry and query processes which use the same screens or report processes which use the same format.

(e) Automated process access diagrams and action tables are derived from their logical counterparts (Fig. 5-13 to 5-16), taking into account changes caused by data store and process adaptations.

(f) Automated processes are implemented (Fig. 7-13 to 7-16) based on their access diagrams and action tables.

7.3 Representation

Physical DFDs may be drawn using the Gane and Sarson or an equivalent diagramming technique. Resources used are written in the bottom of process boxes and on the side of data store boxes.

Automated data stores and views, possibly including constraints, may be represented by relational diagrams and implemented using a relational language. Automated data flows may be outlined using relational diagrams and implemented using automated design tools. Automated processing units may be specified using physical access diagrams and action tables and implemented using a relational language and its associated tools. Manual components may be specified using procedure descriptions, document layouts, etc.

7.4 Approach

7.4.1 Overview

The approach for physical modeling proposed in this book (Fig. 1-3) involves a staged design and development of the data processing system used to implement the logical model.

Such a system is defined by organizational resources: structure, roles and responsibilities, geographical distribution; by processing resources: hardware, telecommunications, software; and by operational procedures which use those resources, as represented by physical DFDs.

Each level of modeling is concluded by a physical modeling stage: the *corporate physical model* is succeeded by domain specific *general physical models,* then by *detailed physical models,* by *detailed physical specifications* and finally, by the *implementation* of each release.

This approach also offers an opportunity to validate and refine the logical model at increasing levels of detail.

7.4.2 Corporate physical model

The *corporate physical model* is developed as part of the corporate strategic plan, based on the corporate logical model (Fig. 5-34).

It consists of the corporate context diagram (Fig. 7-1) and descriptions of its components. It shows the corporate orientation with respect to the distribution of data, processes and associated responsibilities; and the distribution of hardware and software to support them. It provides a common framework for planning systems development throughout the organization.

This broad model is developed by considering factors such as organizational structure, activity levels, capacity of existing and available hardware and software, existing systems, and overall costs and benefits.

7.4.3 General physical model of a domain

The *general physical model* of a domain is developed based on its general logical model (Fig. 5-36).

It consists of the domain context diagram (Fig. 7-2) and descriptions of its components. It is prepared as a conclusion of the corporate systems architecture stage – or as part of the domain preliminary study. It provides a framework for planning development of domain systems.

This model is a refinement of the corporate physical model for the domain under consideration. It takes into account the same organizational, volumetric, resource, risk and cost benefits factors.

7.4.4 Detailed physical model of a domain

The *detailed physical model* of a domain is developed based on the detailed logical model (Fig. 5-38) at the end of the systems architecture stage for the domain.

The detailed physical model consists of the domain context diagram (Fig. 7-2), its subordinate DFDs down to the level of processing units (Fig. 7-3 and 7-4) and descriptions of their components, including preliminary data store specifications (Fig. 7-5). It includes components required to interface with other systems and those required to transfer data from the existing systems which it will replace.

The level of detail provided by this model makes it possible to measure the size of the system and to estimate the required amount of development work. In addition, when the system is too large to be developed in a single stage, the detailed model can be used as the basis for a partition into releases to be installed in successive stages.

7.4.5 Detailed physical specifications of a release

The *detailed physical specifications* of a release apply to processing units and data stores which are part of the release. They include physical access diagrams (Fig. 7-11 and 7-12), physical action tables similar to logical action tables (Fig. 5-15 and 5-16), screen and report layouts (Fig. 7-9 and 7-10) and finalized data store specifications (Fig. 7-19).

Detailed physical specifications are an adaptation of logical specifications, taking into account changes caused by adaptations to data stores and processes.

7.4.6 Implementation of a release

Developing data stores (Fig. 7-6) and especially processing units of a release (Fig. 7-13 to 7-16) is a major step in implementing a system.

In a systems development cycle using a conventional structured approach, this step is undertaken only after detailed physical specifications are fully developed and approved.

However, several tools make it feasible to develop a system by first building a prototype and then enhancing it until it is complete enough to be transferred to production. This results in a more flexible approach, in which implementation starts before specifications are complete, and specifications are refined as implementation progresses, taking user feedback into account.

One approach is as follows. Data stores are developed first, based on preliminary specifications (Fig. 7-5). Prototypes of interactive processing units are developed, based on preliminary screen designs (Fig. 7-9 and 7-10) and access diagrams (Fig. 7-11 and 7-12). Detail logic based on business rules is then added to them. Batch processing units and operational reports are developed in the next stage. When the prototype is fully functional, management information type queries and reports are developed. The system is tuned for performance.

In this approach, users participate in each step, by reviewing and validating physical components as they are developed, and by supplying data and business rules information required to refine those components. The prototype evolves from being a specification of the system to becoming the system itself.

PART IV

Conclusion

Data driven systems modeling derives its power from the fact that the conceptual model describes the real world on which a system is based, rather than the system itself. Thus it provides a stable foundation for designing and implementing the system. Logical and conceptual models bridge the gap to system implementation. The concluding chapter in Part IV argues for an iterative approach based on *CASE* tools and for a preoccupation with other dimensions of systems development.

Chapter 8

Making it Work

> A real-world problem, on the other hand, never is sealed off from any part of the world with absolute certainty.
>
> (D. Hofstadter, *Gödel, Escher, Bach*)

In this book, we have walked through three tiers of models.

We have thoroughly examined the workings of the conceptual model in order to fully understand it. We have experimented with it in order to be able to develop one. We have used the conceptual model as a tool to specify the components of logical and physical models (Fig. 8-1). Then we have explored the process of implementing a system using those specifications.

MODEL TYPE	DATA	<—>	PROCESSES	FOCUS
CONCEPTUAL	Entity-relationship diagram		Business rules	DATA
LOGICAL	Data flow diagram			DATA PROCESSES
	Data store view	Data flow view	Access diagram Action table	
PHYSICAL	Data flow diagram			
• AUTOMATED (Relational)	Data store view	Data flow view	Access diagram Action table	DATA PROCESSES RESOURCES
• MANUAL	File description	Form desc.	Procedure descr.	

Figure 8-1 Specifying the components of the various types of models.

This analytical approach is consistent with the purpose of this book, and it has led us into emphasizing distinctions between the conceptual, logical and physical facets of an information system. However, when applying these techniques to a real-life case, we must keep in mind that these facets relate to one another and that the system itself must be integrated to the real world it purports to describe.

Indeed, we must adopt a comprehensive and integrated perspective and be ready to iterate through the modeling cycle, knowing when to proceed to the next stage and when to retrace our steps to correct earlier inaccuracies (Fig. 8-2).

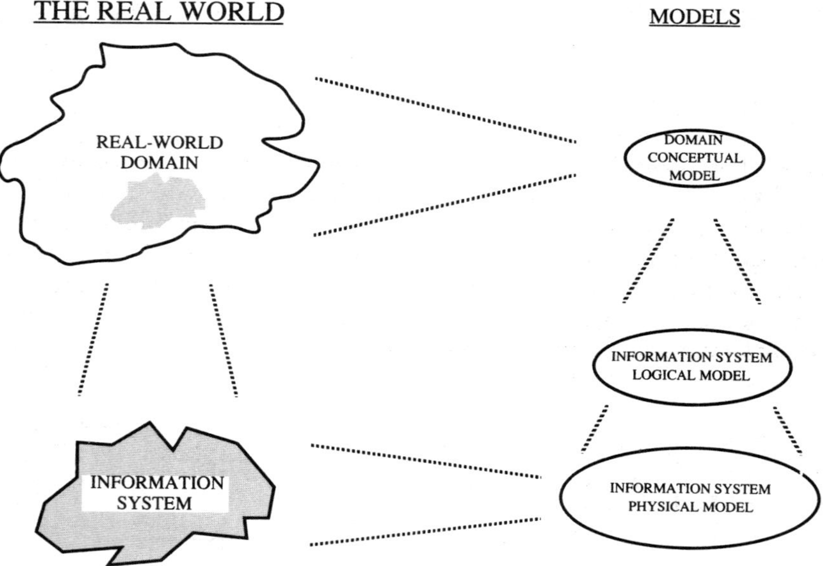

The modeling cycle can be used in different ways:
• Forward engineering leads from a real-world domain to an information system implementation, through stages of conceptual, logical and physical modeling;
• Reverse engineering extracts a domain description from an information system implementation by proceeding in the opposite direction;
• Combining these two approaches is becoming increasingly practical and efficient through the use of re-engineering and prototyping tools.

Figure 8-2 Proceeding through the modeling cycle.

Fortunately, this is becoming more and more practical, thanks to modern integrated *CASE* tools for system design and development. Increasingly, these software tools tie together conceptual, logical and physical descriptions of systems, and implemented systems. They offer an interactive choice of preferences as to which diagramming techniques are used for displaying models.

Models become 'views' on an integrated 'repository' which we can review at leisure in order to examine the facets of the system which are of interest to us. Prototypes become models in this sense, and the system itself becomes the ultimate refinement of its own specification.

Also, we should not forget that the process of inserting a system into an organization has a number of dimensions, one of which is the human dimension, which is not addressed by the present analysis, and which must be taken into account.

Last but not least, we should entertain a healthy confidence that the practitioner's art will always involve being able to combine theory with experience to obtain practical and workable results.

References

Barker, R. (1990) *CASE Method: Entity Relationship Modelling*, Addison-Wesley. Data modeling explained, using the Information Engineering diagramming technique. Offers many hints. Compares conventions.

Chen, P. (1980) *Entity Relationship Approach to System Analysis and Design*, North Holland. Time-honored data modeling approach and conventions.

Coad, P. and Yourdon, E. (1991) *Object-Oriented Analysis*, 2nd edition, Prentice Hall. Develops an object-oriented conceptual model and approach.

Date, C. (1990) *An Introduction to Database Systems*, Vol. I, 5th edition, Addison-Wesley. A classic on databases. Consult it for an in-depth treatment of the relational model.

Date, C. (1985) *An Introduction to Database Systems*, Vol. II, Addison-Wesley. A sequel, which includes a discussion of data models.

DeMarco, T. (1978) *Structured Analysis and System Specification*, 2nd edition, Yourdon Press. A delightful introduction to data flow diagrams. Consult it in connection with the logical and physical models.

Flavin, M. (1981) *Fundamental Concepts of Information Modeling*, Yourdon Press. One of the early books with a data driven understanding of systems.

Gane, C. and Sarson, T. (1980) *Structured System Analysis: Tools and Techniques*, McDonnell Douglas. The source of data flow modeling techniques used in this book.

Hares, J. (1990) *SSADM For the Advanced Practitioner*, John Wiley & Sons. Discusses higher-order normal forms, access path analysis, knowledge bases and other advanced topics. Stimulating and challenging.

Higgins, D. (1982) *Designing Structured Programs*, Prentice Hall. Data driven Warnier/Orr design based on the structure of the program view.

Hofstadter, D. (1985) *Gödel, Escher, Bach: An Eternal Golden Braid*, Basic Books. Brilliantly speculates about the significance of formal systems incompleteness for understanding human thought. A Pulitzer prize classic.

Jackson, M. (1983) *System Development*, Prentice Hall. Processes are based on 'entity' life cycles. Entities are dynamic and evolve through well-defined states. Processes model state transitions.

Kent, W. (1980) *Data and Reality,* North Holland. Asks all the right questions about the nature of data and its connection to the world.

Martin, J. and McClure, C. (1985) *Structured Techniques for Computing,* Prentice Hall. A handbook of diagramming techniques for data and process modeling, including access diagrams and action charts.

Nijssen, G. and Halpin T. (1989) *Conceptual Schema and Relational Database Design: A fact oriented approach,* Prentice Hall. A meticulous approach to conceptual modeling, using the binary model.

Rumbaugh, J., Blaha, M., Premerlani, W., Eddy, F. and Lorensen, W. (1991) *Object-Oriented Modeling and Design,* Prentice Hall. Shows how object-oriented analysis and design mesh into data driven implementation.

Schlaer, S. and Mellor, S. (1988) *Object-Oriented Systems Analysis: Modeling the World in Data,* Prentice Hall. An object-oriented conceptual model with inheritance relationships.

Sowa, J., (1984) *Conceptual Structures: Information Processing in Minds and Machines,* Addison-Wesley. A preview of the future of conceptual, knowledge based, intelligent models.

Tardieu, H., Rochfeld, A. and Colletti, R. (1984) *La méthode MERISE,* Vol. 1: Principes et outils, Les Éditions d'organisation. The basic text about *MERISE* data and process modeling techniques. The source of data modeling techniques used in this book.

Tardieu, H., Rochfeld, A., Colletti, R., Panet, G. and Vahée, G. (1984) *La méthode MERISE,* Vol. 2: Démarches et pratiques, Les Éditions d'organisation. The basic text about the *MERISE* methodology, which simultaneously addresses data and process aspects of systems.

Yourdon, E. (1989) *Modern Structured Analysis,* Prentice Hall. A textbook by one of the founders of this classic process driven approach.

Index